Afghanistan

Preserving
Historic Heritage

The Aga Khan
Historic Cities Programme

# Afghanistan

## Preserving
## Historic Heritage

Edited by Philip Jodidio

PRESTEL

Munich · London · New York

# Contents

Preceding pages, carpenters working to clean
and repair timber doors at the Hazrat-e Bilal
Mosque, Herat.

The restored Timur Shah Mausoleum set within
a public garden adjacent to the Kabul River.

# Preface

HIS HIGHNESS THE AGA KHAN

The Aga Khan Development Network (AKDN) consists of a series of specialized agencies that have been brought into existence over the years since 1957 in response to needs that were identified in many of the developing countries of Asia and Africa. It is rooted in the ethics of our faith, and it serves all the populations we seek to support, without regard to gender, race or faith. The challenge for AKDN is thus to address the development needs not only of countries at peace, but also of nations that that have suffered from war and internal conflict. An element in these interventions that is worth special mention is the emphasis that AKDN has placed on culture as a significant factor for both urban and rural development, helping to alleviate poverty while also contributing to a stronger, richer sense of local and national identity.

It is striking in this regard that nearly one third of internationally recognized World Heritage sites are in the Muslim world, but like most such sites in the developing world they are inhabited by some of the poorest people. Traditional approaches to cultural regeneration — often seeking to simply create museums in such places — fail to address the full potential of complex situations and often become unproductive burdens. The central objective of our work, therefore, is to leverage cultural opportunities in pursuit of poverty alleviation. We do this through a critical mass of programmes — the creation of parks and gardens, heritage conservation, water and sanitation improvements, microfinance resources, open space and infrastructure improvements, and education and health initiatives.

The UN-sponsored Bonn Agreement, intended to recreate the state of Afghanistan after years of conflict, was signed on 5 December 2001. This was the signal that work in that war-torn country could begin. Shortly afterwards, on 21 January 2002, on the occasion of the International Conference on Reconstruction Assistance to Afghanistan, in Tokyo, I announced a multi-year commitment by the Aga Khan Development Network (AKDN) to help rebuild Afghanistan.

It was clear that effective economic and social action in Afghanistan could not have been undertaken without a significant cultural dimension and so the Aga Khan Trust for Culture (AKTC) was the first part of the AKDN system to be fully active there, beginning in early 2002. A focus was placed on the most urgent reconstruction projects related to the urban heritage of the country. As has been the case in other interventions of AKTC, the reconstruction and renovation of the historic patrimony were guided by the intention to contribute to the social and economic development of the country in urban areas. The result of this activity was to create jobs but also to develop technical competence for large numbers of young Afghan people in the techniques of historic preservation and conservation, as well as competencies related to traditional crafts, such as carpet weaving, glass-blowing and tile making. In collaboration with local authorities, in particular in Herat and Kabul, comprehensive historic preservation plans were formulated, not only for specific monuments or residences, but also for public spaces. These plans fully took into account the contemporary use of the buildings and spaces concerned.

Since 2002, AKDN and its partners have channelled over one billion dollars to enhance self-reliance and improve the quality of life of Afghans. Between now and 2020, AKDN plans similar investments in cultural heritage, education, energy, health and poverty alleviation. It remains urgent to drive efforts to sustain and develop Afghanistan's human and social capital. For this purpose, AKDN supports the Ministry of Education's National Education Strategic Plan in over 850 schools and education centres. In health, AKDN's 'Public-Private Partnerships' have provided treatment to over 1.6 million Afghans and trained over 13,000 doctors, nurses and health workers. It is apparent that the work of AKDN is only a part of the international effort to assist Afghanistan in its ongoing reconstruction, and I wish to take this occasion to thank all of the national and local authorities — beginning with President Ashraf Ghani — who have supported our programmes, together with many international organizations cited at the end of this book.

In Afghanistan, a rich cultural heritage in danger of being cast aside in the race to modernity after years of war has been a significant element in the reconstruction not only of buildings, but of awareness and professions that contribute lastingly to a contemporary definition of the country's identity. Far more than a programme of historic preservation, the work of AKDN in Afghanistan has sought to contribute to the lasting redevelopment of the economy, society and culture of the country.

In this context it is equally important to ensure that the rich pluralism of Islam within Afghanistan is respected and sustained for the peace and serenity of all Afghans, as is necessary today throughout the Muslim world.

The Government of Afghanistan's commitment to this vision is something that continues to inspire us all as we work together to improve the quality of life for the people of this country and this region, and for generations yet unborn. Just as fear can be infectious, so, too, is hope.

* * *

# Architecture as a Key to Identity

HIS EXCELLENCY MOHAMMAD ASHRAF GHANI
PRESIDENT OF THE ISLAMIC REPUBLIC OF AFGHANISTAN

This time of global unrest and polarization is an important reminder that the challenge of development is not just one of building effective states and state administrations, but of defining the symbols that people require in order to find comfort and shared purpose in the idea of 'nation'. But nations and national identities are not built simply from abstract concepts. A nation needs to be embodied in physical expressions. Urbanism, architecture and some forms of artistic endeavour can underpin a dialogue among people that helps them constitute a shared identity in the historical and built environment in which they live.

His Highness the Aga Khan has made that discourse possible by establishing the Aga Khan Trust for Culture, and its Historic Cities Programme that focuses on the preservation of historic quarters and buildings together with improvements in the livelihoods of communities. When the history of architectural knowledge in the twenty-first century is written, the Aga Khan's role in advancing the discipline as a manifestation of a country's identity and culture will figure prominently. Today, His Highness the Aga Khan is a dominant player in the preservation and restoration of Islamic architecture. The Aga Khan Trust for Culture (AKTC) has fashioned entirely new ways of seeing, building and using the built environment as a foundation to help countries construct a historically grounded national identity.

What makes AKTC's restoration work unique is its holistic approach to physical conservation, which becomes a platform for complementary initiatives aimed at improving living standards, reviving traditional crafts and raising public awareness. Though attuned to the value of conserving history, the Trust does not seek simply to restore the past in isolation from the wider socio-economic context. Its restoration activities are as much about the practical needs of living communities as they are about historical conservation, and it is the interplay between restoration and functionality that makes the Trust's work both pertinent and meaningful in Afghanistan.

The Aga Khan University in Karachi provides a case in point for understanding the Aga Khan's unique commitment to grounding architecture in identity. After rigorously selecting a qualified firm, His Highness then asked the successful candidate to spend a full year studying Pakistan's historical monuments so that they could fashion a university that would both embody the past and also function as a modern institution that would provide state-of-the art medical training to the doctors and nurses of the future.

Established in 1977, the Aga Khan Award for Architecture, presented once every three years, has provided global recognition to young architects, planners, historical

**Above, upgrading activities in informal residential quarters surrounding Babur's Garden have helped improve living conditions for residents.**

**Below, built on multiple levels, the restored rooftops of the Ikhtyaruddin Citadel in Herat provide ample space for public events and gatherings.**

conservationists and landscape designers working in countries with significant Muslim populations. Inherited Islamic traditions of proportion, symmetry, reflection and innovation are often evident in the selected projects.

And then there is AKTC's remarkable Archnet project, the online library of Islamic architecture built on the basis of five decades of research, documentation and practical applications to the world of Islamic architecture. It would not be an exaggeration to say that the bulk of knowledge about Islamic architectural traditions is consolidated in this one, unique, digital archive. What once required thousands of miles of travel to achieve understanding, is now available online for young people — the scholars, builders, planners and architects of Islam's future. While virtual reality cannot replace the physical presence of place, making such a rich collection of Islam's architectural traditions available to the world at large is surely one of the most noble contributions to global knowledge.

Afghanistan has been a beneficiary of this accumulated architectural knowledge. As Chief Adviser to then President Karzai, I was privileged to facilitate the signing of an agreement between the Aga Khan Development Network (AKDN) and the Government of Afghanistan in early 2002. After forty years of continuous, destructive conflict, the partnership with AKDN has helped reconnect us with our history and traditions by reviving the legacy of knowledge and beauty that was our pre-war past. As a result of the Trust's brilliant restoration of the Ikhtyaruddin Citadel in Herat, funded by the US Ambassadors Fund for Cultural Preservation, what was a heart-breaking ruin is now, once again, a functioning tribute to Herat's place at the heart of Timurid Asia: a central position in world history and trade that Afghanistan will again occupy one day.

His Highness the Aga Khan's commitment to restoring our historic quarters and landscapes has also helped revive and transform precincts within our nation's capital, Kabul. In 2002 there was little sign of life in Babur's Garden. Devastated by years of conflict, the flora and fauna that had once captivated Babur, the founder of the Mughal dynasty, had long since disappeared in the rubble and wreckage of war. Amir Abdur Rahman Khan's *haremserai* lay in ruins, while Babur's grave was on the verge of collapse. The restoration of this important garden, co-funded by the Federal Republic of Germany, is described in detail in a recent publication by the Aga Khan Trust for Culture entitled *Heritage of the Mughal World*, which provides insights on the conservation and careful attention through which the garden was restored to again become the beating heart of the city. The people of Kabul love their garden — more than five million individuals have visited the site since its restoration was completed — and their daily usage and care for the place guarantee that our understanding of the past, present and future will be continually shaped by this historic landscape.

The Trust's ongoing rehabilitation of the Chihilsitoon Garden, generously supported by the Federal Republic of Germany, will be another key addition to the public and cognitive space of Kabul — providing key facilities for recreation, cultural activities and sport. Meanwhile, the partnership between the Government of Afghanistan and the Aga Khan Trust for Culture continues to evolve. A recent agreement that encompasses planning and conservation activities within a heritage precinct along the historic riverfront of Kabul aims to revive the area as the centre of the city's social and economic life. With the late-eighteenth-century Timur Shah Mausoleum as its anchor, the renewal of the historic riverfront will provide an unforgettable reminder of the beauty of traditional architecture and contribute to the revival of social and economic activity in the downtown area.

The range of skills and scales of intervention put into action make AKTC's work unique. The restoration of Stor Palace in Kabul, funded by the Government of India, is a result of disciplined attention to historic and architectural detail, and pushes the boundaries of innovation and design in a context where many would settle for far less. Stor Palace was the setting where Afghan leaders such as King Amanullah and Mahmoud Tarzi — respectively the twentieth-century's most transformational leader and key intellectual — discussed the reforms that shaped our destiny for a century.

These accomplishments should not, however, lull us into forgetting the opportunities that we have missed. Kabul today is a visible manifestation of the failure of public policy. We have destroyed far more of our past than we have been able to save. Babur's "City of Roses" is at present ringed by informal settlements of people forced to the periphery not just by conflict but also by illegal land grabbing, unmanaged speculation, corruption and other forms of social violence. Successive governments failed to pay attention to basic aspects of urban planning and provision of services, whether for traffic management, clean water, or adequate drainage and sewerage, much less building a responsive governance for a 'smart city' that binds rural and urban areas together through shared interests in growth and well-being.

While to date Kabul and our other cities have suffered through a failure of imagination about the critical role of cities within a unifying national vision, not all is lost. Since assuming the Presidency, my colleagues and I have been engaged in a constant examination of the problems in Kabul, with the aim of defining the potential of appropriate urban development as a means to providing the nation with a unifying vision for the future. I am pleased to note that the Aga Khan Trust for Culture has been central in this dialogue about Kabul's role in the nation-building project.

King Amanullah built Darulaman Palace as the cornerstone of a new paradigm of urbanism for the city, aiming to integrate state institutions with civic, cultural and public spaces. His vision was never fully realized, resulting in the isolation of Darulaman Palace from the rest of Kabul. Half a century later, the palace was destroyed in the fighting that followed the expulsion of the Soviet army. But King Amanullah's vision of the functional city is still relevant, and we have restarted the process of relocating most of our state institutions to the quarters around Darulaman Palace.

Restoring a city's past is as much a social undertaking as it is a physical or engineering endeavour. To restore Darulaman Palace, the Municipal Administration, the Ministry of Urban Development and Housing, and the Capital Region Independent Development Authority needed to cooperate and develop a shared vision. This required building institutional relationships as a precursor to wider engagement with the surrounding community. As the government relocates to Darulaman, large state-owned properties in central Kabul can be recovered for civic and public uses. In districts near downtown Kabul, well-thought-through and consultative planning will ensure that development reflects a wider dialogue and considers Kabul's past, present and future. As part of this process, the Aga Khan Trust for Culture will help Afghan institutions prepare a narrative for regenerating Kabul's riverfront area in a manner that is rooted in history, focused on the needs of Afghan citizens and embedded within the overall vision of the nation's capital.

Above, the main entrance lobby of the restored Stor Palace in Kabul.

Below, a foreman secures fastening on form-work for new rammed-earth constructions at the Chihilsitoon Garden in Kabul.

# Fifteen Years in Afghanistan

LUIS MONREAL
GENERAL MANAGER
AGA KHAN TRUST FOR CULTURE

Shortly after the December 2001 Taliban surrender in Kandahar, the Aga Khan Trust for Culture (AKTC) was present in Afghanistan at the behest of the Chairman of the Board, His Highness the Aga Khan. There were three main challenges to be met as quickly as possible. The first of these was to determine a strategy and locations for a long-term commitment to the country, estimated at fifteen to twenty years. The second was to prioritize the work to be undertaken in Kabul and Herat so as to have the maximum positive impact possible for the population. The third initial priority was to begin to create a competent team capable of carrying out the requisite renovation and development work. Specialists, often Afghan expatriates, were identified and asked to return to their country to participate in the reconstruction effort. The actual projects undertaken since then, which are the subject of this book, were developed over time, with sites in Balkh and Badakhshan being added to the originally selected projects in Kabul and Herat.

His Highness the Aga Khan made an initial commitment of $75 million to the reconstruction of Afghanistan at the time of the Tokyo Conference in early 2002. To date, the assistance of the Aga Khan Development Network (AKDN) to Afghanistan has exceeded that original pledge by a factor of ten. With the support of donors and partners, more than a billion US dollars has been channelled through AKDN for the efforts in Afghanistan. In the spirit of the broadly based initiatives of the organization in other countries, the investments made helped to initiate and carry forward rural development, health, education and civil society programmes. AKDN has also been active in the provision of a range of microfinance services, a rapidly growing mobile phone network, and the renovation of a five-star hotel in Kabul. The safeguarding of historic landscapes, structures and neighbourhoods undertaken by the Historic Cities Programme, a part of AKTC, is the focus of this volume. Between now and 2020, AKDN will continue to contribute actively through investments in culture, education, health and energy in order to help alleviate poverty, reflecting the belief of His Highness the Aga Khan in the power of sustained, long-term, multidimensional development that empowers individuals and communities to improve their quality of life.

In 2002, AKTC began the rehabilitation of Babur's Garden, or Bagh-e Babur, a walled and terraced garden containing the tomb of Babur, the founder of the Mughal Empire. AKTC's improvements include the restoration of walls and the Queen's Palace, the relaying of water channels, the reconstruction of a caravanserai to provide space for a visitor's centre, shops and offices, and the replanting of trees favoured by the Mughals. A range of community upgrading activities has also been carried out,

Opposite page, a group of students visiting Babur's Garden as part of an educational programme, Kabul.

Above, a 16th-century miniature painting, contained in an illustrated version of *The Baburnama*, showing Babur entering the Bagh-e Wafa — a garden laid out by the young Mughal prince in Afghanistan.

**Above, rebuilt and expanded over two millennia, the Ikhtyaruddin Citadel stands upon a man-made mound in the Old City of Herat.**

**Below, conservation of the Ikhtyaruddin Citadel by AKTC has enabled the site to be used regularly for public events.**

improving water and sanitation facilities for 10,000 inhabitants of the surrounding residential area, which has been the focus of joint area-planning initiatives with Kabul Municipality.

Since 2003, war-damaged quarters of the Old City of Kabul have been the focus of an AKTC programme to conserve key historic buildings, including houses, mosques, shrines and public facilities. Upgrading work has improved living conditions for approximately 15,000 residents of the Old City in the neighbourhoods of Asheqan wa Arefan, Chindawol and Kuche Kharabat.

In the western Afghan city of Herat, a range of documentation, conservation and upgrading projects has also been carried out since 2005 in the surviving historic sections of the Old City, including the conservation and reuse of the Qala Ikhtyaruddin (Citadel) as a museum, completed with a grant from the US Ambassadors Fund for Cultural Preservation. This programme has been accompanied by supporting efforts to improve urban management and governance in the city. In addition, restoration work has been undertaken on an important Timurid shrine complex in Gazurgah, north-east of the city.

With fifteen years of direct involvement in preserving more than 120 monuments in several regions of Afghanistan, AKTC's programmes have supported communities living and working around historic sites with new economic and social opportunities through investment in conservation and by providing training and capacity building initiatives. In all of this work, AKDN has tried to maintain a balance between conservation that is rooted in a sound understanding of the past, and development based on the aspirations and potential of surrounding communities. Clearly stated, the cultural wealth of the past has been put forward as a base on which to build contemporary Afghan society, particularly in urban areas.

## NUMBERS THAT TELL THE STORY

Although statistics can appear to be somewhat dry, the nature and scale of the efforts of AKTC in Afghanistan can best be understood through the numbers and nature of the improvements made and training provided. Thus, beginning with Kabul and Herat, which were the first points of intervention, here is an overview of what has been accomplished.

**KABUL**

**1**
Mughal garden restored

**3**
public open spaces rehabilitated (including the ongoing Chihilsitoon Garden)

**12**
residential buildings conserved

**15**
historic public buildings conserved

**7.5**
kilometres of underground and surface drains repaired or rebuilt

**134**
houses improved through grants and technical advice

**22,000**
square metres of pedestrian alleyways, walkways and streets paved

**915,000**
workdays generated for skilled and unskilled labour in total

**5454**
young people trained in carpentry, masonry, traditional plastering, tailoring, embroidery, carpet and kilim weaving, horticulture and literacy

**30,000**
residents and more benefited directly from these programmes

**HERAT**

**40**
public buildings and monuments restored and renovated

**5**
public open spaces rehabilitated

**35,000**
square metres of pedestrian alleyways, walkways and streets paved

**60**
houses improved through grants and technical advice

**7**
houses rehabilitated

**75**
apprentices trained by 15 master craftsmen

**120**
skilled labourers trained

**30**
young people trained as carpenters, masons and glass makers

**507,000**
workdays generated for skilled and unskilled labour in total

**BALKH**

**12**
monuments conserved

**2**
public open spaces rehabilitated

**10,000**
square metres of pedestrian alleyways, walkways and streets paved

**68**
apprentices trained by 10 master craftsmen

**110**
men trained as carpenters, masons and tile makers

**170,000**
workdays generated for skilled and unskilled labour in total

**BADAKHSHAN**

**3**
historic buildings conserved

**1**
public open space rehabilitated

**2000**
square metres of pedestrian alleyways, walkways and streets paved

**35**
apprentices trained by master craftsmen

**140**
skilled and unskilled labourers trained

**113**
young people trained as carpenters, masons and plasterers

**105**
women trained in tailoring, weaving and embroidery

**37,000**
workdays generated for skilled and unskilled labour in total

**Students of the Aga Khan Music Initiative (AKMI) rehearsing in the courtyard of the Karbasi House in Herat, restored by AKTC.**

In another initiative to preserve and develop Afghanistan's cultural heritage, AKDN has established schools of classical Afghan music in both Kabul and Herat. The disruptions of the war threatened the disappearance of the country's classical music tradition. Under the *ustad-shagird* training scheme begun in 2003, master musicians teach students, selected on merit, to preserve and pass on this musical tradition. Instruments taught include the *rubab*, *delruba*, *sarinda*, *dutar* and sitar.

A 'Memorandum of Understanding' (MOU) for the conservation and rehabilitation of Kabul's key historic areas is in place between the Government of Afghanistan, represented by the Ministry of Urban Development, and the Aga Khan Trust for Culture. The MOU encompasses a multi-year partnership for urban planning activities and the implementation of a number of projects that will protect and enhance heritage assets of the capital city. This public/private cooperation aims to further develop aspects of heritage management principles outlined in the Government of Afghanistan's Urban National Priority Programme.

The efforts and outputs realized over the past fifteen years could not have been achieved without the dedicated work, vision and engagement of teams of people of various backgrounds, capabilities and skills representing the mosaic of Afghanistan in all its plurality. These teams have come together, sometimes at great personal risk, to restore and lift the pride of generations of Afghans through the preservation of their cultural heritage. The efforts of AKTC were led at the outset by Jolyon Leslie (2004–10) and since 2010 by Ajmal Maiwandi, whose leadership of the Trust's programmes under difficult conditions has been exemplary. The Trust has benefited from having the close cooperation and support of the Government of Afghanistan and a large number of partners and other participants in financing and ongoing work. Due to continue until at least 2020, the work of AKTC in Afghanistan includes the ongoing Chihilsitoon Garden renovation (see pp.130–137), but also recently announced interventions in the centre of the historic city of Kabul and along the Kabul River.

The Aga Khan Historic Cities Programme seeks to foster a mutually rewarding dialogue between tradition and modernity. The vision of AKTC is to invigorate culture as an intellectual, economic and aspirational generator for ideas that positively shape the future in ways that are meaningful and beneficial, and that enhance the quality of life. Culture, in its diversity, remains a source of personal pride that has the power to inspire and unify an entire nation, revealing it, at its best, to the outside world. The work of the Aga Khan Trust for Culture has shown that these projects can have a positive impact well beyond conservation, by promoting good governance, strengthening civil society, encouraging a rise in incomes and economic opportunities, and affirming greater respect for human rights and better stewardship of the environment.

**Left, storm-water diversion pipe being laid at the site of AKTC's rehabilitation of the Chihilsitoon Garden, Kabul.**

**Right, a curved rammed-earth building forming part of extensive public facilities being constructed at the Chihilsitoon Garden, Kabul.**

# A Portfolio of Projects with Diversity and Continuity

CAMERON RASHTI
DIRECTOR, HISTORIC CITIES PROGRAMME
AGA KHAN TRUST FOR CULTURE

The Aga Khan Historic Cities Programme's portfolio of projects in Afghanistan, from 2002 to the present, represents individually and collectively an impressively broad array of built heritage, spanning geographically from Kabul in the east and Herat in the west to Balkh and Faizabad in the north, and comprises historic gardens, mausoleums, religious buildings, schools, residential buildings, former palaces, and historic market spaces and squares.

The portfolio includes public, private and semi-public/semi-private spaces within the context of traditional sites and urban complexes that, in the instance of Kabul, date back to the first century AD but took on a more discernible urban form after the fourteenth century and accelerated with the ascent of Emperor Babur and the Mughal period. Similarly ancient in origins, Herat became a major urban centre in the region, a significant node in the flourishing Silk Route and later a Mughal, and then Timurid, urban centre, together with the satellite village and shrine complex at Gazurgah. The old towns of Balkh and Faizabad have become critical areas of Programme engagement in the north.

The development of this portfolio has been incremental and sequential, based on an initial phase of pilot projects that have demonstrated opportunities not only for resuscitating heritage that is important both internationally and nationally but also for coupling such projects to research, documentation, capacity building and socio-economic initiatives, thus boosting the overall benefit of individual projects. This multi-centric and multidisciplinary approach of the Historic Cities Programme has provided the resilience that has enabled this process to unfold over the past fifteen years. This publication is a testament to the achievements of a very dedicated team in Afghanistan with the essential support of the Government of the Islamic Republic of Afghanistan (GOIRA) and a wide group of international donors. A brief account of the evolution of this set of projects is in order.

Following the cessation of hostilities in Kabul and the December 2001 UN-sponsored conference in Bonn, Germany, to mobilize international assistance for Afghanistan, the expertise and resources of the Aga Khan Historic Cities Programme (HCP) (alongside other AKDN agencies) were deployed with a sense of urgency in early 2002 to assist in this momentous, international process.

As the Historic Cities Programme's mandate is to revitalize derelict or distressed historic sites and districts in ways that spur social, economic and cultural development and improve the local quality of life, its initial projects focused on the conservation and stabilization of key landmark sites in Kabul — Babur's Garden (or Bagh-e

Opposite page, view across the courtyard of the Queen's Palace, a late-19th-century building located within Babur's Garden, Kabul.

Above, the upper terraces of Babur's Garden showing the remains of key historic structures, including the Queen's Palace (centre-top), Kabul.

Below, the same area of Babur's Garden following restoration of the site by AKTC between 2002–08, Kabul.

250 m

**Boundary of AKTC conservation programme
and physical upgrading interventions,
Herat Old City.**

Babur), the Timur Shah Mausoleum, and urban conservation and redevelopment in the Kabul Old City. While the former two sites were complicated but classic conservation projects within prescribed boundaries, the Kabul Old City project was multi-stakeholder and multi-site in nature and called for a balance between urban physical conservation of historic structures with socio-economic initiatives that addressed the quality and upgrading of public open spaces (streetscape, infrastructure, parks, neighbourhood facilities) and the issues of vocational training, job creation and quality of life. These socio-economic and urban redevelopment initiatives were concentrated in the districts of Chindawol and Asheqan wa Arefan in coordination with a specially formed Kabul Old City Commission. Over time, and in response to the demand for engagement in adjacent sites of interest, such as the Chihilsitoon Garden, AKTC's initiatives have resulted in the urban regeneration of large sections of historic Kabul, a process that was renewed in 2016 with an agreement between AKTC and the GOIRA to turn its focus on the Kabul riverfront adjacent to Timur Shah's Mausoleum and a number of other historic nodes. During this process, Kabul's urban needs for both development guidelines and actual regeneration have been addressed not through the mechanism of an inflexible master plan but through the means of a series of action area plans, extendible in both spatial and temporal terms.

In sequential terms, the Programme's technical assistance was extended next, in 2005, to the Old City of Herat, where a multi-year programme of documentation of rare and fragile urban heritage was coupled with conservation interventions on selected sites and planning advocacy to counter the trend — post-conflict — for centrally located, historic structures to be torn down and replaced with higher-revenue-generating structures, normally alien in architectural character to the historic nucleus. To the present, any visitor to the Old City of Herat is struck by the still legible architectural coherence of the city's core, complete with *decumanus maximus* and *cardo maximus* that define its urban centre and with visible traces of its original rectilinear

Left, affected by an infestation of termites in the woodwork of the Abresham Bazaar, coupled with damage to its masonry arches and domes from penetration of water from its roof, the historic structure required extensive conservation, Herat.

Right, along with household goods, hand-spun silk and wool products are produced by weavers located within the restored Abresham Bazaar.

Above, masons work to repair the ribbed dome of the Timurid-era Namakdan Pavilion, Gazurgah, Herat.

Below, traces of ribbed plaster decoration found at the Namakdan Pavilion, known as *karbandi*, enabled restoration teams to restore the original character of the late-15th-century garden pavilion, Gazurgah, Herat.

Right, following the discovery of remains of an irrigation channel during conservation work at the Namakdan Pavilion, the flow of water through the building was restored.

defensive walls. The Qala Ikhtyaruddin fortress on the city's northern edge contrasts in morphology and height with the relatively flat Old City, reinforcing the sense of a multilayered, ancient urban settlement, and here the Programme was active in consolidating and stabilizing its perimeter walls and public access. The historic shrine complex at Gazurgah, just north of Herat, was thoroughly documented and urgent areas of conservation of component parts of the complex were carried out with the generous participation of international co-founders, a list of whom has been provided under the "Acknowledgements" section at the end of this publication.

More recently, as of 2008 as a project centre, HCP's initiatives in Balkh's old town (the eighth/ninth-century Haji Pyada Mosque being perhaps the most internationally recognized structure) have offered the opportunity to assist in conservation, with an international team of experts, of heritage dating back to the Abbasid era. Perhaps the most technically demanding of HCP's conservation and consolidation projects in the country, the project lasted six years and included assistance from the French Archaeological Delegation in Afghanistan (DAFA) and other specialists; an account of its many stages of documentation and structural mock-ups on site are discussed in the section on Balkh and in addition it will be the subject of a separate publication, to appear soon in partnership with the World Monuments Fund and DAFA. Altogether, a total of twelve projects have been undertaken in Balkh to date.

In Yamgan and Faizabad, Badakhshan, project work started in 2011 and continues to today; overall, a total of five projects have been undertaken including the iconic

Nasir Khusrau Shrine, the resting place of the eleventh-century poet-scholar, which sits dramatically on top of the cliff edge on a hilltop. Project work in Faizabad, in conjunction with sister AKDN agencies, has focused on local monuments, such as the Mir Yar Beg Shrine and urban survey and documentation.

A geographic and physical description of HCP's portfolio of initiatives does not provide a complete picture. One needs also to review activities focused on vocational training, capacity building, cultural heritage support and archaeological documentation in close coordination with the Ministry of Information and Culture. These initiatives, while anchored to many of the above 'area redevelopment' or 'action area' projects, in essence transcend specific project site boundaries, as one would expect, and lend themselves to replication in other historic sites and settlements in the country.

Some of these projects are self-contained in terms of specific end-of-project deliverables while most aim to create a reservoir of knowledge and capacity that will allow others — now and in the future — to tap the rich ensemble of Afghan heritage in innovative ways, further expanding the existing base of knowledge. Completed sites such as the Queen's Palace in Babur's Garden, the to-be-completed Chihilsitoon Garden, and the Timur Shah Mausoleum (to name only prime examples) are designed to serve as venues for civil society as spaces for meetings, seminars, training, exhibitions, performances and recreation.

The reader may discern from a review of the projects described in this publication that the architectural traditions exemplified in these projects denote a collective concept as well as a specific spirit of a place, or *genius loci*, despite their situation at considerable distances and times from each other. Continuously refreshed cultural mores of the times, geography, materials and forms of expression of course play a role in such perceptions. This duality provides heritage with a special value and can be considered a central theme of this publication.

Above, the Noh Gunbad Mosque is one of the earliest and most important structures in Balkh, 1965.

Left, extensively altered during the 1950s, the restored Namakdan Pavilion demonstrates the ingenuity and craft of Timurid builders, Gazurgah, Herat.

# KABUL

# INTRODUCTION

Preceding pages, the centre of Kabul is
densely built and contains extensive areas
of historic quarters and monuments
disconnected by recent development.

Above, flanked by a range of historic settlements, monuments and mid-20th-century
buildings, Kabul River continues to be the
focus of speculative development, 1970s.

Below, Kabul Old City as viewed from the
foothills of the Sher Darwaza Mountain,
showing the Timur Shah Mausoleum standing
in a large square garden (left), 1879–80.

## INTRODUCTION

Even before most of the historic fabric of Kabul was laid waste during inter-factional fighting in 1992, the Old City had long been in decline. Architectural remains confirm that a Buddhist settlement, first mentioned by Ptolemy in AD 150, existed in the area of present-day Kabul between the first and fifth century AD. The fortified citadel and walls along the ridge of the Sher Darwaza Mountain bear witness to the turbulent history of the city, control of which passed from Hindu to Muslim rulers in AD 871. At a time when other towns and cities in the region witnessed periods of significant architectural innovation, Kabul remained little more than an outpost during the Ghaznavid and Timurid dynasties. After its destruction by the Mongols in the thirteenth century, Kabul experienced something of a renaissance under the first Mughal emperor Babur, who laid out a number of gardens in and around the city. While the centre of the Mughal emperors was to be in India, Kabul continued to flourish under their rule. In the mid-seventeenth century an extensive covered bazaar, Char Chatta, was built by Shah Jahan's governor, Ali Mardan Khan, who also gave his name to a garden on the south bank of the Kabul River. By the late eighteenth century, when Timur Shah moved his capital from Kandahar to Kabul in the face of unrest following his succession, the city was home to 60,000 people.

Accounts of travellers to Kabul during the nineteenth century describe a dense settlement of mud-walled homes, accessed through narrow alleys divided in parts into sub-districts (*mahallas*) that could be closed off for defensive purposes. Apart from the citadel and homes of rich merchants, the bazaars seem to have been the main landmarks, along with a number of markets (*serais*) used by visiting traders. It was the covered Char Chatta Bazaar that was the target of a punitive raid on Kabul by British troops during the 'War of Retribution' in 1842, who later returned in 1880 to destroy Bala Hissar, the historic citadel which had until then served as the seat of power. This prompted Amir Abdur Rahman Khan to make plans for a new palace on the plain north of the Kabul River, outside the confines of the Old City. By the late nineteenth century Kabul's population had risen to around 150,000, and merchant families who had traditionally lived close to the bazaars began to move out of the Old City. Others followed as new suburbs were laid out from the 1920s onwards to the south and the north-west.

**Typical courtyard residence in the Old City of Kabul decorated with sliding wooden screens, 1919.**

While the historic centre retained its commercial importance for some time, many of the large merchant homes were subdivided, and fell into disrepair. As densities increased, living conditions deteriorated, prompting further movement out to the

**AKTC Area Development Programme, Kabul.**

■  Intervention areas
1  Bagh-e Babur (Barbur's Garden)
2  Timur Shah Mausoleum and Park
3  Asheqan wa Arefan

suburbs. A swathe was cut through the dense historic fabric in the late 1940s with the creation of the 'boulevard' of Jade Maiwand through the heart of the Old City, as part of efforts to modernize the capital. With newly established residential and commercial districts to the north and west of Kabul, many of those who could afford to relocate into more modern and larger homes left the congested centre of Kabul in the 1950s. Sustained by a period of development and growth, economic migrants relocated to the capital in search of employment and the population of the city rose to nearly 500,000 inhabitants by the 1960s. Rural migrants seeking more affordable accommodation began to relocate into rental properties in the Old City. In response to anti-government unrest in the late 1970s, historic residential areas in Chindawol and part of Shor Bazaar were punitively demolished in order to gain better access to the southern part of the Old City.

At this time, as part of the utopian master plan for Kabul, government planners envisioned that the entire historic Old City should be redeveloped with multi-storey apartment blocks between wide freeways running along the base of the Sher Darwaza Mountain. The reality on the ground, however, was of a dense traditional fabric that differed little from that described by nineteenth-century travellers. By the time that the inhabitants fled their homes in the face of inter-factional fighting in 1992, the historic quarters of the Old City were regarded by officials as little more than a slum.

It was into this 'slum' that the many families displaced by the conflict began to resettle after 1995 and, on a more significant scale, in 2002. Since then, war-damaged parts of the Old City have witnessed an incremental process of residential reconstruction that, despite the intentions of official planners, largely follows historic patterns or that of 'informal' hillside settlements.

In this context, in 2002 AKTC commenced a multi-year partnership with the Government of Afghanistan focused on revitalizing historic quarters and public sites in Kabul. Built on more than thirty years of experience working with impoverished communities across the Islamic world, AKTC's Area Development Programmes aim to promote physical conservation as a means to improve living conditions and provide economic opportunities for communities living and working in and around historic areas. In collaboration with local authorities, AKTC's programmes have entailed extensive urban conservation, planning, upgrading and socio-economic initiatives in the Old City of Kabul, the rehabilitation of Mughal emperor Babur's Garden, and conservation of Timur Shah's Mausoleum and the reclamation of its public garden. Subsequent projects have included the restoration of the historic Stor Palace and more recently AKTC has been engaged in rehabilitating the Chihilsitoon Garden, a twelve-hectare public site in the south of Kabul. With additional projects currently in the planning stage, AKTC's reputation as one of Afghanistan's most capable international partners in the cultural sector has been built on more than fifteen years of work to safeguard Afghan heritage and improve living and socio-economic conditions.

Above, the upper terraces of Babur's Garden showing the partially collapsed perimeter wall and the Queen's Palace, 1922.

Below, Mughal emperor Babur describes constructing an 'avenue garden' in his memoirs, *The Baburnama*, believed to refer to the central water axis of Babur's Garden in Kabul.

# PHYSICAL CONSERVATION AND RESTORATION

# BABUR'S GARDEN

## HISTORY AND CHARACTERISTICS

In the foothills of the snow-peaked Hindu Kush mountains and the fertile alluvial plains of the Kabul River basin, Zahir-ud-Din Muhammad ("Defender of the Faith") commonly known by his nickname "Babur" (believed to derive from *Babr*, Persian for "tiger") — a young Uzbek prince exiled from his native Fergana region in present-day Uzbekistan — laid the foundations of an empire that subsequently became known as the Mughal dynasty. In 1495, at the age of twelve, Babur ascended to the throne of the small principality of Fergana. Like his father, Babur set his sights on extending his rule over Timur's capital, Samarkand, which he managed to occupy briefly on three occasions. Having unsuccessfully attempted to conquer Samarkand and losing control of his native Fergana in the process, Babur travelled south though the Hindu Kush with a small entourage of followers and captured Kabul at the age of twenty-one, in 1504.

In Kabul, on the south-western foothills of the Sher Darwaza Mountain, Babur set out what might be the 'avenue' garden he describes in *The Baburnama*. The layout of the garden included running water, flowers and fruit trees: most of the elements that came in time to be associated with later Mughal funerary gardens, such as those of Humayun, Akbar, Jahangir and Shah Jahan. When he died in 1530, Babur's remains were transported from Agra to Kabul and were interred within a grave on an upper terrace of the garden around 1540. His successors came to pay their respects at this grave, with Babur's grandson Akbar visiting in 1581 and 1589, and his great-grandson Jahangir instructing during the course of a visit in 1607 that a platform (*chabwtra*) be laid around the grave, an inscribed headstone erected and that the garden be enclosed by walls. Shah Jahan dedicated a marble mosque during a visit to the site in 1647, when he also gave instructions for the construction of a gateway at the base of the garden, which later archaeological evidence suggests was never built.

The site subsequently seems to have fallen into disrepair, as Kabul's political and economic importance in the region was inextricably linked to the rise and collapse of the Mughal dynasty. When Charles Masson visited the site in 1832, and prepared a drawing of Babur's grave enclosure, he noted that the tombs had been left to decline and their stones had been taken and used in the enclosing walls. As part of a wider programme of investments in Kabul, Amir Abdur Rahman Khan (r. 1880–1901) rebuilt the perimeter walls of the garden and constructed a number of buildings for his court within the site, thereby transforming an environment that had until then been defined largely by trees and water. Further transformations occurred in the 1930s, when

Preceding pages, laid out on the slopes of the Sher Darwaza Mountain, Babur's Garden is divided into stepped terraces of sixteen levels, with his grave located near the top of the site.

Opposite page, an oasis of tranquillity surrounded by informal residential development; native species of fruit trees and flowers have been planted in the restored garden.

Above, a watercolour rendering of the central avenue of Babur's Garden by James Atkinson, 1839.

Top, at more than 1.6 kilometres, the reconstruction of the compacted-earth perimeter wall around Babur's Garden employed local masons applying traditional building techniques.

Middle, reconstruction of the central water channels, chutes and tanks in Babur's Garden was based on detailed archaeological evidence.

Bottom, water flows again through the reconstructed channels and tanks in Babur's Garden.

Nadir Shah remodelled the 'central axis' of the garden in a European style, with three fountains in stone pools. It was at this time that Babur's Garden was officially opened to the public, and a large swimming pool was constructed on the site of a graveyard north of the Shah Jahan Mosque.

Babur's Garden was much transformed and in a poor state of repair by the time that inter-factional fighting broke out in Kabul in 1992. The conflict quickly engulfed the area around the site, which lay at the front lines between factional fighters, who cut down trees to limit cover, stripped and set fire to buildings and looted the water pumps.

**WORK UNDERTAKEN**

In March 2002, the Aga Khan Trust for Culture (AKTC) signed a 'Memorandum of Understanding' with the then Transitional Administration of Afghanistan for a comprehensive programme of rehabilitation of Bagh-e Babur. The decision to select Babur's Garden for rehabilitation was made on the basis of its importance as a public garden for the inhabitants of the city, together with the historic significance of the site as a key registered national monument and within the wider history of Afghanistan. The goal of the work was to restore the original character of the landscape and conserve key buildings, while ensuring that the garden, which is the largest public open space in Kabul, continues to be a focus for recreation for the inhabitants of the city.

As it was at the front line between warring factions in the 1990s, extensive efforts were required to clear the site of unexploded ordinance and war debris and to mobilize and train a competent team of local professionals. In support of counterpart institutions, including Kabul Municipality and the Ministry of Information and Culture, a joint coordinating committee was established and tasked with facilitating rehabilitation work.

Surrounded by 'informal' hillside residential quarters built on public land over the course of three decades of war, another key challenge for the restoration team was to mobilize the local community and ensure their active participation in and support for the rehabilitation work.

Babur's Garden comprises a walled area of approximately eleven and a half hectares, within which the principal historic structures are Babur's grave and other historic graves, a marble mosque dedicated in the seventeenth century by Shah Jahan, and a *haremserai*, or Queen's Palace, and a small pavilion that both date from the late nineteenth century. Built along a slope, the site is divided into stepped terraces containing sixteen levels of various sizes, traversed by ramps and stairs. At its centre, extending from the lower entrance to the upper reaches of the site, the garden is divided longitudinally by a wide formal avenue, known locally as the "central axis". This area is the organizational spine of the site and contains the bulk of the archaeological remains and historic buildings of the Mughal garden, including water channels, tanks and chutes lined with marble.

Although it is not clear how Babur originally defined the extent of his garden, the perimeter walls that now surround it follow the tradition of enclosure of formal Persian gardens. Jahangir's instruction in 1607 that walls be built around several gardens in Kabul included the construction of walls around Babur's Garden. The scale and alignment of these walls has doubtless changed, but surviving sections of compacted-earth (*pakhsa*) walling were surveyed in 2002. With many sections found to be close to collapse, nearly 1.6 kilometres of walls (parts of which are nearly eight metres high and over two metres thick) were rebuilt or repaired by hand using traditional techniques and materials.

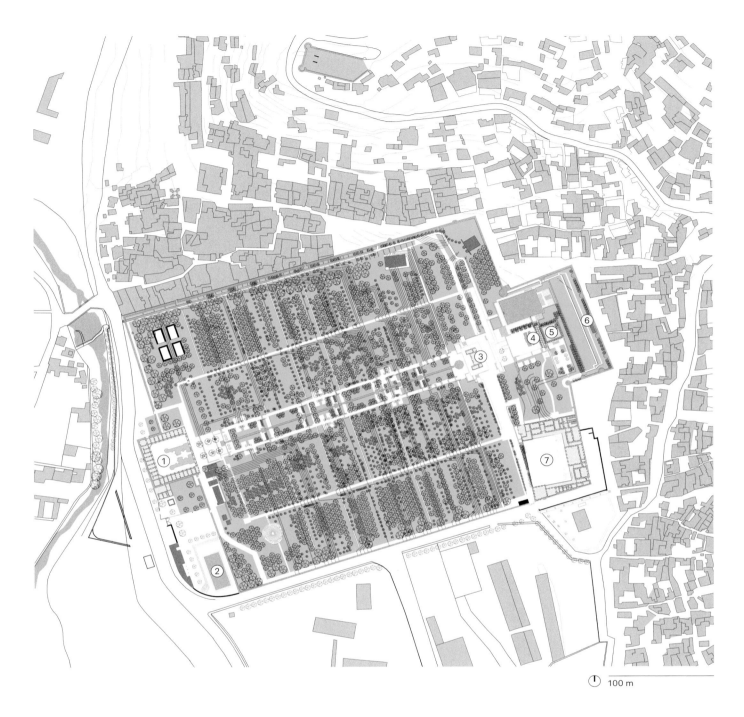

In order to understand the original nature of the landscape, six seasons of joint
archaeological excavations were undertaken by the German Archaeological Institute
and the Afghan Institute of Archaeology. Architectural elements, from gravestones
to parapets and waterfalls, were found to have been altered and reused in a random
manner throughout the garden, suggesting a subsequent disregard for their decorative or symbolic value. The dismantling of three twentieth-century fountains enabled excavation to take place along the length of the central axis, where remains
of eight rectangular tanks linked by channels, sections of terracotta pipe and stone
retaining walls at the edges of terraces were found. Fragments of three carved,
marble, waterfall elements of matching dimensions, which had been reused as gravestones, were also discovered. Together, these finds enabled the team to reconstruct

**Key facilities and monuments.**

1  Caravanserai complex
2  Swimming pool
3  Garden pavilion
4  Shah Jahan Mosque
5  Babur's grave enclosure
6  Perimeter wall
7  Queen's Palace

Above, clearance of debris from the destroyed Queen's Palace, prior to its restoration.

Below, masonry vaults being reconstructed using traditional techniques and specially prepared square bricks, Queen's Palace.

Right, craftsmen work to lay local sandstone on the terrace of the Queen's Palace.

the central axis and its main water channel, allowing water to flow once more through the site, as it did in Babur's time. This has been achieved without significantly disturbing the surviving archaeological remains, which were protected and backfilled after thorough documentation.

In addition to archaeological evidence, historic descriptions, sketches and images of the garden were used to restore the character of the landscape that originally captivated Babur. The focus of landscaping activities has been on reviving the key elements in the original concept — planting, grading and the restoration of running water along the spine of the garden. Underlying this work was the intention to provide visitors with an exciting visual experience of the garden, as they progress up through the site. Having passed through the lower entrance on the bank of the Chardeh River and entered the courtyard of the new caravanserai, the visitor glimpses the ascending garden through an arched gate in the reconstructed stone wall of the Shah Jahan gateway. Passing through this gate, it is possible to perceive the full extent of the orchard terraces of the garden, rising more than thirty-five metres up the hillside.

The visitor proceeds through the garden by means of pathways and flights of stone stairs on either side of the central axis, along which water flows through a series of channels, waterfalls and pools. This central watercourse is flanked by an avenue of plane trees, as depicted in an early nineteenth-century watercolour of the area by James Atkinson, directing views up the spine of the garden towards the pavilion and providing the deep shade that has long characterized this verdant space.

Each terrace along the central axis forms in itself a small garden, planted with pomegranates, roses and flowering shrubs between areas of stone paving around a pool of water fed from the terrace above. Babur's Memoirs have provided an invaluable source of information about the trees that he planted in gardens in and around Kabul. Based on this description, areas closest to the central axis contain pomegranates, apricots, apples, cherries and peaches, between which are small grassy meadows. At the outer edge of each terrace, copses of walnut trees have been planted along the perimeter walls, over which they will in time be visible from outside the garden.

At the source of the water channels along the 'central axis', a large octagonal tank (replicating the original that has been preserved underground) is flanked by four large plane trees around an area of stone paving. The modern swimming pool that had encroached upon the terrace north of the pavilion was removed and a new swimming pool facility was built outside the garden enclosure, near the lower entrance from the city. On the level above the pavilion, the marble-clad western wall of the Shah Jahan Mosque represents an important visual element, as do the rebuilt drystone retaining walls that run across the width of this part of the garden. Cypresses have been introduced to the north of the mosque, while planes and indigenous roses have been replanted alongside the dry trunks of the massive plane trees that once provided shade at this level.

With the original level of Babur's grave terrace restored, the platform is now approached by marble stairs leading up from a formal flower garden to the south, surrounded by a circle of wild cherry trees. Between the outer and inner grave enclosures, Judas (*arghawan*) trees blossom once a year in spring, while plane trees have been planted around the outer enclosure and along the terrace above, where they provide shade near the grave of Ruqaiya Sultana Begum, against a backdrop of towering mud-plastered perimeter walls.

Babur's grave has seen significant transformations since his body was exhumed from Agra for reburial in Kabul, in accordance with his wishes. Apart from the carved headstone erected on the instructions of Jahangir in 1607, which contains an elaborate chronogram that confirms the date of Babur's death in AH 937 (AD 1530–31), few original elements of the grave seemed to have survived. The intricately carved marble grave enclosure recorded in Masson's drawing had apparently collapsed by the time of Godfrey Vigne's account of a visit to the garden, published in 1840, while Burke's photographs from the 1870s show fragments scattered over the grave terrace. Later transformations in the grave area included the erection in the last years of the nineteenth century of an arcaded outer enclosure — subsequently demolished — and the levelling of the southern end of the grave terrace in the 1930s, when the swimming pool was built. In the ensuing years, Babur's headstone had been enclosed in a concrete frame and the grave itself embellished with coloured marble and onyx and covered by a framed shelter.

Based on archaeological excavations and a review of earlier documentation, the work undertaken over the course of the project aimed to re-establish the original character of the grave area in a manner that conformed to international conservation practice. The thirty-one marble fragments found in the grave area yielded important evidence as to the style and workmanship of the original enclosure around Babur's grave. Together with documentary material, the fragments have enabled the reconstruction of the enclosure, carved from Indian Makrana marble used in the original structure, which has been erected *in situ* on the original grave platform. Measuring 4.5 metres square, the elevations of the reconstructed enclosure comprise a central arched opening on the southern elevation flanked by pairs of marble lattice (*jali*)

Above, the caravanserai building at the entrance to Babur's Garden was constructed on the site of a destroyed late-19th-century structure.

Below, a new swimming facility was constructed on the external perimeter of Babur's Garden, replacing a dilapidated late-1970s pool within the site.

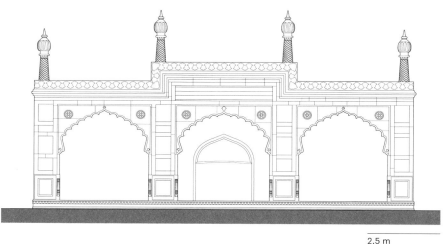

2.5 m

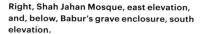

**Right, Shah Jahan Mosque, east elevation, and, below, Babur's grave enclosure, south elevation.**

**Below, the reconstruction of Babur's grave enclosure was based on visual and archaeological evidence including discovery of key sections of the original marble enclosure during archaeological excavations.**

1 m

screens. Now replanted with Judas trees, the area between the marble screen and the outer masonry enclosure provides a tranquil space in which visitors can pay their respects; and here, among others, the grave of Babur's son Hindal also survives.

Immediately west of Babur's grave enclosure and visible from the site of his tomb, the white marble mosque dedicated by Shah Jahan during his visit to Babur's grave in 1647 is arguably the most important surviving Islamic monument in Kabul. The building retains a fine inlaid marble inscription above its main elevation reading: "Only a mosque of this beauty, the temple of nobility, constructed for the prayer of saints and the epiphany of cherubs, was fit to stand in so venerable a sanctuary as this highway of archangels, this theatre of heaven, the light garden of the God-forgiven angel king who rests in the garden of heaven, Zahir-ud-Din Muhammad Babur the conqueror."

Historic photographs indicate that a number of other buildings were erected around the Shah Jahan Mosque during the reign of Amir Abdur Rahman Khan, when the structure was covered with a traditional earth roof, later replaced by a pitched roof of steel sheeting. By the time the Italian Archaeological Mission began conservation work in 1964, it was deemed necessary to erect a structure of reinforced concrete and brick, over which the marble facing was reassembled. Subsequent lack of maintenance, together with direct war damage, resulted in corrosion of the reinforcement and leaching of salts from the concrete, affecting both the structural marble elements and facing.

Following a detailed survey, conservation of the mosque was initiated in 2003 with the removal of the modern roofing and laying of traditional lime concrete, and

replacement of cracked marble structural elements. Missing sections of the parapet were replaced with original marble elements rediscovered elsewhere in the garden, and the external elevation of the *mihrab* wall was refaced, using some of the original marble pieces that had been laid as paving around the mosque. Staining on the marble elevations was cleaned and graffiti removed, but surface damage sustained during the fighting in the 1990s has been left visible.

The garden pavilion, built at the turn of the century as a place for the royal family to entertain guests, partially covered a large square tank that is mentioned in accounts of Shah Jahan's visit in 1638, and which also appears in nineteenth-century illustrations of the garden. It was looted and burned during the factional fighting in 1992, and initial repairs were begun in 2003 by UN-Habitat and the Afghan organization DHSA. The restoration of the pavilion was completed by AKTC in 2005, and since then it has been used for a range of official functions and cultural events.

While Babur might have camped on platforms similar to that found beside the pavilion, the Queen's Palace (*haremserai*) seems to have been the first permanent residential structure in the garden. Built in the 1890s by Amir Abdur Rahman Khan in a local style permeated by European influences, the complex provided secluded quarters for the royal family around a central courtyard open to the west, with sweeping views of the garden terraces below and across the western plains of Kabul to the Paghman Mountains. Used as a residence for the German legation during World War I, the complex subsequently served as a school and a military store, before being looted and burned during fighting in 1992.

Following the clearing of unexploded ordnance and mines, the collapsed sections of the *haremserai* roof were removed and the entire complex surveyed. Following consolidation of the ruined structure, reconstruction work began in early 2006. While respecting the architectural character of the original building, it was possible to incorporate a range of alternative uses into the reconstructed complex and integrate

Top and middle, the Shah Jahan Mosque is considered by many to be the finest Mughal-era structure in Afghanistan.

Bottom, Babur's grave enclosure reconstructed.

new services and a range of materials. Since its restoration, the Queen's Palace, with its large courtyard, has become the focus for public and cultural events in the garden, generating substantial revenue used for the upkeep of the site.

Photographs of the garden from around 1915 identify a double-storey caravanserai structure built around a courtyard at the base of the garden adjacent to the river. Although the caravanserai no longer existed, archaeological excavations revealed foundations of an earlier structure corresponding to a passage in the *Padshahnama* referring to a building commissioned by Shah Jahan in which the destitute and poor should "eat their food in those cells sheltered from the hardships of snow and rain". This was the inspiration for a new caravanserai complex constructed on the site to house a range of modern facilities required for contemporary visitors to Bagh-e Babur. Drawing on traditional built forms and brick-masonry techniques of the region, it houses an exhibition and information centre, offices, commercial outlets and public facilities.

The restoration of one of Afghanistan's most important historic sites and the largest public garden in Kabul has transformed the previously decaying and partially destroyed site into an authentic Mughal-era garden and a resource for the millions of inhabitants of the city. Following its conservation in 2008, Babur's Garden was added

Top left, the promenade at the base of the Queen's Palace is frequently used for large outdoor events, including the exhibition of local handicrafts.

Top right, public exhibitions held at the Queen's Palace attract thousands of Afghans from a wide cross-section of society.

Bottom left, a performance of the traditional *attan* dance during New Year festivities at Babur's Garden.

Bottom right, cultural programmes are frequently held within the various buildings or outdoor spaces of Babur's Garden.

to the tentative list of UNESCO World Heritage sites. Investments in conservation and rehabilitation continue to attract Afghan and international visitors to the garden and have generated significant employment among the neighbouring communities, whose own investments in self-built housing have been enhanced by infrastructure upgrading. An important secondary objective of this work has been the provision of over 735,000 workdays of employment for on average 350 skilled and unskilled labourers from the surrounding communities.

Conceived as royal property, the fortunes of Bagh-e Babur until the mid-twentieth century depended on investments made by Afghanistan's rulers. After the era of royal patronage, when the site became a public park, its gradual degradation bears out the challenge of meeting the costs of its upkeep from public funds. Realizing that the management and operations of the restored garden posed further challenges, an independent Trust was established jointly with local authorities in order to manage and operate the site. The seventy-five full-time staff members of the Bagh-e Babur Trust (BBT) has ensured that the garden remains accessible to the more than 5.3 million Afghan and international visitors since 2008 and that revenue collected through visits and the hire of facilities is reinvested towards the operation of the site. The establishment of the BBT and its successful management by an Afghan team with direct oversight by the Afghan authorities has provided an important precedent for the sustainable management and operations of historic sites across Afghanistan.

Many visitors to Bagh-e Babur remark that the site represents a symbol of cultural recovery in Afghanistan. The challenge continues to be that of finding a balance between the symbolic and the actual, to retain the unique character of the landscape and monuments while ensuring access to the public for recreation and education and contributing to the recovery of the wider area around the garden.

The restored Queen's Palace building and its landscaped courtyard provide high-quality facilities for a range of social, cultural and educational events.

# Burj-e Wazir Mausoleum

**Remains of the Burj-e Wazir, partially submerged beneath accumulated rubble.**

### HISTORY AND CHARACTERISTICS

The Burj-e Wazir, or Minister's Tower, is an imposing funerary structure located on a stone outcrop above the historic settlement of Gazurgah outside the northern perimeter walls of Babur's Garden in Kabul. Built in the eighteenth century (late Mughal era), the mausoleum is believed to contain the remains of a prominent local figure, as indicated by the discovery of an intricately carved, red-sandstone gravestone within the building and several other fine marble graves in the immediate area of the structure.

Typical of important masonry structures, four identical arched openings (*iwans*) lead to a small, domed square grave chamber at the centre of which a red-sandstone gravestone was excavated from beneath building rubble. Remains of large sections of painted and gilded stucco decorations were also discovered within the grave chamber. In-depth investigation of the building indicates that the masonry mausoleum may have been built on the foundations of a seventh-century multi-levelled Buddhist stupa, which still retains finely laid flat stonework on two of its external elevations. A theory further supported by the discovery of a stone arched opening leading to a small stone-domed space at the base of the stupa.

While the structure had been extensively damaged in the armed conflict in the early 1990s, photographs from the turn of the twentieth century show the tower in a ruined state. As the structure was further threatened by modern encroachments built using stone and fired bricks removed from the tower, conservation work started with the preparation of a detailed physical survey of the site.

### WORK UNDERTAKEN

In tandem with documentation work, a team of archaeologists was engaged to identify the remains of the Buddhist-era structure and to undertake excavations at the perimeter of the stupa in order to establish whether additional structures had been built adjoining the site. While excavations established that the structure had stood independently, it became clear that structural stabilization work of both the Buddhist-era structure and the Mughal-era funerary tower were required. A structural breast wall was built in areas where the finished stonework of the stupa had been destroyed, followed by the careful consolidation of finely laid stone elevations. In order to protect the site from the elements and to provide new structural 'piers' for the consolidation of remaining areas of brick masonry, it was decided to reconstruct the funerary tower on the basis of extensive physical and photographic evidence. New sections of

masonry were carefully laid adjacent to the original structure and treated in a manner that would enable visitors to distinguish between old and new brickwork. Once the arches and masonry dome had been rebuilt, a timber substructure was constructed and finished using galvanized metal sheeting. The site was further protected with the construction of a low stone-masonry wall topped with a steel railing. Rising above the village of Gazurgah, the restored Burj-e Wazir forms an imposing landmark in southern Kabul. The project also provided an excellent opportunity to train young conservation architects and a team of archaeologists in documentation, archaeology, restoration and project planning activities.

Top left, the restored funerary structure is located on a stone outcrop above Babur's Garden.

Top right, in order to prevent further damage to the original remains of the structure, collapsed sections of arches were rebuilt using traditional materials and techniques.

Above, detailed surveys of surviving areas of the structure enabled an accurate reconstruction of the monument.

Below, first-floor plan and section.

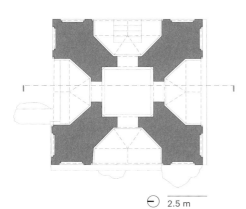

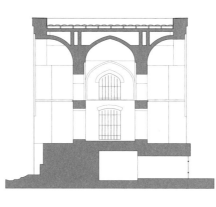

2.5 m

# TIMUR SHAH MAUSOLEUM

## HISTORY

One of the largest surviving Islamic monuments in central Kabul, the mausoleum of Timur Shah marks the grave of the son of Ahmad Shah Durrani, who effectively created the modern state of Afghanistan in the late eighteenth century. Born in 1746, Timur Shah served as governor of Herat before facing off a military challenge to the throne from his elder brother, and then moved his capital from Kandahar to Kabul. After his death in 1793, his son Zaman Shah laid him to rest in a garden on the banks of the Kabul River, but it was not until 1817 that the construction of the mausoleum began. Zaman Shah was supplanted by his brother Shah Shuja and work on the mausoleum, disrupted in the battle for succession, was never completed. As a result, the final finish of the outer dome remained incomplete and small areas of internal plasterwork are the only indication that the rough internal brickwork may have originally been intended as a sub-base for a final layer of decorated plaster finish. Photographs from the late nineteenth century show that the garden (*chahar-bagh*) in which the mausoleum of Timur Shah stood was by then much reduced in extent. In 1904, as part of efforts to modernize the capital, Habibullah Khan constructed a large secondary school, the first in the country, on land to the north-east of the mausoleum. The Habibia College formed part of a range of Neoclassical buildings that stretched in time along both banks of the Kabul River. In 1965, a section of this range was demolished and a municipal park created between the mausoleum of Timur Shah and the river.

## CHARACTERISTICS

Timur Shah's Mausoleum comprises an octagonal structure with two intersecting cross-axes organized on six levels. Above a crypt, in which the grave stands, is a square central space surrounded by an octagonal structure, with four double-height arches (*iwans*) on the main elevations. On the first floor, there are sixteen brick-vaulted spaces of varying size, encircling the central space, with a flat roof above, surrounding the sixteen-sided drum under the domes. Following the central Asian tradition, the mausoleum has an outer dome constructed on a high drum above a ribbed inner dome.

## WORK UNDERTAKEN

Surveys of the structure in 2002 revealed that part of the upper dome had partially collapsed and that rainwater had penetrated parts of the supporting drum. This

Opposite page, the construction of the Timur Shah Mausoleum was abandoned at the end of the 18th century and was then damaged during the conflict, until, in 2005, it was restored by AKTC.

Above, the large square *chahar-bagh*, within which Timur Shah's Mausoleum was constructed, has been steadily built upon since the early 20th century, 1879–80.

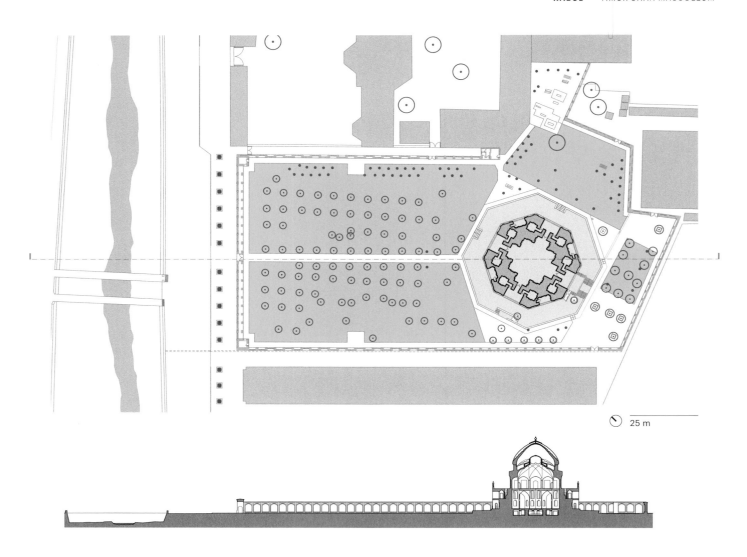

**Above, Timur Shah Mausoleum and Park, site plan and section.**

**Below, the remains of a public garden surrounding the mausoleum was occupied by temporary shops located within metal shipping containers.**

area was therefore the focus of the initial conservation work, once the damaged roof sheeting and timber structure had been removed. Examination of the upper dome revealed that it had been built in stages, using 'layers' of brick masonry laid in relatively weak lime mortar. After the erection of a bamboo platform over the lower dome, and installation of two temporary tension-reinforcement belts around the drum, a reinforced-concrete beam was poured around the inside, anchored into the brickwork with forty-eight stainless-steel anchors. Unstable sections of brickwork in the upper dome were removed, and repairs undertaken to match the original structure, using specially produced bricks laid in lime mortar. The original geometry, comprising six layers of brickwork at the springing, reducing to two at the apex, was reproduced in the repairs.

As the final external finish of the upper roof had originally remained incomplete, a new geometry was devised for its profile, based on a harmonic curve that matched the proportions of the main structure. A total of thirty-two laminated timber rafters, measuring up to thirteen metres, were produced to support a new 'shell' roof, which now spans the repaired dome. Timber boards were then screwed in a circumferential pattern over these rafters, prior to the fixing of galvanized sheeting.

While work proceeded on the main dome, repairs were carried out on the flat roofs and supporting vaults. Areas of facing brick on the elevations were also repaired, as

Above, the double-skin dome of the mausoleum had been damaged by artillery fire and required urgent conservation and reconstruction.

Left, teams of masons work to clean and repoint the exposed brick elevations of the mausoleum.

Right, the construction of a low octagonal platform around the mausoleum enabled the redirection of rainwater away from the foundations of the building.

Above, the repaired finial being raised to the apex of the dome.

Below, prior to the installation of galvanized iron sheeting, timber planks were fixed to rafters.

Right, curved rafters spanning the length of the masonry dome were constructed on site using laminated timber, lifted above the structure and installed by hand.

were the soffits of the main vaults, where there was high-quality brick masonry. In order to protect the lower sections of masonry and facilitate public access, a seven-metre-wide brick platform was built around the mausoleum.

During the course of the conservation work, negotiations took place for the re-location of the two hundred or more informal traders who had encroached on what had been the garden around the mausoleum. A range of options was explored aimed at incorporating the traders into a new development in or adjoining the garden of the mausoleum, but these were not endorsed by Kabul Municipality, who relocated the traders in 2005. Since then, a perimeter wall has been constructed to protect the site, which has been planted with an orchard of mulberry trees — matching those seen in historic photographs of the site — and laid out with paths for pedestrian access through the garden.

Since its restoration, the central space of the mausoleum has been the setting for lectures, seminars and exhibitions, and a recent agreement with the authorities has established that the space and reclaimed garden will be used for cultural events on a regular basis. Despite the challenging physical and institutional context in which the project was realized, it stands as an example of how an important historic monu-ment can help to encourage a wider process of regeneration in a fast-changing urban setting.

Left, decorated column bases were originally constructed using shaped bricks cut to size.

Right, since its restoration, the mausoleum continues to be used for appropriate public functions.

Below, the restored mausoleum is one of the most iconic monuments in central Kabul, and the surrounding park provides much-needed green space in a congested part of the city.

# KABUL OLD CITY PROGRAMME

## INTRODUCTION

Historically defined as the area contained by the citadel of Bala Hissar and the Sher Darwaza Mountain to the east and south and the Kabul River to the west and north, the Old City of Kabul is composed of historic residential and commercial quarters. Of these, the residential quarter of Asheqan wa Arefan is particularly important to the history of urbanism and the rich building tradition of the region. As in other quarters of the Old City, families of widely differing means have historically lived side by side, with no evident grouping of homes of the wealthy in a particular area. In places where related families inhabited adjacent homes, sections of alleys had doors installed to enable them to be closed off for defensive reasons.

While there is an ingenious variety in the pattern of building, most traditional homes centre on a secluded courtyard, with summer quarters oriented to the north and a south-facing area for use in the winter. Many homes have half-basements used for storage, and constructed of stone masonry, as are the foundations. Walls at the ground-floor level are mainly of mud brick or monolithic compacted earth (*pakhsa*), while a timber-framed system with mud-brick infill (*sinj*) is commonly used for the upper levels. Traditionally, the main courtyard elevations comprised carved timber shutters that could, according to the season and need, be raised vertically within a timber-frame structure. Flat roofs are supported on uncut timber joists, and finished with a mud-straw finish (*kahgil*). In the absence of written records, it is the decorative style of plaster or woodwork that provides clues to the age of a dwelling.

Based on initial surveys of surviving historic homes in Asheqan wa Arefan during 2002, several were identified for possible conservation, based primarily on an assessment of their architectural value and vulnerability. Over the subsequent seven-year period, more than twelve important residential buildings, a large public garden and fifteen historic public buildings — including mosques, shrines, madrasas, traditional hammams, and educational facilities — were systematically restored by AKTC in the war-affected quarters of Asheqan wa Arefan, Chindawol, Pakhtafurushi, Shanasazi and Kuche Kharabat. Collectively these historic quarters are home to more than 30,000 people in one of the most densely populated areas of Kabul.

In addition to the conservation of important architectural heritage, this work has enabled the AKTC team to both deepen their understanding of traditional construction techniques and to develop the skills of a cadre of craftsmen. More than a hundred carpenters, plasterers and masons, trained by AKTC, many of whom live in the

Opposite page, the Peshawari Serai is one of few remaining historic commercial premises in the Old City of Kabul.

Above, limited public services and an absence of investment in infrastructure has contributed to poor living conditions in the Old City. Significant time is spent collecting and transporting potable water.

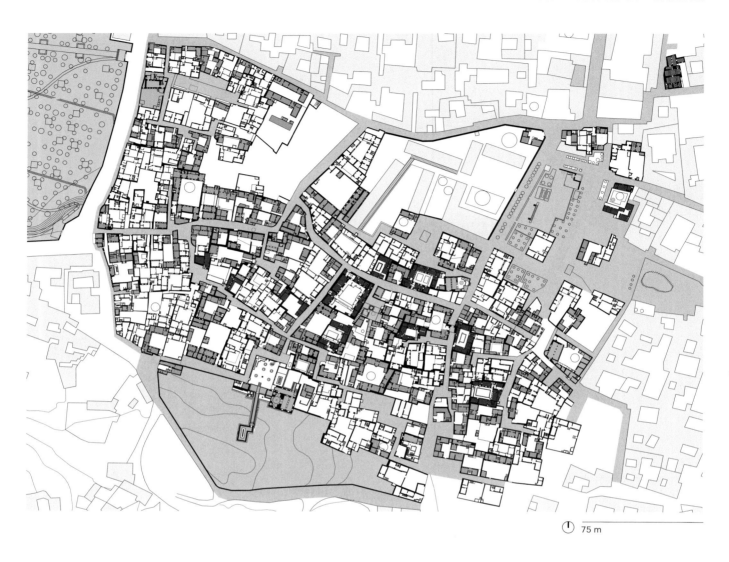

**Above, Asheqan wa Arefan neighbourhood: conservation and upgrading improvements.**

◻ Conservation of religious buildings
◼ Conservation of public buildings
◼ Full-scale residential conservation
◼ Small-scale residential repairs
◼ Building advice
◼ Public access and infrastructure improvements
◻ Open public space
◻ Open green space rehabilitation

**Right, socio-economic surveys conducted within the Old City enable a better understanding of living conditions.**

75 m

Old City, continue to find regular employment — often engaged by local residents for the regular upkeep of their properties.

Much of the fragile stock of traditional housing in the Old City is subdivided and residents, half of whom are tenants, have access to only the most rudimentary services, due to decades of under-investment and neglect, as well as more recent conflict-related damage. In order to address the abject conditions facing the majority of residents in this area, AKTC has provided sustained support for the repair or construction of drains, paving of alleyways and streets, and safer water supplies, improving living conditions and extending the benefits of the conservation programme to nearly 15,000 inhabitants of the Old City.

In parallel with physical restoration activities, a system of small household grants was instituted to assist house owners who had embarked on repairs of traditional or infill homes, but might not otherwise be able to afford to complete such work. In addition to making available essential materials and tools, on-site building advice has been offered in more than eighty instances to owners through this scheme. Aimed at ensuring that the surviving stock of traditional houses does not deteriorate further, and that living conditions (including facilities such as bathrooms) within homes are improved, the household grants have had a significant impact within the neighbourhood.

As important as the physical outcome of conservation and rehabilitation work in the Old City has been, the opportunities provided permitted residents to develop their skills and to find employment. As part of a vocational training initiative aimed at improving family livelihoods, more than 1500 women from the neighbourhood have attended courses in tailoring, embroidery and weaving, along with classes in basic literacy. Over the course of the programme, more than 350,000 workdays of employment was generated for skilled and unskilled labour, most of whom were selected from among communities in the Old City.

**Left, the presence of wholesale markets in the Old City has accelerated speculative commercial development, often resulting in historic fabric being destroyed and replaced with modern constructions.**

**Right, a typical street in a residential area in Asheqan wa Arefan with timber screens on the upper floors of historic, enclosed, courtyard houses facing outwards.**

# Asheqan wa Arefan Shrine

The Asheqan wa Arefan graveyard is one of the largest burial sites in the Old City of Kabul and the location of one of its most important shrines.

## HISTORY

The historic residential neighbourhood of Asheqan wa Arefan, named after the graves of two brothers reputed to have introduced Islam to Kabul during the third Islamic Caliphate, in the seventh century, is located directly to the west of the citadel of Bala Hissar in the Old City of Kabul. Historic shrines where revered figures are buried become places of pilgrimage where people offer prayers. They are often associated with healing sicknesses or mental conditions, helping the impoverished or offering protection to the weak.

As with other burial sites of figures revered in Afghanistan, the area around the shrine of Asheqan wa Arefan — translated from Dari as meaning "lovers and mystics" — has been transformed over time into an expansive graveyard populated with both the tombs of the well-to-do and the simple graves of the poor. People continue to visit the shrine to offer prayers or pay their respects to this day and the site is important to the religious practices and social customs of the community. Together with an adjacent mosque, the historic complex is home to an important Sufi brotherhood.

## CHARACTERISTICS

With the exception of a two-storey summer and winter mosque built to the west of the shrine in the early twentieth century, the remaining structures of the complex are single-storey, wood-frame (*sinj*) constructions, with extensive use of woodwork, including lattice screens, carved columns and decorated wooden ceilings. The complex is located on a promontory above the Asheqan wa Arefan neighbourhood and is comprised of three distinct levels, the lowest being its courtyard and entrance, where the grave of Khwaja Abdus Samad (Aref) is located. The next level, an open north-facing portico, is accessed from a set of stairs in the courtyard and leads, via an elongated semi-submerged corridor lined with fine wooden lattice screens, to the grave of Khwaja Abdus Salam (Asheq) — located at the highest level of the complex and in the midst of the graveyard to the south of the site.

## WORK UNDERTAKEN

The conservation project was vital in building confidence within the community during the initial stage of AKTC's programme in the Old City of Kabul in 2002. Building on the experience gained during the conservation of smaller mosques in the area, work was initiated on the Asheqan wa Arefan Shrine complex in late 2005.

Left, a carpenter stripping layers of modern paint from the wooden decoration of the shrine.

Middle, conservation of the shrine was carried out by craftsmen familiar with traditional construction materials.

Bottom left, intricate timber latticework screens (*jali*).

Bottom right, latticework screens were carefully cleaned and repaired, before being treated with linseed oil and reinstalled.

0.25 m

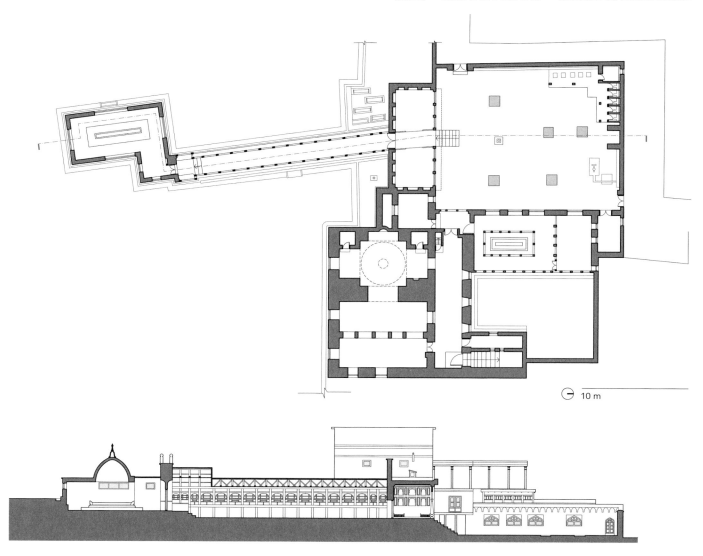

**Asheqan wa Arefan Shrine, ground-floor plan
and section.**

Found to be in a poor state of repair, the distinctive colonnaded entrance and passage that leads to the grave of Khwaja Abdus Salam (Asheq) required extensive structural repairs, while the lower grave of Khwaja Abdus Samad (Aref), which retains its traditional wooden enclosure, was re-roofed, as were those of the adjoining summer and winter mosques. A stone retaining wall was built along the length of the corridor leading to the grave of Khwaja Abdus Salam (Asheq) in order to protect the timber screens, which were cleaned and repaired, along with the finely carved timber entrance door. During the course of repairs to the plasterwork of the portico, a series of decorated plaster niches were uncovered and restored. The entire roof over the lower grave of Khwaja Abdus Samad (Aref) was rebuilt and its internal plaster and marble decoration restored. Extensive repairs were also carried out on the roof of the adjacent summer mosque, which retained fine decorated plasterwork on the prayer niche ($mihrab$), the domed winter mosque beneath, and its long corridor.

The courtyard of the shrine, which provides an important focus for residents of the area and visitors alike, was landscaped and improvements made to the public water supply and ablution facilities located at its perimeter. Rehabilitation work was completed in late 2007 and the site was transferred back to local custodians who continue to maintain and operate the site.

Above, the entrance portico to Asheqan wa Arefan Shrine, with its series of decorated plaster niches, was uncovered during the course of repairs and restored.

Left, visitors to the shrine are led into a long corridor decorated with timber screens before ascending to the burial chamber of Khwaja Abdus Salam.

Right, an engraved *hamsa* (Hand of Fatima) attached to the main entrance of the shrine.

# Uzbekha Mosque

**Children collect water from the courtyard of the Uzbekha Mosque before its restoration.**

## HISTORY AND CHARACTERISTICS

While the history of the Uzbekha Mosque remains vague, the construction located in the centre of the Asheqan wa Arefan neighbourhood probably dates to the late nineteenth century, when there would have been a significant presence of the Uzbek community in the area. The typology of the building is typical of a historic mosque structure found in Kabul, with an upper summer prayer space (originally open to the east) divided by two rows of decorated timber columns above an enclosed and well-insulated winter mosque on the ground floor. As with other mosques in the Old City, the courtyard is used as a temporary prayer space in warmer months. In addition to providing water for ablutions, the well located in the courtyard of the mosque is an important focus for the surrounding community.

## WORK UNDERTAKEN

In order to develop an understanding of traditional construction techniques, physical surveys were conducted on the Uzbekha Mosque — a site that had been extensively damaged due to conflict. As one of the first conservation projects carried out by AKTC in the Old City of Kabul in 2002, the engagement enabled the AKTC team to build a constructive relationship with the recently resettled community, who became key advocates of the wider conservation programme. When conservation work began, few local craftsmen were found to have sufficient experience in the traditional building techniques employed in the Uzbekha Mosque. It was thus necessary to embark on an intensive programme of on-the-job training for masons, plasterers and carpenters.

During the course of initial repairs to the timber roof of the mosque, intricate moulded plaster decoration was found on the walls — hidden beneath layers of modern plaster and oil-based paint — and preserved using traditional techniques. Careful removal of paint from timber columns and arches supporting the roof revealed finely carved, wooden, decorative elements, which were left exposed and sealed using locally available linseed oil.

Although not an original feature of the historic mosque, glazed timber screens on the second-floor courtyard elevation of the mosque were repaired and reinstalled in order to enable use of the upper prayer space during colder months. The traditional hypocaust heating system (*taba khana*) under the floor of the winter mosque was also rebuilt and reinstated, using flat stone plates laid over low brick walls. In addition to the reconstruction of rooms around the courtyard, required for storage and

to house the custodian of the site, the water supply was improved and facilities for ablution were upgraded.

The restoration of the Uzbekha Mosque was completed in early 2005 with the landscaping and paving of the courtyards and has since been in use by the community.

**Top left, the restored Uzbekha Mosque provides space for worship and consultative community gatherings.**

**Top right, damaged areas of the timber ceiling of the summer mosque were replaced.**

**Above, sections of fine plaster decoration, uncovered during conservation work, were cleaned and repaired.**

**Below, first-floor plan and section.**

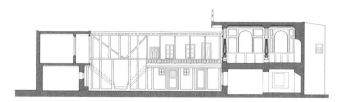

5 m

# Sedukan Mosque

The Sedukan Mosque continued to be used by the local community prior to restoration.

### HISTORY AND CHARACTERISTICS

Located in the Asheqan wa Arefan neighbourhood, the small historic Sedukan Mosque retains key characteristics of other nineteenth-century community mosques in the Old City of Kabul, including a colonnaded open summer prayer area built above a ground-floor mosque with traditional under-floor heating for use in winter. The name Sedukan (three-shops) is most probably a geographic reference to several commercial premises located at a junction of narrow pedestrian streets adjacent to the mosque. The two-storey building is accessed through a small courtyard lined with an ablution space and room for the custodian of the site. A well, located next to the entrance, provides water for worshippers and potable water for the wider community. As with other mosques, where religious donations or *waqfs* provide for the upkeep and maintenance of the buildings, large areas of the *mihrab* wall of the upper summer mosque were painted over time. Based on the deeply rooted religious beliefs of Afghans and the provision of funds for the upkeep of religious sites, the vast majority of historic monuments that remain unaffected by war or lack of maintenance throughout Afghanistan are those serving religious purposes; such as mosques, shrines, or madrasas.

Constructed using a mixed masonry and wood-frame (*sinj*) technique, with a flat timber roof supported on two rows of decorated timber posts, the Sedukan Mosque was in poor condition at the time of surveys conducted in 2003.

### WORK UNDERTAKEN

Following a detailed physical survey and documentation of the building, which highlighted the elaborate carved craftsmanship on the internal wooden posts, conservation work began in 2004. This entailed rebuilding part of the collapsed southern wall of the mosque, followed by the removal of accumulated earth from its roof and replacement of damaged rafters. Re-roofing work entailed laying wooden decking above the rafters before the application of a layer of waterproofing material, followed by a thick layer of compacted mud (*ghoragil*) and finished with a finer layer of mud-straw plaster (*kahgil*). Sufficient slopes for water run-off were provided and downspouts were constructed redirecting snowmelt and rainwater into drains located in the courtyard.

Structural consolidation work included stabilization of stone foundations and replacement of infill brickwork where required. Stripping of interior and exterior paintwork revealed fine details of the original timber craftsmanship, which were repaired

0.5 m

Top left, protective mud plaster being applied to external masonry elevations.

Top right, clearance of debris was followed by the reconstruction of damaged sections of the roof over the mosque.

Bottom left, detailed drawing of intricately carved timber columns and arches at the Sedukan Mosque.

Bottom right, a carpenter at work repairing woodwork elements.

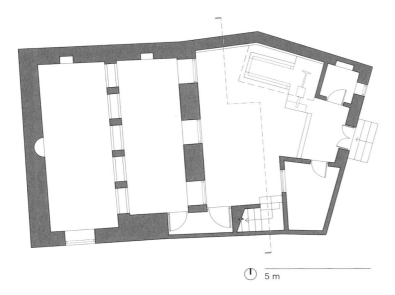

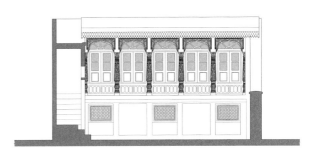

①  5 m

Above, ground-floor plan and section.

Below, left, the small community mosque is frequented by residents of the Asheqan wa Arefan neighbourhood, who contribute to its upkeep.

Right, restoration work included the reconstruction of the roof and internal spaces, followed by the cleaning and repairing of the decorated woodwork.

and preserved. This was followed by the repair and replacement of damaged timber elements, rehabilitation of ablution facilities, interior flooring and the paving of the courtyard with fired brick. Linseed oil treatment was applied to all exposed areas of timber for protection. Fine mud-based plasters (*simgil*) were used for interior and exterior wall finishing.

The conservation work offered craftsmen an excellent opportunity to develop their skills in repairing moulded plaster and carved timber decoration. Surveyors and site architects were also able to benefit from practical first-hand experience on the project.

Above, the main elevation of the restored mosque.

Below, a repaired timber lattice screen installed at the entrance to the mosque.

# Chuqurak Mosque

**The Chuqurak Mosque was in risk of collapse prior to restoration.**

**HISTORY AND CHARACTERISTICS**

The Chuqurak Mosque is situated on the southern edge of Asheqan wa Arefan neighbourhood in the Old City of Kabul and represents a typical example of a small community mosque embedded in the historic fabric of the area. While it is difficult to determine a date of construction, based on the building technique and quality of craftsmanship, it was probably built in the early part of the twentieth century. Historic structures built in the Old City of Kabul using traditional construction techniques (*sinj*) and building materials available locally require constant upkeep. Over time, this leads to gradual transformations in historic structures, including expansion of existing buildings or demolition and construction of new sections, making it difficult to provide accurate attributions.

As with many other historic structures in this area, the building had been damaged during inter-factional fighting and had since fallen into disrepair. Having seen other examples of conservation in the neighbourhood, community members approached AKTC requesting support for the rehabilitation of their mosque as part of a multi-year Area Development Programme.

**WORK UNDERTAKEN**

Conservation work commenced in 2005 with the clearance of debris from the site, making possible a detailed physical survey. Measures required to restore the building included stabilization of stone foundations, removal of excess earth from above the roofing allowing the replacement of damaged rafters, and reassembly of the structural timber frame and replacement of infill brickwork where required. Structural work was followed by the cleaning, repair and replacement of sections of damaged timber decorative elements and the partitioning of the upper floor to create living quarters for the custodian of the site. Internal elevations of the mosque were levelled by applying traditional mud-straw plaster (*kahgil*) and finished with a fine mud plaster (*simgil*).

External work required rebuilding of the boundary walls, which also included a small corner shop, and construction of toilets and ablution facilities for worshippers. Landscaping activities entailed laying stone paving and planting in the courtyard and the digging of a well for water supply. As part of the restoration process the Chuqurak Mosque and other sites restored by AKTC have been registered as protected monuments with the Department of Historic Monuments of the Ministry of Information and Culture. The building continues to be used by the community.

Top left, visible from the street, the restored mosque provides a glimpse into the historic character of the Old City.

Top right, restoration work entailed structural repairs to the timber-frame construction of the mosque.

Middle left, the external perimeter wall of the mosque was reconstructed to incorporate ablution facilities.

Middle right, traditional mud plaster was used to finish external elevations.

Bottom, ground-floor plan and section.

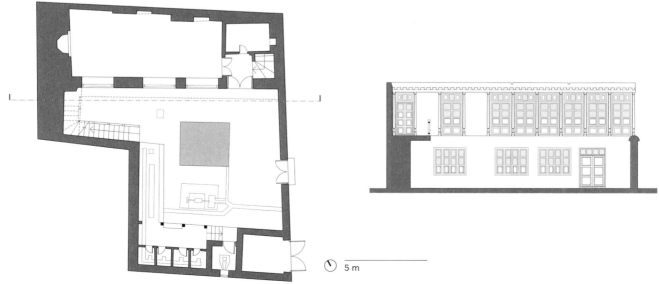

5 m

# Dewan Begi Mosque

**The Dewan Begi Mosque continued to be used by the community prior to restoration.**

### HISTORY AND CHARACTERISTICS

The Dewan Begi Mosque is situated on the western side of a busy shopping street which is the main access road to the residential neighbourhood of Asheqan wa Arefan. Interviews with local elders indicate that the word Dewan (legal court) and Begi (an Uzbek name) may suggest that the mosque was named after a local judge of Uzbek descent named Beg. The complex consists of several spaces for worship, located within an older (possibly late-nineteenth-century) single-storey building on the western boundary of the site and a separate two-storey building on the northern side — which both open onto to a large courtyard with ablution facilities and a central green space.

The single-storey mosque has an unusual typology when compared to other mosques from a similar date due to the fact that both the winter and summer prayer spaces are located on the ground floor. In order to access the winter mosque at the back of the building, worshippers have to pass through the summer mosque. Architecturally, the double insulated space of the winter mosque makes it easier to heat, while the open wood and glass facade of the summer mosque allows ventilation for cooling purposes. The fact that the spaces can be used separately is indicated by the construction of a second prayer niche (*mihrab*) in the wall separating the two spaces.

### WORK UNDERTAKEN

Survey and documentation of the Dewan Begi Mosque started in 2007. Damaged during the conflict, the roof of the open prayer space situated on the upper level of the two-storey building had collapsed and required comprehensive reconstruction. This involved incorporating existing wooden posts with newly constructed posts and rafters and finishing the roof with protective compacted mud and mud-straw plaster. The staircase leading to the second floor was upgraded and secondary prayer spaces on the ground floor were consolidated and made usable.

Conservation work undertaken on the older one-storey structure to the west of the site included the removal of accumulated debris from above the roof and the systematic repair and replacement of damaged rafters. This was followed by the application of protective layers of mud plaster and the installation of downspouts for redirection of rainwater and snowmelt into the courtyard. Several layers of paint applied to the external elevations of the one-storey building were carefully removed, revealing the mosque's original timber fenestration, which was repaired and preserved.

Internal spaces were cleared of debris and load-bearing walls were repaired and consolidated using wooden ties before being finished with a fine mud plaster (*simgil*). A damp-proof layer was installed beneath the flooring, which was finished using a traditional mixture of compacted mud and gypsum and made ready for the laying of furnishings. Newly produced timber doors and windows were installed and sealed using linseed oil. As with other mosques restored by AKTC, provisions were made for the construction of ablution facilities and a deep well that provides water for both worshippers and the community. Landscaping work included paving a large section of the courtyard with local stone.

**Left, the upper floor of a later addition to the mosque, which had collapsed during the civil conflict, was reconstructed using traditional techniques and materials.**

**Right, a previous two-storey addition to the mosque provided space for worship and living facilities for the custodian of the site, seen here after reconstruction.**

**Below, ground-floor plan and section.**

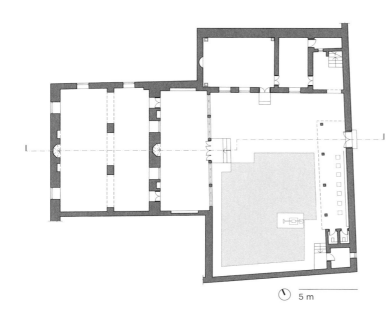

5 m

# Chahardah Masoom Shrine

**The Chahardah Masoom Shrine was first surveyed in 2004 prior to its restoration by AKTC.**

### HISTORY

The Chahardah Masoom Shrine is situated at the end of Kuche Kharabat, the traditional 'musicians' quarter' that adjoins the historic citadel of Kabul, Bala Hissar. Still an important place of pilgrimage, the name of the shrine suggests that fourteen graves might originally have existed on the site. It is said that a historic Qur'an had been kept in the shrine and, during an epidemic in the reign of Amir Abdur Rahman, was carried on an elephant through the city, resulting in an end to the plague affecting the inhabitants. Possibly as a recreation of this occasion, an important religious relic stored within the shrine is carried through the Old City during religious occasions (Nawrouz and Muharram) in a ceremony called "Alam Kashi".

At the centre of the shrine, there is an octagonal platform bearing four children's graves, enclosed by an intricate lattice screen made of timber. Along with other graves that lie within this internal space, the four graves might have formed part of a larger cemetery that still extends to the south and east. Over time, the association of the shrine with small children has meant that women who are not able to conceive children offer prayers at the shrine, while others with ill or disabled children pray for their recovery.

### CHARACTERISTICS

There are indications that the original shrine, built at the base of a steep rocky hillside containing the children's graves, was expanded at a later date to include a separate space for prayer to the north accessed by a large staircase. The original wooden screens (*pataii*) of the shrine area were retained as internal screens when the building was expanded. An arched opening links the shrine space with an elongated prayer space with a prayer niche (*mihrab*) on its western facing wall. Wooden screens are repeated on the northern elevation of the mosque facing the courtyard, where there is an arched brick-masonry building used for cooking food (*langar khana*) during religious festivals.

The present structure of the shrine, probably dating from the late nineteenth century, was badly damaged during the conflict that raged through this neighbourhood when many homes and religious buildings were looted and burned.

### WORK UNDERTAKEN

Rehabilitation work on the Chahardah Masoom Shrine began in 2007 with extensive surveys of its existing state. During the initial stages of conservation work, the roof

Top left, due to extensive structural damage, the roof of the shrine was rebuilt using traditional building techniques.

Top right, damaged sections of the timber screens were removed for repair.

Middle left, assembled as a 'kit of parts', large sections of the woodwork were carefully dismantled, repaired and reinstalled as part of restoration activities.

Middle right, carpenters work to reconstruct missing sections of an intricate latticework screen.

Bottom left, detailed drawing of intricately carved timber screens.

Bottom right, restoration work entailed the careful removal of layers of modern paint, revealing the natural colour and texture of the shrine's fine timber woodwork.

0.5 m

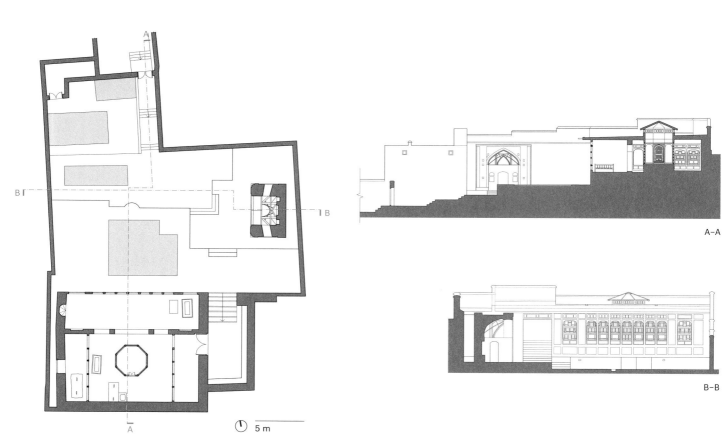

A–A

B–B

5 m

was stripped and key structural timber elements were dismantled to allow for repairs. This permitted the reconstruction of damaged stone walling on the east and south walls of the shrine, and the improvement of drainage from the steep hillside above the complex.

The removal of the roof made it possible to dismantle the central screen, parts of which were cleaned and repaired before being reinstalled. Once the base of the structural frames (most of which proved to be affected by rot) had been replaced, it was possible to refit the rafters over the entire building, fix timber boarding and lay a traditional earth finish prior to the first snowfall. Internal stone elevations of the shrine area were repaired and pointed using a lime-based mortar. Two sections of wooden screens (*pataii*) to the east and west of the octagonal enclosure of the shrine were cleaned. Structural consolidation work entailed the repair of sections of the brick-masonry partition between the shrine and the prayer area to the north, which, together with repair work on the *mihrab* wall, was finished using gypsum plaster. Layers of paint were removed from the main external elevation of the building and the wooden fenestration was repaired and preserved using locally available linseed oil. Internal floor areas of the building were finished with paved brick.

The last stage of conservation work entailed the restoration of the *langar khana* (kitchen), which included the stabilization of stone foundations and repair of the damaged sections of brickwork on its walls and dome. Compatible bricks were produced and used to repair destroyed sections of the building, resulting in the restoration of its original character. With conservation work completed, the courtyard area was paved using local stone. The provision of a well and the upgrading of existing ablution facilities rendered the site usable by worshippers.

Opposite page, above, ground-floor plan and sections. Below, in addition to the conservation of the shrine, physical work included the rehabilitation of the terraced landscape.

Left, built into the mountain, residents of the Kuche Kharabat area seek respite in warmer months by visiting the shrine.

Right, view of the restored octagonal lattice-screen chamber housing several small graves.

# Goldasta Mosque

**The abandoned ruins of the Goldasta Mosque
prior to conservation.**

## HISTORY

Located in the Tandoorsazi quarter — the part of the Old City where traditional clay ovens were once made — the Goldasta Mosque is an exquisite early nineteenth-century religious complex that draws on a range of regional decorative influences. The name Goldasta literally means "an arrangement of flowers", which may be a reference to the double-column cusped-arch opening at the entrance of the structure, which resembles a floral arrangement. Despite the damage wrought during inter-factional fighting, the Goldasta Mosque was protected by local residents. Since their return to the area, these people prevented the looting of the valuable timber elements and further damage to the plaster decoration. With barely the resources to undertake repairs to their war-damaged homes, however, resettling residents did not have the means to restore their mosque, which continues to provide an important focus for the community.

## CHARACTERISTICS

Effectively comprised of a summer and a winter prayer space, the single-storey mosque was built using a mix of mud and fired-brick masonry, and roofed by timber rafters over which a traditional earthen roof was laid. The main prayer area, which would have been used in the winter months, lies along the western side of the building, with a central prayer niche (*mihrab*) that retains fine plaster decoration and an inscribed marble panel. Most of the roof over this area has collapsed, resulting in damage to the external masonry walls. The summer prayer space is an open-terraced veranda accessed by a staircase from the courtyard. This space is enclosed by a fine, timber, double-column colonnade, which has survived largely intact. This area retained part of its roof, together with the characteristic diagonally laid timber ceiling of the era, as well as traces of the nineteenth-century moulded and carved plasterwork.

Unlike other more typical mosques, there is extensive use of carved or cut marble within the building, including bases of timber columns and inlay in the high wooden skirting that lines the walls of the summer and winter prayer spaces. Surveys indicate that designs on the marble slabs inlaid within the skirting may have been salvaged from other historic sites and recycled for use in the mosque. The reuse of architectural elements or materials is common in the Old City of Kabul and other historic areas.

Top left, carpenters work on site, carrying out repairs to the fine double-column colonnade enclosing the summer prayer area.

Top right, construction of timber ceiling over the summer prayer area.

Bottom left, preparation of a plaster mould for use to repair damaged areas of decoration.

Bottom right, intricate plaster reliefs being cleaned and repaired.

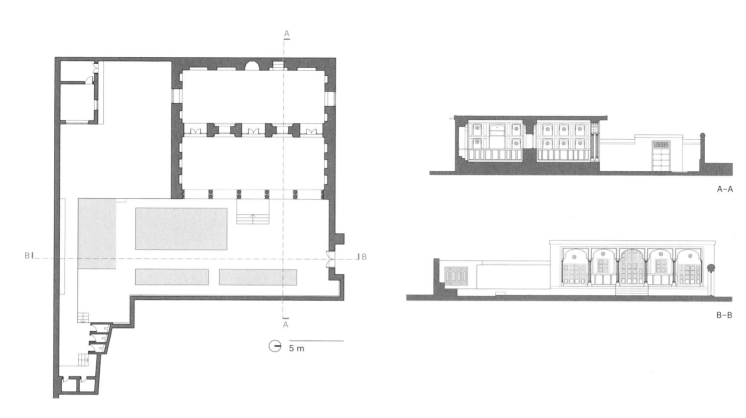

**Above, ground-floor plan and sections.**

**Below, detail of the double-column capitals and cusped arches built using local cedar wood.**

## WORK UNDERTAKEN

Following initial clearance of rubble and the storage of reusable building elements and materials from the Goldasta Mosque, the entire structure was surveyed and documented in detail. The first stage of conservation work entailed removal of damaged and unstable parts of the brick-masonry walling, followed by essential repairs and consolidation using fired bricks. At this stage, detached sections of decorated gypsum plaster were removed from the internal surfaces of walls, before being documented and safely stored.

Double rows of timber beams (*katiba*) were fixed along the top of all structural load-bearing walls in order to mitigate damage in case of seismic activity, after which roof beams were relaid and fixed in place. Timber boards were then laid across these beams providing a decking for the application of a traditional layered mud-straw roof. The timber colonnade, which had settled as a result of damage to its foundations, was subsequently dismantled using temporary supports, repaired, and reattached to its marble column bases. Timber boarding (some of which was retrieved from the original structure) was fixed to the ceilings of the winter and summer prayer areas. With the structure of the mosque repaired, conservation focused on the restoration of the internal finishes, including extensive areas of moulded plaster. In addition to cleaning and repairing existing areas of plaster, new moulds were prepared and used to replaster areas that had been completely destroyed. When the bulk of the internal plasterwork was restored, the floor of the external prayer area was paved with fired bricks, and the internal space paved with traditional lime concrete. The construction of ablution facilities, a water well, and a separate space for the custodian of the site preceded the paving of pedestrian areas in the courtyard using locally available stone.

In reference to the name of the mosque, areas were prepared directly opposite the main elevation of the building for the planting of beds of roses.

Conservation activities provided an opportunity for on-the-job-training for craftsmen and Afghan professionals in traditional building practices and techniques.

Above, view of the restored mosque showing the elevated summer prayer area.

Below, view of the restored mosque showing timber arches and plaster decorated niches.

# Pakhtafurushi Madrasa

**Pakhtafurushi Mosque prior to conservation.**

## HISTORY AND CHARACTERISTICS

The Pakhtafurushi Madrasa was built in the early twentieth century as an extension to one of the largest communal mosques in the Old City of Kabul and takes its name from a complex of 'cotton bazaars' located adjacent to the site. Built around a large courtyard planted with mulberry trees, two single and double ranges of fifty-two interconnected spaces — built using brick-masonry domes — had nearly all collapsed when the complex was surveyed in 2003. With large openings towards the courtyard, skylights built into domes and clerestory windows where possible, the internal spaces of the madrasa benefit from an abundance of natural light making it an ideal place for study. The massive masonry walls provide insulating thermal mass and the high spaces of the construction, with several openings, enable rapid ventilation — both features ideally suited to the climate of Kabul where temperatures fluctuate significantly between seasons.

## WORK UNDERTAKEN

An agreement was signed with the Ministry of Hajj and Religious Affairs in 2005 for the madrasa's restoration, with the intention that it should serve the surrounding neighbourhood as an early childhood centre — incorporating religious education and possibly health services. A second building attached to the north-west corner of the main mosque, containing toilets and ablution facilities, had been identified as being in need of essential repair and reconstruction work.

Focusing on the structural stabilization of the partially destroyed structure, rehabilitation work entailed consolidation of stone foundations, repair to networks of arches supporting the domes, and ultimately the reconstruction of a majority of all fifty-two domes in fired brick using traditional masonry techniques. Once the domes were constructed, an external layer of lime mortar was applied in order to waterproof the building. Rainwater and snowmelt were redirected into downspouts and a channel was built in the courtyard that contained and enabled the flow of water away from the building. Newly produced timber windows and doors were installed in existing arched openings and the external gypsum plaster decoration was restored using traditional techniques. Internal spaces and the courtyard were paved with durable fired brick, laid in slopes to direct water towards surface drains.

The final stage of work entailed cleaning and repairs to the public ablution facilities, the existing septic tank and surrounding areas to the west of the toilet block. Additional remedial repairs were carried out on the roof of the adjacent main mosque

in order to stabilize the structure and prevent further deterioration. Since completion of work in 2007, the madrasa is being used as a facility for the religious education of some 250 youths. About 150 of these students live in adjacent neighbourhoods, while the madrasa provides boarding for the remaining students whose families live outside Kabul.

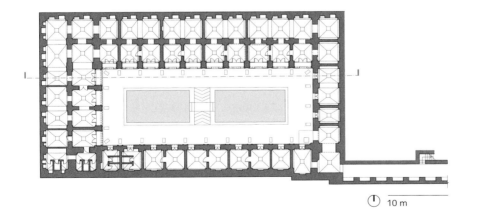

10 m

Top, used by local children for religious education, the restored madrasa is organized around a central courtyard planted with mulberry trees.

Above, built using thick masonry walls and domes, the internal restored spaces of the madrasa are ideally suited to the climatic conditions of Kabul.

Left, ground-floor plan and section.

# Shanasazi Mosque and Hammam Complex

**Above, the ruined Shanasazi Hammam was being used as a waste dumping site before its restoration.**

**Below, left abandoned due to its condition, the Shanasazi Mosque required extensive structural repairs.**

### HISTORY AND CHARACTERISTICS

Located in the area of the Old City associated with the production of wooden combs (*shana-sazi*), the conservation of the Shanasazi Mosque and Hammam complex formed part of a wider programme of work undertaken by AKTC in the Shanasazi quarter of the Old City. The Shahnasazi Mosque is believed to originally date from the late eighteenth century and consists of the main mosque building, an outdoor summer mosque attached to its southern facade and a smaller building, which can be accessed via a separate courtyard on the eastern boundary. A second two-storey building accessed from the east is used as additional prayer space and a religious education facility. Together with the traditional Shanasazi Hammam, located adjacent to the northern wall of the mosque, the complex provides much-needed services for the community. Traditional bathhouses, or hammams, play an important role in urban centres across the region, where few homes traditionally had washing facilities, causing residents to rely on communal spaces. With the provision of piped water to homes, the demand for these facilities decreased, but a significant proportion of families who live in the overcrowded conditions associated with historic quarters still do not have access to adequate washing facilities at home.

The Shanasazi Hammam follows a typical configuration of semi-submerged rooms grouped around two major brick-domed spaces, which would have been kept at different temperatures, together making up the communal bathing areas. A series of open tanks from which water would be scooped by bathers is placed between these central spaces. Sourced from a well on the site, water is heated in a large bronze vessel situated over an *atish khana* (literally, fire-room), a subterranean space beneath one of the outer walls of the bathhouse, where wood fires are lit. Heat and smoke from the *atish khana* is led through a hypocaust system of masonry ducts (*taba khana*) running under the main spaces of the hammam, which serves to maintain the temperature and humidity that is characteristic of such traditional bathhouses.

### WORK UNDERTAKEN: MOSQUE

Following a detailed physical survey of the mosque building in 2009, structural repair work was undertaken entailing the strengthening and stabilization of stone foundations, the rebuilding of collapsed masonry walls, and reconstruction of the roofing structure. During removal of timber wainscoting and ceiling woodwork, more than twenty-five carved timber joists dating from an earlier mosque on this site were discovered together with white marble column bases in the Mughal style. The main

elevation of the mosque, containing intricately carved timber columns and arched fenestration, was carefully repaired *in situ*. Later additions on the main elevation and internal walls of the mosque were removed, revealing original characteristics of wooden and plaster decorative elements that were systematically conserved. Exposed sections of masonry walls were finished using traditional fine mud plaster (*simgil*) and gypsum plaster applied to the *mihrab* niche. The internal floors were levelled and a lime-based mortar was applied as a moisture-proof finish, enabling the custodians of the mosque to install locally procured furnishings in the area. In the courtyard, several Mughal-era, marble, column bases unearthed during excavations were incorporated in new stone paving. Ablutions and toilet facilities were built and an existing well was upgraded on the perimeter of the courtyard.

In 2011, repairs were completed to a smaller building that adjoins the main building to the east. This double-storey structure, which probably dates from the early twentieth century, is an integral part of the Shanasazi Mosque complex and has been in use since for religious instruction and prayer.

**Partial reconstruction of domes and an internal view of the hammam after completion.**

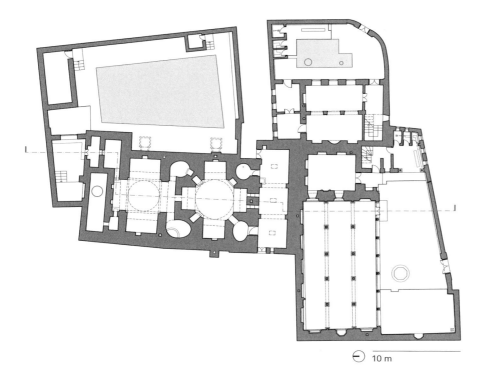

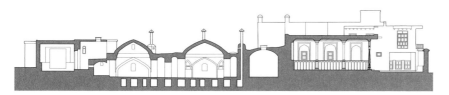

## WORK UNDERTAKEN: HAMMAM

In 2008, agreement was reached with the owner of the Shanasazi Hammam in the Old City of Kabul to reconstruct and recommission the derelict property as a community-managed facility. Rehabilitation work started with the clearance of accumulated debris and waste so that the condition of the existing structure could be assessed. Excavations revealed two brick-domed spaces surrounded by smaller rooms for private bathing and services. Once cleared of waste and rubble, the system of under-floor ducts for heating the hammam was found to be largely intact. A boundary wall was constructed before structural repairs were carried out on damaged sections of brick-masonry domes and external load-bearing walls. On completion of the external building work, the hypocaust flooring, chimneys and vents were reconstructed. Internal elevations of the hammam were replastered using a damp-proof lime mortar and marble flooring was installed throughout the space.

With all facilities required to operate a traditional hammam put in place and the conservation of the mosque completed, both facilities are open to residents of the surrounding neighbourhoods. Several hundred women and children make use of the hammam on a weekly basis on payment of a modest fee. Moreover, the revenue generated is reinvested in upgrading of drainage in the surrounding neighbourhood, extending the benefits of the operation to a wider area.

Opposite page, restoration of the mosque entailed structural repairs, followed by the conservation of timber fenestration and plaster decoration, as well as landscaping work.

Top left, ground-floor plan and section.

Top right, conservation of the elaborate timber columns and arched windows required replacement of damaged sections of the cedar woodwork resulting in a clear distinction between original and newly constructed areas.

Above, believed to have been remodelled in the mid-20th century, the internal space of the mosque has a contemporary character, with square columns and wooden panelling on its walls.

# Ulya Madrasa

**The Ulya Madrasa and Mosque continued to be used for religious education prior to its restoration.**

### HISTORY AND CHARACTERISTICS

The construction of the Ulya Madrasa was endowed by the mother of Afghan king Amir Amanullah Khan (r. 1919–29), on the occasion of his ascension to the throne in 1919. Located in the Shor Bazaar quarter and built on the site of an earlier religious structure, the madrasa represents one of few remaining examples of public architecture from the 1920s in the Old City. Built at a time when Afghanistan had established steel-manufacturing facilities, reflected in the use of steel trusses, pressed-iron roof sheeting and decorated metal air-extraction vents, the building represents the convergence of traditional architectural form and modern materials.

The building is comprised of a large open space enclosed by load-bearing masonry walls and steel-truss roof. Probably inspired by the large factories being built at that time, the extruded open section of the main space is contained at either end by two traditional constructions in the form of masonry towers associated with fortifications. These heavy 'book-end' towers are in stark contrast to the lightweight steel materials used elsewhere in the building. Moreover, this contrast and differences in the type and size of masonry used may point to the fact that the towers — or at least one tower — possibly precede the date of the madrasa constructed by the king's mother. It would not be unusual for later buildings to incorporate elements of a previous structure, particularly when they can serve a purpose — in this instance, as a minaret for the call to prayer. The typology of the building generally reflects standard one-storey mosques, with a larger summer and a smaller winter prayer space facing a wall with a prayer niche (*mihrab*) and an external landscaped space.

A small three-step marble pulpit (*minbar*) is located adjacent to the *mihrab* of the main prayer space. Resembling a mosque more than a madrasa, which would generally contain smaller spaces for study and living quarters, the building was used by the community for prayer with the east-facing veranda supported on metal columns and offering additional prayer space during warmer months.

Despite significant damage and being a clear danger to the community using the site, residents intervened to protect the building during the course of a municipal road-widening project that threatened to destroy a section of the structure.

### WORK UNDERTAKEN

As part of AKTC's wider Area Development Programme in the Old City, conservation activities commenced in 2009 with the preparation of a detailed physical survey, followed by the removal of debris and rubble from the site.

Ad hoc temporary structures were carefully demolished and work commenced to strengthen and consolidate sections of the building that had been damaged. This included reconstructing sections of brick-masonry walls and stone foundations and enabled the carpentry, steel repair and installation work to begin. A new perimeter wall was built and facilities for use by worshippers and custodians were incorporated in the site. Large sections of the metal roofing and the steel trusses had been damaged beyond repair and these elements were reconstructed on site, where a

Above, children from the local community receive instruction on the veranda of the madrasa.

Left, built as a congregational mosque able to house up to 400 worshippers, original ventilation covers were repaired and reinstalled as part of the work done.

Right, carpenters work to construct new joinery under a newly constructed steel roof, resembling its original early 20th-century steel trusses.

Above, the restored madrasa provides the largest congregation prayer space in the Old City and is often used for community gatherings.

Opposite page, ground-floor plan, east elevation and section.

steel workshop was established as part of the project. New corrugated-steel sheeting was applied on wooden decking attached to repaired steel trusses. Gutters were installed and downspouts enabled the redirection of rainwater and snowmelt into soak-away pits in the yard. As a final element, original decorated ventilation stacks were repaired and were installed on the roof along with newly produced elements. Broken or missing steel columns in the veranda were replaced and steel trusses were fabricated and installed as part of reconstruction of the covered area. Internal finishes required the application of a lime-based plaster, followed by laying appropriate flooring. Fabrication and installation of wooden doors and windows followed and a new wooden ceiling was installed — suspended from steel trusses — enabling better insulation facilitating the use of the space in colder months.

The courtyard was carefully landscaped with stone-paved pathways, trees and plants, preserving existing graves in parts of the site. Pathways connect the main building with the newly built ablution and sanitary facilities on the southern perimeter, and to the rooms built for custodians of the site near the western perimeter wall.

Following the completion of comprehensive restoration and landscaping, the Ulya Madrasa was handed back to representatives of the Shor Bazaar community and the site continues to be used for community gatherings, prayers and religious education.

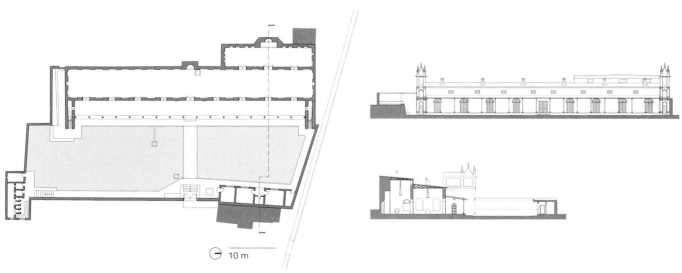

10 m

# Wasay House

**The Wasay House was close to collapse prior to restoration.**

## HISTORY AND CHARACTERISTICS

The Wasay House is located in the densely populated quarter of Asheqan wa Arefan, and is one of the few historic homes to have survived intense conflict and periodic neglect, retaining the fine timber and plaster decoration that was characteristic of traditional homes in the area. This is one of the oldest houses identified and it was close to collapse, only the south-facing range of the original courtyard complex had survived. Occupied continuously by descendants of the same family since the late eighteenth century, it is thought that parts of the Wasay House underwent several phases of transformation and expansion. For extended families, the local custom is to add rooms or expand houses to accommodate male children who tend to stay in parental homes after marriage. This results in homes that undergo frequent change. While sections of some homes might indeed be older, traditional mud-brick and timber-frame (*sinj*) construction requires significant upkeep. Comparative examination of photographs from the late nineteenth and mid-twentieth centuries suggests that many homes in the Old City were replaced or expanded using traditional techniques. As a result it is very difficult to give accurate date attributions to buildings in the Old City of Kabul.

Historic photographs of the dwelling enabled the project team to ascertain the original decorative scheme, on which basis the documentation and restoration of war-damaged parts of the internal moulded plaster decoration — including a series of recessed niches (*chini khana*) used for the display of porcelain — and timber screens was made possible within the main space on the first floor.

## WORK UNDERTAKEN

The building, has served as a demonstration of repair, conservation and infill techniques to other homeowners, and as a test bed for training craftsmen and young professionals. While only the south-facing range of the original courtyard complex had survived, this structure retained fine decorative details on the main elevation and inside the upper space.

As the house was occupied at the time of documentation, a series of single-storey rooms were built across the courtyard to the south in order to house the family during the course of the conservation work. When this work commenced, the first task was to remove thick layers of earth material from above the roof, prior to installing temporary props beneath the timber structure, which had undergone serious deflection due to the added weight, causing structural failure in a mud-brick gable

Left, following the removal of accumulated debris and damaged areas of the masonry walls, the timber-frame structure of the house was lifted into place using hand-operated jacks.

Right, carpenters work to reconstruct missing sections of an intricate latticework screen.

Below, detailed elevation.

0.5 m

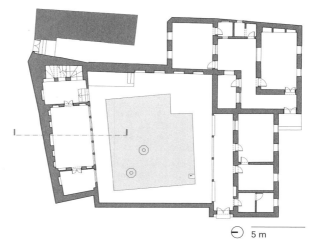

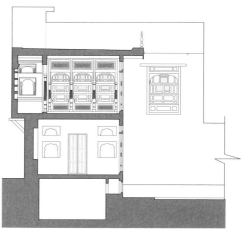

Above, the Wasay House was restored to be used as originally intended, with an upper living area with sliding screens for use in warmer months.

Below, over the course of AKTC's conservation programme in the Old City, community gatherings were often held in restored premises in order to demonstrate the benefits of conservation.

Top right, ground-floor plan and section.

Opposite page, built using a combination of woodworking techniques, the Wasay House is arguably one of the finest historic homes in the Old City of Kabul.

wall. Adding layers of mud-straw plaster to the roof of a dwelling is a common practice that prevents water from seeping into the building. But this traditional technique requires owners to also remove layers of plaster every ten years, failing which, the added weight of layers of plaster risks causing structural failure.

Once the gable wall was rebuilt, the timber frame was gradually shifted back in stages close to its original position, to regain its stability. To limit damage to plaster decoration in the upper space, sheets of soft polyurethane foam were fixed over the walls during the course of shifting the frame. Once upright, excess plaster and whitewash was carefully removed by hand, exposing sections of fine moulded decoration. This enabled the reconstruction of a replica decoration surviving on the internal east elevation of the space. As with many homes of this era, a series of recessed *chini khana* could be found in the main space, which was divided by carved timber screens. Following restoration of the internal plaster, work began on repairs to the two levels of sliding timber panels (*pataii*) that make up the south elevation of the house. Damaged sections of carved woodwork were replaced in places, and new shutters were made from cedar wood (*archa*) and installed. Following the completion of conservation, the dwelling was returned to its owners, who presently occupy the house.

Here, as in other conservation projects, the documentation of the building has enabled a better understanding of the diversity of construction and decorative techniques used in the Old City over the past 120 years.

# Shukur House

The Shukur House retained much of
its internal original decoration prior to
conservation.

## HISTORY AND CHARACTERISTICS

The Shukur House had been occupied by the same family since the late nineteenth
century and was only abandoned at the onset of conflict in Kabul. Returning from a
refugee camp in 2004, the owners had lost hope of being able to reoccupy the family home due to the amount of damage incurred in their absence. As the family had
grown in number over the years, it was not possible for all members to live in the
same building. Support was provided by the AKTC team for the construction of an
infill unit using traditional materials, consisting of two rooms and a kitchen, across the
courtyard from the original historic house. Once the owners had built an extension
to their home and could vacate the historic section of the building, rehabilitation work
commenced with a detailed physical survey of the property.

Built on a comparatively small plot for homes of the era, the steep parcel made
it difficult to orient the internal spaces of the house towards the south where they
would benefit from natural sun in winter months. Demonstrating the ingenuity of
traditional builders, this obstacle was partially resolved by changing the orientation
of the upper level of the house — perpendicular to the lower floor — facing exposed
elevations to the north so that the space could be kept cool in warmer temperatures.
While the ground floor necessarily needed to adjust to the topography, the upper
floor was given a more beneficial layout.

## WORK UNDERTAKEN

Restoration work required complex structural retrofitting and stabilization of the traditional wood-frame construction. Large sections of the masonry walls had to be replaced with fired brick and the upper floor of the house was rebuilt, retaining original
architectural elements. Chronic structural problems had forced occupants to fill
openings with mud brick for fear of collapse of a wall. These areas were consolidated
and historic windows were reinstalled enabling the upper floor to benefit from cross-
ventilation in the warmer months. Internal gypsum plaster decoration was carefully
cleaned and damaged sections repaired using fine mud plaster (*simgil*). Timber
columns and screens were cleaned, repaired and preserved using linseed oil. Conservation work was completed in 2005 and the dwelling was retuned to its owners,
who presently occupy the house. As part of the conservation process, historic homes
restored by AKTC in the Old City are registered as national monuments with the
Ministry of Information and Culture, providing protection against further destruction
and technical support for maintenance.

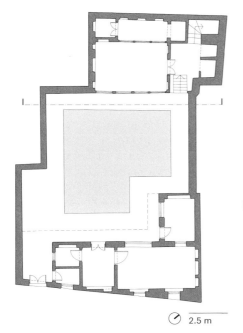

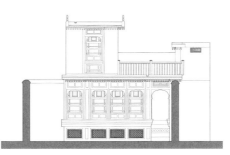

Top left, repair to the timber-frame construction of the house entailed removal of damaged sections of timber and retrofitting of wooden reinforcement.

Top right, built into a sloping hillside, the Shukur House benefits from multiple orientations, with the upper floor facing north.

Above, the main living quarters have deep recessed niches for storage of household items.

Left, ground-floor plan and section.

2.5 m

# Ruhullah House

**The Ruhullah House is one of the largest historic homes in the Old City, seen here prior to restoration.**

### HISTORY AND CHARACTERISTICS

The Ruhullah House is a fine early twentieth-century family home, with carved timber decoration on the external elevations and exquisite moulded plaster decoration in the rooms of the southern wing. Even in its partially collapsed state, the Ruhullah House stood out from the surrounding fabric, with its large courtyard and decorated timber screens — some of which retain their original coloured glass — and fine internal plasterwork. Looted and abandoned during the inter-factional fighting, the building was in very poor condition when first surveyed in 2003.

Like many other merchant houses in the Old City, most of which have now disappeared, the dozen or so rooms of the dwelling were built at different times, and show the evolution of decorative styles since the early 1930s. The grandfather of the present owner, who may have been the original builder, served as an imam in King Nadir Shah's court, and is said to have commuted from the Old City to the Arg Palace by camel. The distinction of the owners of the house is further borne out by the domed baths (hammam), complete with an ingenious water supply system. The present owner Haji Ruhullah, now in his early seventies, recalls weekly family bath days in the hammam space. For most residents of the neighbourhood, animals were an important part of life in the house. A small stable was constructed in the basement, where the current owner's father kept two horses and raced a flock of pigeons from the roof.

### WORK UNDERTAKEN

The rehabilitation of the Ruhullah House entailed the rebuilding of the eastern wing, the reconstruction of its roofs, and the restoration of the timber screens on the south and north courtyard elevations. Work commenced with the removal of debris and careful dismantling of timber architectural elements for repair in a carpentry workshop established in the courtyard of the building. Decorated wooden structural posts and fenestration was stabilized *in situ*, cleaned and repaired before wooden joists were reattached internally to support floors and the roof. Infill walls were reconstructed and existing sections of masonry walls with stucco decoration were stabilized and repaired. Roofing was constructed using traditional methods and materials before face boards and timber railings were installed. Exposed surfaces of timber decorative features were preserved and missing sections of sliding shutters were fabricated and installed.

Restoration work was completed in 2006 and the house was returned to its owners, who had been living in another area of the city.

Above, built within the dense fabric of the Old City, the restored house is organized around a private internal courtyard.

Below, a carpenter's apprentice at work repairing timber screens.

Right, ground-floor plan and section.

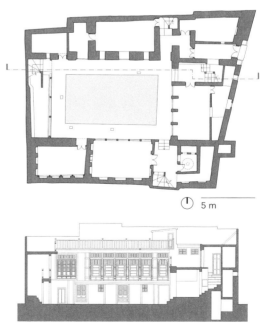

5 m

# Jelan House

### HISTORY AND CHARACTERISTICS

Built in the historic fabric of the Asheqan wa Arefan neighbourhood, the Jelan House is an excellent example of a modest early twentieth-century family home, with three wings and a veranda on the eastern side organized around a central courtyard. The rooms on the second floor are either decorated with fine moulded plaster, as on the southern side, or timber screens (*pataii*) which form the facade on the northern wing. As the main residential quarter in Kabul in the late nineteenth and early twentieth centuries, where working classes would have lived and worked, the construction of such homes would have employed the same craftsmen as those working on larger, state-funded projects. It is believed that the carpenter of the Jelan House was later employed on the construction of the Darulaman Palace, which, if accurate, would mean that the house was built in the 1920s. Abandoned during the conflict in Kabul, it was partially occupied at the time when AKTC conducted initial surveys in 2004.

### WORK UNDERTAKEN

With residents continuing to occupy the house during conservation, work proceeded in phases requiring the completion of one segment and the relocation of the family into restored quarters — before the next section of the building could be restored. Rehabilitation of the Jelan House entailed the removal of debris and careful dismantling of timber structural elements for repair. Decorated timber posts and screens were stabilized and repaired *in situ*. Where damaged, infill walls were reconstructed and existing sections of stucco decoration were stabilized and repaired. Roofing was constructed using traditional methods and materials and timber railings were installed. Timber decorative features were preserved and missing sections of sliding shutters and screens were fabricated and installed. Restoration work was completed in 2007 and the house was returned to its owners, who presently occupy it.

The Jelan House was partially occupied by multiple families prior to restoration, who remained in the residence throughout all the conservation work.

Left, the Jelan House and all of the other sites restored by AKTC have been registered with the government as national heritage, providing a measure of protection against future changes to its character.

Above, returned to its occupants following restoration.

Below, damaged sections of decorative stamped plaster were consolidated *in situ*.

Bottom, ground-floor plan and section.

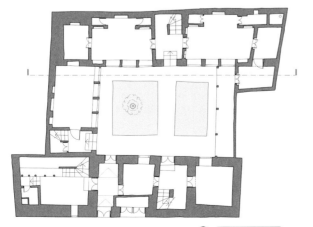

5 m

# Shekeba House

**The Shekeba House prior to restoration.**

### HISTORY AND CHARACTERISTICS

The Shekeba House is accessed from a narrow, winding street in the Asheqan wa Arefan neighbourhood, where a number of historic homes were restored by AKTC. This compact early twentieth-century family home is arranged around a central courtyard. It was built in at least two distinct phases — as evident in the changes in floor levels between various wings of the building. The plan reveals three staircases leading to the different wings, making it possible for members of the same family to occupy it separately. Named after the current owner who purchased the property in 2002, the house features carved timber decoration on external elevations as well as internal timber partition screens (*pataii*) and moulded plaster decoration.

### WORK UNDERTAKEN

As with other historic homes restored by AKTC, the main cause of damage in structures built using traditional methods is subsidence of masonry walls or deterioration of timber structural elements due to a general lack of maintenance. Areas affected by the intense conflict in Kabul were often abandoned for an extended period, which resulted in further deterioration of structures that might otherwise have been easily repaired. Traditional homes use the *sinj* construction technique and are built as a 'kit of parts', with timber-frame elements and wooden fenestration fabricated in workshops and then installed *in situ* on top of masonry walls, where the final layers of masonry infill and roofing are applied. Full-scale conservation of traditional structures requires the careful removal of damaged masonry and the repair of the timber 'skeleton' of the building before the application of new masonry and final finishes. The Shekeba House required extensive rebuilding of the eastern wing, which had subsided, and the reconstruction of an entire timber screen on the south courtyard elevation. Over the course of AKTC's work in the Old City, wooden architectural decoration, including screens and shutters, was salvaged from dozens of destroyed properties that were beyond repair. These items were often repaired and reinstalled in historic homes that were being conserved and that had similar architectural features. Building and conservation work was completed in 2006, when the property was handed back to its owner. Since then the property has changed hands again and is currently being used as a permanent storage for a collection of historic architectural artefacts and decorative items intended for public display.

Above, internal living spaces are separated by timber screens, which can be opened to create larger spaces or closed to provide privacy.

Left, first-floor plan and section.

Below, stamped plaster decorations were cleaned and consolidated as part of restoration activities.

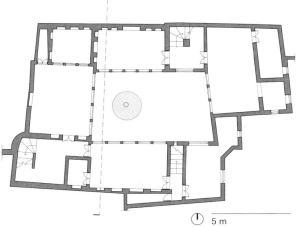

5 m

# Rambu House

**Above, the Rambu House was spared the worst during the conflict that destroyed large parts of the Old City. However, lack of maintenance and having remained vacant for prolonged periods resulted in damage to the structure of the house, which was in a poor state prior to conservation.**

**Opposite page, the restored house will enable a younger generation of occupants to better understand and become custodians of their built heritage.**

## HISTORY AND CHARACTERISTICS

The Rambu House is an extraordinary late-nineteenth-century family home, with carved timber decoration on all four courtyard elevations, as well as fine moulded plaster decoration on both floors. Located in the historic fabric of the Asheqan wa Arefan neighbourhood, which is documented as having the highest concentration of historic structures in the Old City, the house is organized around a central courtyard and accessed through an arched opening on a narrow street. Upon entering the property from the congested pedestrian thoroughfare, visitors are often surprised by the unexpected scale and grandeur of this building. While the uniform elevation of the courtyard suggests that internal spaces are linked as a single dwelling, four separate staircases lead to individual units that may have been occupied by up to twenty members of the same family. Courtyard houses enable families to carry out their daily routine in the privacy of their homes and are widespread throughout the Islamic world. As with other homes in the area, the rooftop area of the Rambu House is also used regularly by the family for airing laundry, drying foods and — as is generally the case for inhabitants of the Old City — for keeping and flying trained pigeons. Like the Ruhullah House, the Rambu building also contains an area for bathing (hammam) that was only available at the time in affluent homes. A basement level running the length of the building that is partially below grade would have been used for the storage of foods, goods and possibly for housing animals.

## WORK UNDERTAKEN

At the time surveys were conducted in 2003, nine households inhabited the Rambu House. The building was in a poor state of repair and presented safety concerns for the families living there, and restoration commenced in 2006. As with other homes restored by AKTC, the project was divided into phases enabling families to continue to occupy various segments of the house during the conservation process. Condition assessments had revealed severe structural problems in the western wing of the property, which became the focus of the first phase of building. Damaged sections of the house were temporarily propped up using jacks and scaffolding, while affected areas of masonry construction were removed and rebuilt. Timber posts and joists were examined for decay and replaced where necessary before a protective layer of tar was applied to sections embedded in masonry walls to prevent future damage. Wooden boards were placed above timber joists and covered with a layer of straw-matting, before a final layer of compacted mud was applied to internal floor areas and

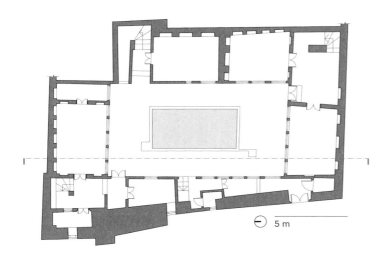

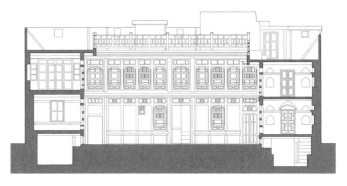

Above, ground-floor plan and section.

Below, conservation work to the street elevations of houses restored by AKTC contributed to preserving the quality of public spaces in the historic quarters in the Old City.

finished with a mud-straw plaster on the roof. Compacted mud has traditionally been applied in thick layers as a thermal insulation material, offering good resistance to the transfer or loss of heat.

Once the masonry elements of the building had been consolidated and the structure provided with a roof, conservation work focused on internal plaster decoration and timber fenestration. Original sections of the woodwork were carefully dismantled and transferred to a carpentry workshop established in the courtyard of the property, where they were cleaned, repaired and later reinstalled. Sections of the facade that could not be removed for structural reasons were repaired *in situ* and sections that had been damaged beyond repair were replaced with newly constructed cedar elements. Once all the wooden elements had been repaired and installed, linseed oil was applied as a protective layer against damage from rain. As with many homes of this era, a series of recessed niches used for the display of porcelain (*chini khana*) was found in the main space. Together with other areas of plaster decoration, these were carefully cleaned and conserved. Sections of plasterwork that had become detached from the masonry walls were consolidated *in situ*.

Sections of the building that had been fully conserved were returned to the occupants and work commenced on areas they had vacated. In this manner the conservation project was completed in mid-2007, after which the courtyard area was repaved. In addition to conserving the historic property, new toilets were added and an existing well in the courtyard was upgraded.

**Above, occupied by nine families unable to relocate, restoration work was phased, enabling the families to remain on the premises during conservation.**

**Below, restoration work provided an opportunity for training young craftsmen and apprentices in traditional building techniques.**

# Akram House

A large family home, the Akram House had been damaged in the conflict and was vacant prior to conservation.

## HISTORY AND CHARACTERISTICS

Located on a corner near the Asheqan wa Arefan Shrine, the Akram House occupies one of the largest plots in the neighbourhood and is comprised of three wings arranged around a large internal courtyard. As with other large properties owned by distinguished families, this house benefits from a separate bathing (hammam) area and a small stable located at its entrance. Built in the early twentieth century, its original owner is believed to have been a banker working for the Ministry of the Interior. The three wings of the house are accessed by separate staircases, making the residence ideal for housing visitors or an extended family. A high retaining wall encloses the southern perimeter of the courtyard, separating the house from other residential properties located on a substantially higher level. This difference in levels may have prevented the owners from building the fourth wing of the house that would have enclosed the courtyard.

Like many other properties in the area, the building had been damaged during the conflict in 1993 and since then had fallen into disrepair.

## WORK UNDERTAKEN

As part of AKTC's multi-year conservation programme in the Old City, the Akram House was initially surveyed in 2003, with conservation and structural repair work commencing in 2007. The construction of a new stone retaining wall at the southern boundary became necessary in order to stabilize the neighbouring property on the hillside. Rebuilding and conservation work focused on stabilizing masonry foundations and walls, followed by the conservation of fine plaster decoration and timber crafted fenestration. Sections of plaster decoration that had become detached from the masonry walls were preserved and reattached following consolidation work. Wooden structural elements were stabilized *in situ*, with detachable screens and shutters dismantled and repaired before being reinstalled.

Restoration work was completed in 2009 with the paving and landscaping of the inner courtyard. An agreement was reached with the owners of the Akram House, who had been living outside the Old City since the 1990s, to enable AKTC to use the premises as a vocational training centre in the area. The property serves to enable students from the Asheqan wa Arefan neighbourhood to receive training in traditional crafts such as flat weaves (*kilim*), sewing and embroidery, along with supplementary literacy courses.

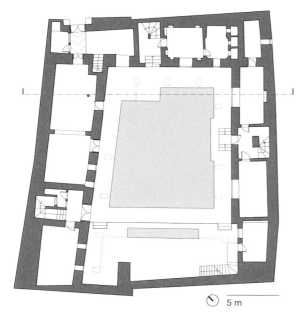

Above, arched timber screens were repaired on site and reinstalled prior to the application of a finishing layer of plaster on the main elevation and the roof of the house.

Below, ground-floor plan and section.

Following pages, since 2009, the Akram House has been used to provide crafts training and literacy education to young girls and women from the community.

5 m

# Khaluddin House

**Built into the hillside, the Khaluddin House prior to restoration. Unusual for historic residences in the Old City, decorative elements in the house included plastered and inlay woodwork ceilings.**

## HISTORY AND CHARACTERISTICS

Located on a hillside in the Asheqan wa Arefan neighbourhood, bordering the Akram House to the north, the Khaluddin House has panoramic views over the Old City of Kabul. Accessed via a narrow passageway, the original three-sided historic house had been extensively damaged — with only the southern part surviving at the time AKTC carried out survey work in 2003.

The southern wing consists of two floors, both of which have a main living space that opens onto the courtyard, with smaller rooms attached to its sides. On the ground floor, the traditional heating system (*taba khana*) and a fireplace were found but were not functioning at the time. The main living space on the first floor contains two smaller spaces (*pesh khana*) on opposite sides, which are separated by timber partition screens (*pataii*). Traditional niches (*chini khana*) with richly decorative plasterwork containing different coloured mirrors are set inside the mud-plastered walls. Connected to the north side of this room is another space that contained fine plasterwork and a specially decorated ceiling (*hakkaki*) where small intricate pieces of wood are joined to form a larger field pattern. One of the smaller spaces also contained a decorated plaster ceiling, unique among the houses restored by AKTC in the Old City, which regrettably had been destroyed prior to conservation.

## WORK UNDERTAKEN

Restoration by AKTC started in 2006 with the stabilization of the south wall, followed by the repair or replacement of timber facade elements and repair work to the roof structure and covering. Internally, the chimney and fireplace on the ground floor were repaired, and ceilings and walls were replastered. On the first floor, special attention was paid to the restoration of the fine plasterwork and repair of the damaged or missing sections of decorated timber. Teams of carpenters established a workshop on the second floor of the house, enabling them to dismantle damaged sections of the woodwork and replace missing or repaired elements. During the final stage, the courtyard was paved with local stone and landscaped with greenery. Restoration work was completed in 2008 when the property was registered as a historic monument and handed back to its owners.

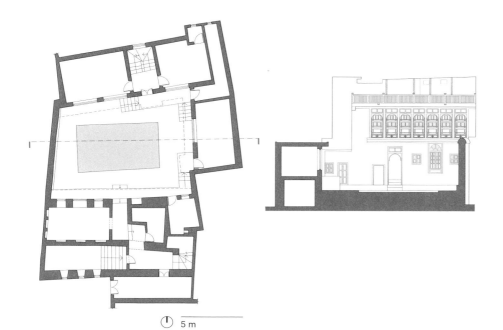

Top left, carpenters work to restore timber partitions.

Top right, layers of modern paint had to be carefully stripped before repairs could be undertaken on decorative plaster elements.

Bottom left, ground-floor plan and section.

Bottom right, the restored elevation of the main house.

⏱ 5 m

# Muneeb House

Initially surveyed in 2003, the structure of the Muneeb House was found to have been damaged during the conflict in the area. The multi-level home retained large sections of its original timber screens.

### HISTORY AND CHARACTERISTICS

The Muneeb House is located to the north of the Asheqan wa Arefan Shrine and is one of the smaller historic houses in the area, consisting of three wings of two to three-storeys that enclose a small courtyard. As with other houses in the Old City, limitations related to the irregular plot presented problems for a building with a square courtyard. In the Muneeb House this problem was elegantly resolved by the original builders through gently tapering the western range of the building. Varying the thickness of the external load-bearing wall also helped make the spaces more rectilinear in this wing of the building. Badly damaged during inter-factional fighting in the early 1990s, the Muneeb House was in need of extensive repair when AKTC carried out property surveys in the area in 2003.

### WORK UNDERTAKEN

Work on the house started in early 2007 with the removal of doors and windows, followed by stabilization of the structural load-bearing walls and roofs. A condition assessment had shown that the upper floors of the south wing, stretching over the street and forming a passageway for the public, had to be entirely rebuilt. Rooms on the roof level, which traditionally served as an extension of the living space during the summer months, were reconstructed using traditional building methods.

In order not to lose usable space through the construction of internal staircases, an external wooden veranda — accessed from the courtyard by an open staircase — was constructed with direct links to living spaces. Though in bad condition, all three facades showed fine timber decoration with elements of the highest craftsmanship on the east-facing facade. Repairing these timber screens (*pataii*), and in particular their intricate latticework and finely carved wooden frames, was a major challenge for AKTC's carpenters and craftsmen. After finishing rebuilding and conservation work, the existing well in the courtyard was repaired and a water pump was installed to provide a clean water supply. Paving of the courtyard and installation of surface drains allowed for the collection of surface water for washing and cleaning. Registered as a historic monument, the restored Muneeb House was handed back to the owner in 2008.

Above, courtyard elevation of the Muneeb House after restoration.

Left, a craftsman laying mud bricks between the timber-frame construction, a technique widely used in traditional homes in the Old City.

Right, view of interlinking spaces on the second floor of the restored house.

Below, first-floor plan and section.

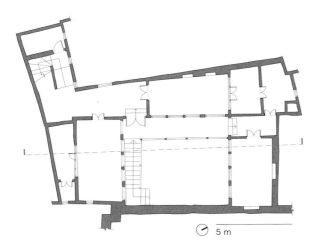

5 m

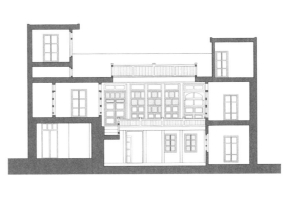

# Amin House

**Owned by the descendants of the original builder, the Amin House prior to conservation.**

### HISTORY AND CHARACTERISTICS

Located directly opposite the Akram House in the Asheqan wa Arefan neighbourhood, the Amin House dates from the early twentieth century and continues to be inhabited by the descendants of the carpenter who originally built the house, replacing an earlier single-storey dwelling on the site. The three-storey structure includes a basement that is partially below grade and that was used for storage. The main elevations of the house were constructed with characteristic, vertical, sliding, timber shutters (*pataii*). Intended as two separate dwellings with independent access stairs, the house was occupied by the original owners at the time of the survey and eventual conservation. Damage caused by the conflict and the subsequent period of neglect had resulted in extensive decay and staining of upper areas of the main timber elevation, which had remained exposed to rain.

### WORK UNDERTAKEN

Following a detailed survey and condition assessment, conservation work began in early 2004. The first stage of work on the Amin House involved removing infill materials, including damaged sections of partition walls and the roofing, from areas of the building that had subsided, in order to carry out repairs to the timber-frame structure.
The next phase required mechanically raising the timber-frame construction in order to rectify settlement in the foundations that had affected the stability of the structure. This was followed by repairs to the load-bearing mud-brick external walls and replacement of infill masonry between the timber-frame structure (*sinj*) of the upper levels. The house was re-roofed using traditional techniques and materials, before moulded plaster and carved wooden decoration and ceilings were carefully cleaned and consolidated. Before the building could be returned to its owners, the courtyard was paved with fired bricks and a well was built to provide residents with clean water.

Conservation work on the Amin House took place in phases, with the family remaining in it, providing the opportunity to document oral history related to the development of the dwelling and the wider area. Information gathered in this process formed part of a larger oral history project conducted in the Old City.

Experienced craftsmen previously trained on similar projects conducted by AKTC were able to complete conservation of the Amin House in less than six months. Projects similar in scale and complexity required more than a year at the onset of AKTC's work in the Old City in 2002, demonstrating the significance of on-the-job training provided for local craftsmen and apprentices.

Left, the restored Amin House provides shelter for the sixth generation of the same family.

Above, masons and carpenters lay a new protective roof over the residence.

Below, internal walls being repaired or renewed where necessary.

Bottom, ground-floor plan and section.

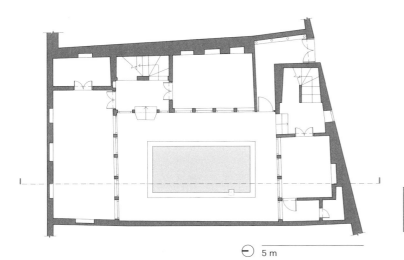

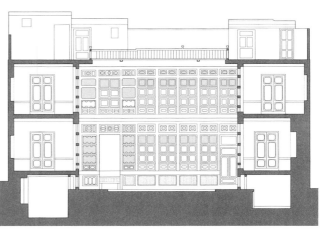

5 m

# Qala-e Moeen Afzal Khan

Above, the Qala-e Moeen Afzal Khan is an important example of fortified residences prevalent across Afghanistan.

Below, built in the early 20th century, the fort was occupied by warring factions and damaged extensively during the early 1990s.

### HISTORY AND CHARACTERISTICS

Dating from the early twentieth century, the Qala-e Moeen Afzal Khan is a large fortified residential complex located near Babur's Garden. It was built by Afzal Khan, who was a deputy minister (*Moeen*) at the Ministry of the Interior during the reign of King Amanullah Khan and later under Nadir Shah. Typical of fortified homes (*qala*) found outside the Old City in Kabul, at a time when vast swathes of the city remained as gardens or agricultural land, the house has an extended residential block with interlinking rooms (on two floors) and two symmetric two-storey towers (*burj*) at the corners of the high perimeter wall. While members of the family would have had access to the large square garden at the centre of the complex, a separate visitor's entrance and associated entertaining spaces were located near the main entrance to the *qala*.

Built using a mix of materials, including compacted mud (*pakhsa*), mud and fired bricks, and timber joists, the house retains key characteristics associated with traditional building techniques and typologies, though it was influenced by European architecture of that era. Photographs taken of Babur's Garden in the 1920s show the fortified property in the distance, where it stands as one of two buildings in the area — surrounded by large tracts of agricultural land. In the second half of the twentieth century the residence was used as a school and later divided and sold separately, before sustaining heavy damage during the conflict in 1993–94, when it had been transformed into the headquarters of a local armed faction. A one-storey dwelling was built sometime in the 1970s on the south-eastern corner of the internal garden of the *qala*, destroying a segment of the fortification wall.

### WORK UNDERTAKEN

As part of supporting conservation around Babur's Garden, AKTC surveyed the property in 2005 and shortly afterwards undertook the conservation of the historic residential complex. In agreement with the current owners of the subdivided property, internal partition walls were dismantled commencing a phase of clearance and removal of debris and rubble. While some work had been carried out after 2002 on the main residential block, the southern tower of the *qala* required structural consolidation and partial reconstruction. From the remains of the original architectural features, it was possible to restore the southern tower to its previous character. Segments of a high perimeter wall built with compacted mud was partially reconstructed and restored. Because it was not possible at the time, the second

Left, one of two restored residential towers, partially connected to a compacted-mud wall enclosing its large garden.

Right, spaces within the fort have been used to train members of the surrounding community in vocations such as tailoring, carpentry and masonry.

Bottom, site plan and elevation, main residence.

residential tower was reconstructed in 2011, completing the restoration of what remained of the original dwelling. As a fine example of residential architecture of the early twentieth century, the complex was registered as a historic monument with the authorities.

10 m

5 m

# Shutorkhana Hammam

The Shutorkhana Hammam is one of several historic public baths located in the Old City, seen here prior to conservation.

## HISTORY AND CHARACTERISTICS

The Shutorkhana Hammam is one of only three surviving traditional bathhouses in the Old City, only one of which was operational at the time AKTC conducted a survey of the building. The name refers to an open market located adjacent to the site that dealt with the sale and exchange of camels (*shutor*). A privately owned facility, it had fallen into disrepair when the area was depopulated, and suffered direct damage during the subsequent conflict. In residential parts of the Old City, where living conditions are generally poor, twenty per cent of the inhabitants do not have access to bathing facilities, while a majority of those that do have these facilities at home face chronic shortages of water or lack the materials with which to generate heat. Access to a public bathhouse positively impacts family health and hygiene.

The hammam follows a typical configuration, with rooms that are partially below grade grouped around two major brick-domed spaces covering the communal bathing areas that are kept at different temperatures. In between these central spaces, a series of open masonry tanks allow users to access hot or cold water during the course of bathing. Water was sourced from a well on the site, and heated in a large copper vessel situated over an *atish khana* (literally, fire-room), a subterranean space under one of the outer walls of the bathhouse, where wood or other fuel fires are lit. Heat and smoke from the *atish khana* were led through a hypocaust system of masonry ducts (*taba khana*) running under the main spaces of the hammam. This system serves to maintain the temperature and humidity that is characteristic of such traditional bathhouses.

## WORK UNDERTAKEN

Having obtained agreement from the owner of the ruined hammam for its reuse by the community, the semi-underground structure was excavated and surveyed.

A significant amount of rubble and earth was cleared from the site, before damaged parts of the masonry structure could be dismantled and fully repaired, along with ancillary spaces around the central domed chambers. Upon completion of the external building work, the hypocaust flooring, chimneys and vents were reconstructed. Internal elevations of the hammam were replastered using a damp-proof lime mortar and marble flooring was installed throughout the space. Following the construction of a new vaulted entrance area and changing rooms, the hammam was made ready for public use.

The Shutorkhana Hammam is visited by up to 250 people on weekdays, with about 400 on Fridays. The proceeds of the lease of the hammam are used for additional upgrading work within this neighbourhood, based on priorities set by the community. The Shutorkhana Hammam is an example of how rehabilitated historic buildings can meet the contemporary needs of urban communities.

**Left, the restored hammam has been operated under a community led initiative entailing the reinvestment of proceeds towards upgrading activities in the area.**

**Right, physical work included the partial reconstruction of semi-submerged masonry domes.**

**Below, ground-floor plan and section.**

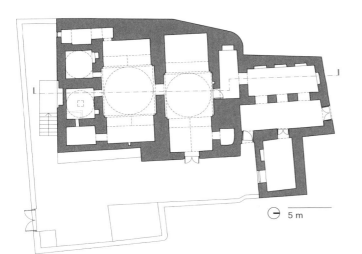

5 m

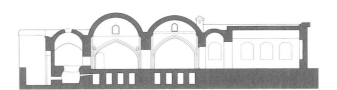

# Bagh-e Qazi

Above, the historic Bagh-e Qazi, located adjacent to the Asheqan wa Arefan neighbourhood, had fallen into extensive disrepair and was used as a waste dumping site.

Below, parts of the site were used to construct temporary wholesale storage buildings, which remained unused due to environmental problems, including chronic flooding.

### HISTORY AND CHARACTERISTICS

Named after a famous judge, the 3.5-hectare Bagh-e Qazi (Judge's Garden) is the largest public green space in the congested centre of the Old City. Qazi Dawlatshahi began his career in Herat as a judge, imam and, crucially, as private tutor to young Prince Timur in the mid-eighteenth century. When his pupil ascended the throne and became known as King Timur Shah, the Qazi followed him to Kabul and became one of his trusted advisers. He was eventually promoted to the position of Supreme Judge (*qazi-ul-qozat*) and his legacy was remembered through the garden he established in the Old City of Kabul. After Mohammad Nadir Shah's ascendance in 1929, the garden was used as an ice reservoir and later converted into an ornamental garden and planted with numerous trees. The garden sustained heavy damage during the conflict in the early 1990s, when the adjoining historic fabric was extensively destroyed and the area became largely depopulated. In 2009, a large portion of the site was occupied by temporary structures used to store and distribute grain, while the remaining area was used by local authorities and the surrounding community as a waste dump.

### WORK UNDERTAKEN

Reclamation activities had to be divided into two phases; the first phase on the parcel of land that had been used for waste, and the second on an adjacent property where more than three hundred traders occupying temporary structures awaited relocation to permanent sites by Kabul Municipality.

Over the three years required to transform the site into a public park, work included the removal of thousands of tons of waste and rubble, to be replaced by rich agricultural soil on a site that had been contaminated by significant pollution. The construction of a wall around the perimeter of the garden was followed by the demolition of three hundred ad hoc buildings, paving the way for the levelling of earth upon which a sports field was eventually created. A large water reservoir was built to feed a newly established network of surface irrigation channels linked with paved pedestrian pathways throughout the site. Gardeners worked to replant the site with species of hardy trees (mulberry, eglantine, poplar and oleaster) and plants that could withstand high levels of ground pollution and thrive in the rocky composition of the soil. Visitor facilities were upgraded and a nursery was established to support future planting in the park.

The reclamation of Bagh-e Qazi resulted in the transformation of a derelict site, which presented significant environmental and health concerns for the inhabitants of the Old City, into a public garden that could be used by the more than 30,000 inhabitants of the area for recreation and sport.

Above, the project has contributed to significant improvement in the environmental quality of the area.

Left, as part of rehabilitation activities, a perimeter enclosure wall was constructed to prevent further dumping of waste.

Right, hardy local species of flowers and trees, including mulberry, were planted in areas were the polluted earth had been replaced with suitable agricultural soil.

# STOR PALACE REHABILITATION

## HISTORY

Built as a one-storey garden pavilion in an orchard to the west of the royal Arg Palace during the reign of Amir Abdur Rahman Khan (1880–1905), Stor Palace (also known as the Qasr-e Storay or Place of Stars) was expanded on at least three known occasions. Stor Palace was Afghanistan's first Foreign Ministry building following the signing of the Treaty of Rawalpindi in 1919, by which Afghanistan became an independent sovereign state reclaiming its right to administer its foreign affairs from British authorities. Part of the building was subsequently used as an office by the intellectual and reformer Mahmoud Tarzi, who became Afghanistan's foreign minister. The palace housed offices of the Ministry until 1965, when most functions were relocated to a modern marble-clad building built to the north. Since that time the palace had been in use intermittently, most recently to store used equipment and documents.

Poor workmanship and the use of inappropriate materials during the third phase of the expansion of the palace had resulted in extensive damage to the roof area and the main elevations of the building. Ad hoc internal partitions created using material recycled from other buildings had caused extensive damage to decorated wooden ceilings, which had been painted over several times. By the time a physical survey and condition assessment were prepared by AKTC, the palace was dilapidated, with many areas of the building affected by structural problems and damage resulting from water seepage from the roof. The area surrounding the palace had been transformed into a road and re-asphalted on several occasions without removal of previous layers of road construction, resulting in the partial covering of the palace beneath forty-five centimetres of asphalt. This resulted in extensive damage to lower sections of the brick-masonry construction, which, together with vibrations caused by the regular traffic of heavy vehicles, had caused areas of the palace to subside.

## CHARACTERISTICS

Originally built as a single-storey pavilion enclosed by a deep-set arcade in the late nineteenth century, the first extension to the pavilion involved the construction of a two-storey brick-masonry building with an arcaded portico during the reign of Habibullah Khan (1905–19). This construction was located to the east of the original pavilion, significantly expanding the functional area of the palace by providing two large spaces for gatherings, accessed through a symmetric 'imperial' staircase. Radically transforming the architectural character of the modest nineteenth-century pavilion, the extension was built using high-quality materials such as pressed-metal

Opposite page, view of the restored Stor Palace building and the fine cast-iron decorative elements used along its terraces.

Above, built as a late-19th-century pavilion, the palace was expanded ahead of Afghanistan attaining its independence in 1919, and on at least two occasions afterwards, 1925.

Below, the palace remained partially used and extensively transformed by ad hoc repairs prior to conservation.

ceilings, elaborately decorated woodwork on low panels along walls, fenestration, and fireplaces. Fireplaces were made using colour-glazed gypsum tiles decorated in floral patterns and polished-brass decorative elements, which were also used to support railings along the main staircase. Cast-iron elements were used to create railings attached to metal columns on the balcony of the second floor, accessed through an exquisite cast-iron spiral staircase for service staff. On the ground floor, a large arched portico on the eastern elevation was used for dropping off guests, who entered the building through a marble staircase.

A second extension, built to the west of the pavilion in 1915, added further functional space by providing a large formal gathering hall. Complementing the architectural design of the first extension, the hall was organized around a central double-height space with clerestory windows surrounded by a lower perimeter zone leading to a marble stage area. One of only a handful of buildings in Kabul to use counter-weighted sash windows on the ground floor, hand-operated steel mechanical levers enabled control of the clerestory windows near the ceilings. Accessed separately from an entrance with a portico on the western elevation, the hall was connected to the rest of the building through an open-terraced colonnade.

Added as 'book-ends' to the original pavilion, the two phases of expansion incorporated the main external elevations of the smaller pavilion within the large gathering hall and the split-level staircase space. Introducing modern construction technology, both extensions employed structural metal decking, I-beam reinforced 'jack arches', and steel roof trusses.

Further expansion work carried out in the 1940s did not conform to the quality or standards of earlier extensions. Two circular masonry 'turrets' were added on the western elevation of the building, enclosing the arched portico. At the same time, a second floor was built above the original pavilion, completely encasing the nineteenth-century structure. Materials used for this intervention were recycled from

**Above, restoration work involved stripping modern paint from the decorated timber ceilings.**

**Left, extensive structural repairs were made to the roof of the building.**

**Right, above, the timber ceiling above the main reception hall was repaired and treated with beeswax.**

**Right, below, restoration work within the building entailed removal of paint from marble and stone surfaces.**

other structures. Brick sizes varied and wooden beams and coverings were found to be remnants of doorframes and panels.

Finally, it is understood that alterations to the main elevation undertaken in the 1970s entailed the repointing of external brickwork with cement-based mortar.

### WORK UNDERTAKEN

Based on the preparation of a detailed condition assessment in 2013, a comprehensive programme to conserve and rehabilitate Stor Palace was designed and implemented by AKTC. In order to establish the sequence and extent of the various phases of expansion work and enable the formulation of an accurate design programme, a comprehensive physical survey of the existing building was carried out using three-dimensional laser-scanning technology. Information gathered through the process was analysed and a programme of building archaeology was created and implemented in order to establish a baseline for the beginning of conservation activities.

Conservation and reuse designs prepared by AKTC aimed to highlight the distinct architectural features of the various phases of expansion in a manner that enabled visitors to discern the characteristics and styles of each period. Conveying the history of the building through a reading of its architectural characteristics — including the most recent work undertaken by AKTC — became the guiding principle of the conservation project.

**Modern cement pointing had to be removed from the external brick elevations, before the surfaces were repointed using a mixture of lime-mortar paste and brick dust.**

Above, a canopy was constructed over the entrance into the main reception hall in an area of the building that had been expanded in the mid-20th century.

Below, designed to link a series of multifunctional spaces, the palace extends more than ninety metres in length.

Left, main spaces are surrounded by a deep, shaded colonnade that prevents direct heat gain in warmer months.

Right, the roofscape of the building reflects its multiple phases of expansion and had to be extensively reconstructed as part of rehabilitation work.

Below, a spiral staircase allows for service of the second-floor rooms.

To this end, the structural consolidation of existing walls, floors and roof trusses became the first priority of the rehabilitation activity. In areas where significant damage had occurred, sections of the building were carefully dismantled and reconstructed using comparable materials. Large areas of the roofing structure that had been damaged or that had been built using inappropriate details were strengthened through the insertion of reinforced-steel framing. Once the structural elements of the roof were consolidated, timber decking was added and protected with a layer of tar-paper. Corrugated galvanized metal sheeting was applied to the roof and a network of gutters and downspouts was added.

Simultaneous to civil and structural work, AKTC teams carefully removed inappropriate elements from within the palace, revealing the original features of the building, which were cleaned and repaired. Sections of internal plasterwork that had become detached from masonry walls were cleared and conservation teams worked to clean and repair intricate wooden decoration. Architectural elements, such as cast-iron railings and stairs, were dismantled and removed to a specially designed workshop for cleaning. Other features that could not be relocated off site were cleaned *in situ* and protected during construction using plastic and foam. Following the construction of an intricate network of scaffolding, separate teams of masons worked to remove cement-based pointing from all external fired-brick elevations. Once completed, the main elevations of the building were repointed using traditional mortars matching original materials. Pointing styles and techniques associated with the different phases of construction were incorporated, making it possible to distinguish sections of newer construction from earlier areas.

Internally, historic features — including coffered timber ceilings and fenestration, cast-iron and brass elements, decorated fireplaces and original marble floors — were meticulously cleaned, repaired and protected. Inbuilt furniture, including large decorated wood-frame mirrors and cabinetry, was also cleaned and protected with beeswax. Thick layers of paint were removed from the surface of pressed-metal ceilings, followed by repair of areas corroded by rust, before the application of filler material and repainting of the ceiling on the ground floor. Although damaged, the pressed-metal ceiling located on the first floor of the palace was not corroded, making it possible to leave the burnished metal exposed.

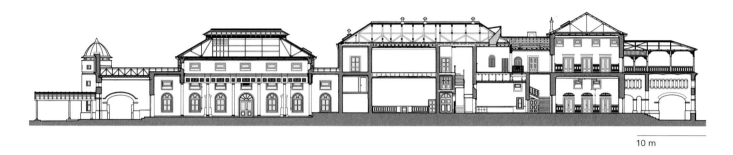

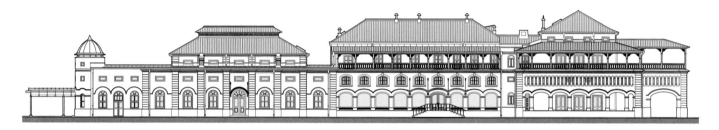

10 m

**Preceding pages, main reception hall following restoration.**

**Above, latitudinal section and south elevation.**

Newly constructed elements were only considered where they would significantly enhance the use of the building, and then only when the construction could be distinguished from the original historic architecture. New entrance canopies were added enabling staff and visitors of the Ministry to safely access the building. A free-standing wooden construction at the entrance to the main hall serves to provide a reception space, while the upper section of the construction is used to control lighting and sound systems during functions in the hall. Lighting systems were designed to be functional and require very little electricity. Uniform modern LED lighting fixtures, providing ambient indirect light, were procured and installed inside. The selection of suspended lighting fixtures was based on reducing their visual impact within the space and in relation to the highly decorated ceilings. External floor-based up-lights have been installed around the perimeter of the palace, highlighting its austere brick elevations. A state-of-the-art and highly efficient underground heating system was installed throughout the building, making it possible to retain original architectural decorations on walls and the ceilings. Sufficient electrical, sewage and water infrastructure was added to enable the simultaneous use of sections of the palace for multiple, independent functions.

Landscaping activities aimed to redress the relationship of the palace to its immediate environment, including its integration with two large garden areas to the south. Asphalted areas that had increased the ground levels by more than forty centimetres around the palace were removed, followed by the construction of stone-paved pathways and a one-way road network — transforming the space around the palace into a large pedestrian-friendly zone.

This high-quality restoration of an important monument established a significant architectural precedent for both Afghan and international professionals, in a post-conflict development environment that often does not encourage innovation.

Above, layers of modern paint were removed from the surface of embossed metal ceilings, restoring their original finish.

Left, oxidized brass railings were restored to reflect the original character of the building.

Right, above, steel elements used to construct a new entrance canopy were fabricated locally.

Right, below, the design of the entrance canopy reflected the arched openings of the palace.

# CHIHILSITOON GARDEN

### HISTORY AND CHARACTERISTICS

Chihilsitoon Garden is a 12.5-hectare public site, located four kilometres south of Babur's Garden, on the same range of foothills of the Sher Darwaza Mountain. Historic documents are believed to refer to this area as early as the sixteenth century, describing an outpost where Mughal troops were stationed in orchard gardens below a hillside settlement along the Kabul River.

A panoramic sketch produced in 1876 by a British military cartographer shows a hillside residential cluster in the same area, surrounded by large trees, possibly indicating a formal garden on the site. Historic maps from the same period refer to the settlement as "Hendaky", which was also the name of the small pavilion built on a stone outcrop above the garden by Amir Abdur Rahman Khan (r. 1880–1901) for his son Habibullah at the end of the nineteenth century. With a royal pavilion on the site, it is believed that this was the time that the garden was delineated and a wall constructed at its perimeter. Early twentieth-century photographs of the pavilion show an elongated rectilinear building (with one circular end) surrounded by a deep arched veranda with forty columns (*chihil-sitoon*) built above a series of terraced platforms with views onto the Chardeh plain. With newly built royal residences (*arg*) at the centre of the city, the pavilion remained unoccupied and occasionally served as a state guesthouse. The most prominent visitors who stayed in the building were members of the British Boundary Commission (charged with negotiating the northern boundaries of Afghanistan).

Upon his ascension to the throne in 1904, Amir Habibullah Khan (r. 1901–19) expanded the site, establishing at its centre a formal axial garden with marble fountains and paved walkways. As part of this work, the pavilion was expanded into a two-storey double-height rectilinear building, retaining only twelve of the original forty columns of its covered veranda and, ironically, renamed it the Chihilsitoon Palace. The flat roof of the original pavilion was replaced by a system of pitched roofs, and the shallow, fan-shaped flights of steps gave way to heavy lateral staircases with cast-iron railings.

The palace was damaged during the armed conflict that led to the succession of Nadir Khan (r. 1929–33), but later repaired and reused as a summer palace and state guesthouse. The building was once again transformed during the reign of King Mohammad Zahir Shah (r. 1933–73) when two squat towers were added and the external facades of the building were modernized. Used at that time primarily as a state guesthouse, dignitaries who resided within the Chihilsitoon Palace included heads

Opposite page, a vast nursery space has been developed to support the planting of indigenous trees and flowers at the Chihilsitoon Garden.

Above, the Chihilsitoon Garden and Palace seen here in an early 20th-century photograph, 1925.

Below, built as a garden pavilion with forty columns, the Chihilsitoon Palace was expanded on two separate occasions before being largely destroyed during the civil conflict in Kabul.

of state, most notably US President Dwight D. Eisenhower (1959) and Soviet Premier Nikita Khrushchev (1955, 1960).

By the 1960s and 1970s, due to the increasing importance of the building as a place of accommodation for foreign diplomats, the government further invested in adding spaces for receptions, banquets and state dinners. A modern L-shaped building was constructed to the east of the palace, which provided additional space for accommodation and banqueting services. The Chihilsitoon Palace remained a hub for government activity in the 1980s, mainly used to convene press conferences with local and foreign media. During the initial days of the Soviet occupation in 1979–80, President Babrak Karmal reportedly took refuge in the Chihilsitoon Palace and was guarded by tanks and anti-aircraft guns. During the conflict that ensued, the building was targeted and heavily damaged. The site remained unused in the years that followed, and was further destroyed and looted during the conflict in Kabul in the early 1990s.

Chihilsitoon Garden — as it is defined today by a low brick wall — seems to have been greatly reduced in size by the construction of roads around its perimeter. Historic descriptions indicate that the garden had extended to sloped areas to the east of the site, where a pigeon tower had been built on a stone outcrop. Since the 1980s, informal settlements have been erected on these hillside areas by those displaced by conflict or economic migrants. While historic photographs depict the garden as being overgrown, planted with deciduous vegetation including mulberry and plane

**Left, destroyed sections of the palace being repaired by masons as part of ongoing rehabilitation work.**

**Right, above, carpenters preparing timber-frame doors and windows, which will be installed in existing and newly constructed buildings.**

**Right, below, a worker prepares existing surfaces for structural retrofitting and repair.**

trees, in the 1950s and 1960s species of evergreen pine and cedar trees were heavily planted in pockets throughout the site. The frequent use of buildings located within the garden for royal or state functions meant that Chihilsitoon Garden remained intermittently accessible to the public throughout the twentieth century. During the period in the late 1970s, when the president's offices were located within the palace, the garden was closed altogether to the public. The central formal garden, which had included large areas of lawns planted with indigenous flowers and shrubs and sandstone pathways and stairs, was in disrepair at the time of surveys conducted by AKTC in 2014. Unlike Babur's Garden, where the natural landscape was heavily scarred by the ravages of conflict, large parts of the horticulture of Chihilsitoon Garden survived periods of neglect and intentional destruction.

Sloping gently towards the north, the garden has historically been irrigated by a surface channel sourced from the Logar River some five kilometres to the south. More recently, disposal of household waste (generated by the spread of informal settlements along the hillsides) in the channel has polluted the water source, which is no longer suitable for irrigation purposes — particularly in a public garden with large groups of children. Since 2002, the site has been cleaned and irrigated using water mechanically extracted from deep wells, ensuring its partial use by the community mainly for recreation and sport. Yet insufficient services and the absence of management oversight have prevented women and young children from entering the site. Based on the successful rehabilitation and sustainable operation of Babur's Garden, in 2015 AKTC commenced a multi-year rehabilitation programme in Chihilsitoon Garden with the intention of providing high-quality public spaces for social and cultural interaction, educational programming, and sport and recreational activities.

Left, newly constructed rammed-earth buildings will provide a range of visitor and operational facilities for the garden.

Right, above, teams of workers prepare areas of rammed-earth construction.

Right, below, provisions have been made to enable rehabilitation work to continue unabated throughout colder months, including the erection of large hangars over construction areas.

**A rendered master plan of Chihilsitoon Garden showing visitor facilities and the sequence of spaces, including a formal garden at the centre of the site, which provides visitors with a wide variety of experiences.**

1   Main entrance / administrative block
2   Secondary pedestrian entrance
3   Outdoor amphitheatre and exhibition space
4   Chihilsitoon Palace
5   Annex and auditorium
6   Sports fields and facilities

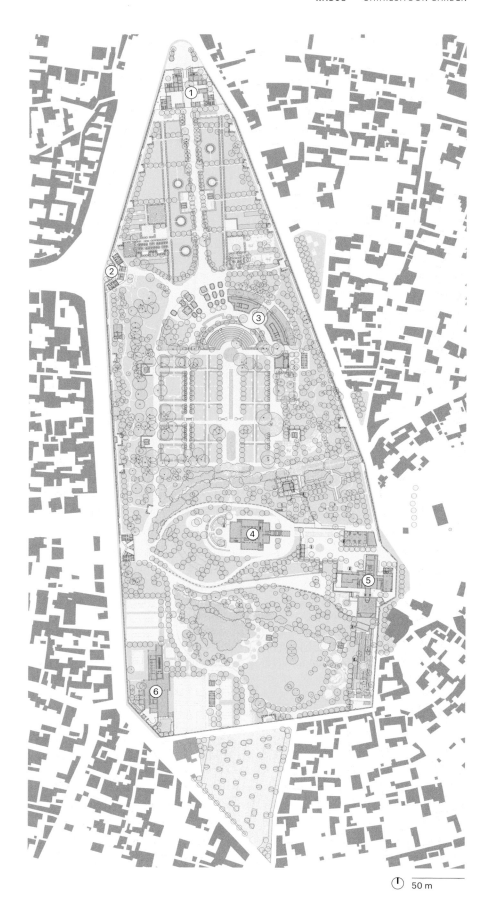

50 m

## WORK UNDERTAKEN

A tripartite agreement with Kabul Municipality and the Ministry of Information and Culture has ensured the active participation of Afghan institutions in a rehabilitation programme through the formation of a coordinating body. Furthermore, the agreement provides the legal basis for the establishment of a management structure for the garden after rehabilitation work is completed. Chihilsitoon Garden will be managed by the newly formed Kabul Historic Gardens Trust, which will have a mandate to operate the city's historic public gardens, building on nearly a decade of experience gained through the sustainable operation of Babur's Garden.

Following the preparation of a detailed physical survey and the finalization of an organizational plan for the site, architectural and landscaping designs include provisions for the construction of new buildings and open spaces. In addition to constructing new buildings for these purposes, existing buildings (including Chihilsitoon Palace) will be restored and made functional for public use. Based on detailed surveys and responses to questionnaires completed by visitors to other gardens, including

Above, administrative building, latitudinal section and elevation studies.

Below, left, local stone being prepared for use in pathways and as cladding on buildings.

Below, right, masons laying dressed stone near the amphitheatre.

Babur's Garden, sufficient provisions have been made for public services such as food and beverage areas, public toilets and visitor facilities.

Landscape designs call for the integration of a variety of disparate spaces, used for different purposes, within a wider network of paths and services that allow for a diverse set of experiences within a rational system of circulation and usage — such as separate areas for sports activities and family picnic sites, an outdoor amphitheatre, and the historic formal promenade (containing original marble fountains), which will be restored and made functional again. In order to support the continued use of the site for sports activities, a distinct zone has been designated to contain cricket batting areas, volleyball fields and football pitches. Additional services have been provided to enable sports teams access to changing facilities and showers, promoting the use of the sports fields for competitive matches. In addition to supplying saplings for maintaining the stock of trees and plants within the garden, a commercial horticulture nursery will be constructed in order to generate additional revenue towards the upkeep of the garden.

In order to promote traditional building techniques, new buildings within the garden will be built using ecologically sustainable reinforced rammed-earth construction. Found to have been used in parts of Afghanistan as far back as the second century AD, rammed-earth structures are highly suitable to the climatic and ecological environment in the region. Reinforced with a variety of material, including bamboo, steel rebar and concrete-frame structures, buildings constructed with rammed earth

**Assembly of lightweight, steel-frame roofing structure.**

are able to withstand moderate earthquakes. While capable of withstanding wide variations in temperature, the characteristics and workability of the material enable a wide range of rich architectural designs.

New structures will provide essential space for the administrative and maintenance teams of the garden, while increasing the capacity of the site to hold multi-purpose events and gatherings. An indoor auditorium will be built as an extension to the existing annex space, which will provide a facility for welcoming up to three hundred people year-round for conferences, presentations or performances. A gallery and visitor centre will be added within the site, enabling cultural organizations and individual artists to exhibit their works to the public. The multi-purpose space can also be used to display and market handicrafts and locally produced merchandise. Retail, food and beverage premises have also been included in the design of new structures in order to ensure that sustained revenue for the operation of the garden can be generated through the hire of these spaces. Provisions have been made for on-site utilities, which will ensure that the garden is properly maintained with limited usage of water and electricity, and septic systems that will filter wastewater through subsurface leach fields.

When complete, the rehabilitated Chihilsitoon Garden will provide users with high-quality landscapes and building spaces capable of containing and promoting the rich and diverse forms of social, cultural and economic expression manifested in Afghanistan.

Above, a newly constructed outdoor amphi-theatre will provide spaces for public and cultural events within the garden.

Below, a computer-generated view of public exhibition spaces currently being constructed at the Chihilsitoon Gardens.

# AMIR ABDUR RAHMAN MAUSOLEUM AND MOSQUE

### HISTORY AND CHARACTERISTICS

Zarnegar Park in central Kabul is thought to originally have been part of an orchard garden laid out by Ulugh Beg, Babur's uncle, in the fifteenth century. In the late nineteenth century, Amir Abdur Rahman Khan commissioned several buildings on the site, comprising a garden pavilion and several residences, including the Zarnegar Palace. After the amir's death in 1901, his son and heir Habibullah Khan transformed the pavilion into a mausoleum, which has since been referred to as Amir Abdur Rahman Khan's Mausoleum. With its onion-shaped central dome, elaborate brick minarets and parapets, this building is an early example of the Indian architectural style in a public building in Kabul.

During the reign of Amanullah Khan, the mausoleum was used as a public library, and reportedly looted during the uprising in 1929 that drove him from power. In the Zarnegar Chamber, located in a separate building to the south of the existing mausoleum that gives the park its current name, Afghanistan's independence was proclaimed in 1919, after the signing of the Treaty of Rawalpindi. Used by the Ministry of Education until the 1960s, the Zarnegar Pavilion was demolished on the orders of Zahir Shah when the municipal park was created. Other structures that stood on the site seem to have fallen into disrepair after the death of Amir Abdur Rahman Khan, and only one part of the Gulistan Serai, a single-storey building with distinctive external plaster decoration, survives and is now used by the Municipality as offices.

### WORK UNDERTAKEN

Since the mid-1990s, the building was used as an office for the Department of Historic Monuments which, in 2005, requested AKTC's support in conserving the mausoleum. Physical surveys were prepared for the mausoleum and a small triangular mosque adjacent to it, which also dated from the late nineteenth century. It was found that infiltration of water from the roofs of both buildings and around the gutters and downpipes had caused extensive damage within the structures.

When urgent conservation work began on both structures in 2005, modern concrete slabs were removed and damp areas below the concrete were left to dry out before structural repairs were carried out to damaged sections of the masonry domes beneath. Once complete, the cavities between domes were backfilled with brick fragments and a layer of porous lime concrete was laid before being finished with flat fired-brick paving. Damaged sections of iron sheeting over the main brick dome and the two porte cochères of the mausoleum were repaired, along with downpipes and

Opposite page, conservation work on the mausoleum included repairs to the roofing and restoration of the original painted colours of the building.

Above, the form of the Amir Abdur Rahman Mausoleum was inspired by 'onion'-domed buildings commonly associated with Russian architecture, 1925.

Below, Zarnegar Park prior to rehabilitation.

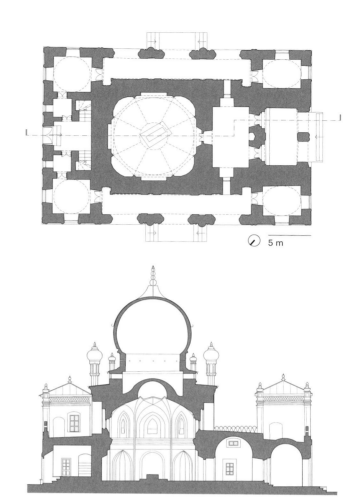

5 m

Above, masons prepare fixings for installation of decorative brickwork on the mosque located adjacent to the mausoleum.

Below, public toilets were constructed using traditional forms and materials.

Right, ground-floor plan and section.

gutters on both structures. Following repairs to the roof of the mausoleum, modern whitewash was removed from parts of the main elevations, exposing layers of ochre and blue paint, which are thought to be part of the original colour scheme of the pavilion built by Amir Abdur Rahman Khan. Sections of decorative plaster decoration on the facades were also cleaned, and timber windows and doors repaired or replaced.

In addition to the conservation of these monuments, AKTC implemented a land-scape rehabilitation project within Zarnegar Park resulting in the planting of saplings — including planes (*panja-chinar*), almond and mulberries, along with flowering shrubs, such as indigenous roses. Newly laid stone paving created an axis on the south side of the mausoleum, leading to a new entrance that was created on the south perimeter of the park. In addition, stone slabs were laid to create pathways up the slopes of the two raised mounds that existed in the park, where seating areas were created for visitors. A new deep well and installation of a water pump linked to underground piping and surface channels enabled effective irrigation across the park. A shallow well was fitted with a hand pump for use by the public, including worshippers at the newly restored mosque.

At an early stage of the rehabilitation programme, it was clear that the absence of public toilets was a major issue on a site visited by thousands of people a day during the summer months. In response to these needs, two separate blocks of toilets where built in locations within the park where access would be easiest for maintenance.

Above, the mausoleum of Amir Abdur Rahman is situated within Zarnegar Park, which was rehabilitated by AKTC.

Left, a durable baked-brick surface was laid over a waterproof layer of lime concrete on the roof of the mosque.

Right, local stones laid on edge were used to construct a durable pathway within the park.

# MILMA PAL MOSQUE

## HISTORY AND CHARACTERISTICS

Dating from the late nineteenth century and built as part of a wider programme of work in Kabul, the Milma Pal Mosque is located within the Bagh-e Bala, a landscaped hillside area believed to have originally been laid out as a Mughal garden. Together with the Bagh-e Bala Palace, which was the favoured summer residence of Amir Abdur Rahman Khan towards the end of his life, the architecture of the Milma Pal Mosque represents a synthesis between the Afghan vernacular and European design influences that characterizes royal buildings of that era.

The building is arranged as a large open space subdivided into ten interlinking bays grouped in two rows of five bays each, with two larger central bays on axis with the prayer niche (*mihrab*). The internal painted plasterwork around the *mihrab* and on the main elevation of the building is a fine example of simplified decorative work that draws on much older patterns. Built using a combination of fired bricks (arches) and mud bricks (domes), a galvanized metal roof had been added in the mid-twentieth century.

Flash floods from the steep hillside above the mosque caused the accumulation of soil and debris behind the western *qibla* wall, resulting in the build-up of moisture in the masonry walls causing extensive damage to internal plasterwork. Compounded by the seepage of water into mud-brick masonry domes from leaks in the metal roof, which resulted in the partial collapse of the central dome, emergency consolidation and conservation work commenced in 2009 with the preparation of detailed surveys and a condition assessment.

## WORK UNDERTAKEN

In order to prevent further damage to internal spaces, the first stage of work focused on repairing the galvanized metal roof of the mosque. The previous corrugated sheeting — much of which had fallen into disrepair, due to poor fixing and lack of maintenance — was stripped in phases, in order to enable a detailed examination of the uncut timber joists beneath. Repairs were carried out to strengthen the wooden substructure, over which new timber boarding was fixed and sections of existing and new corrugated metal roofing was reattached. Lengths of coping and corner edges around the metal roofing were redesigned to prevent penetration of water and to allow for run-off into fixed points linked to surface channels on the ground.

Once the roof of the building had been repaired, internal conservation work was carried out on the partially collapsed dome that was rebuilt with mud bricks produced

Opposite page, the main elevation of the late-19th-century Milma Pal Mosque prior to restoration.

Above, galvanized iron roofing erected over the mosque had been damaged, resulting in the collapse of one of the mosque's domes due to water seepage.

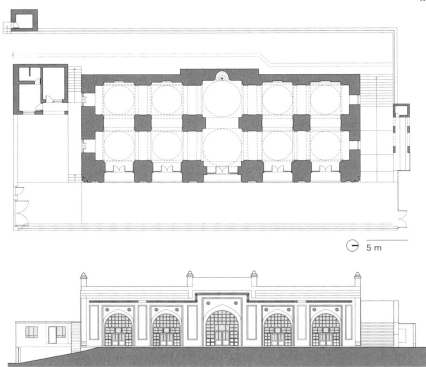

⊖ ‾‾‾‾ 5 m

**Top, ground-floor plan and main elevation.**

**Left, newly formed iron sheets being laid above timber planks.**

**Right, damage to the timber substructure on the roof of the building was repaired.**

on site using soil collected during clearance work. Areas of damaged decorative plasterwork around the *mihrab* and on the main elevations of the building were carefully consolidated and repaired. Damp sections of undecorated plaster that had separated from the *qibla* wall were stripped and the area left to dry, before new plaster finishes were applied. The timber fenestration of the mosque was carefully cleaned and repaired followed by the application of a final layer of whitewash on internal and external elevations. In order to prevent future seepage of water into masonry walls at the back of the mosque, the area was paved using flat stones and a drainage channel was added to divert water away from the building.

Above, situated on a terraced platform along a steep site, work entailed the construction of water diversion drains for flash floods.

Left, a craftsman at work inside the mosque repairing timber woodwork.

Right, sections of decorative plaster damaged by rainwater were repaired.

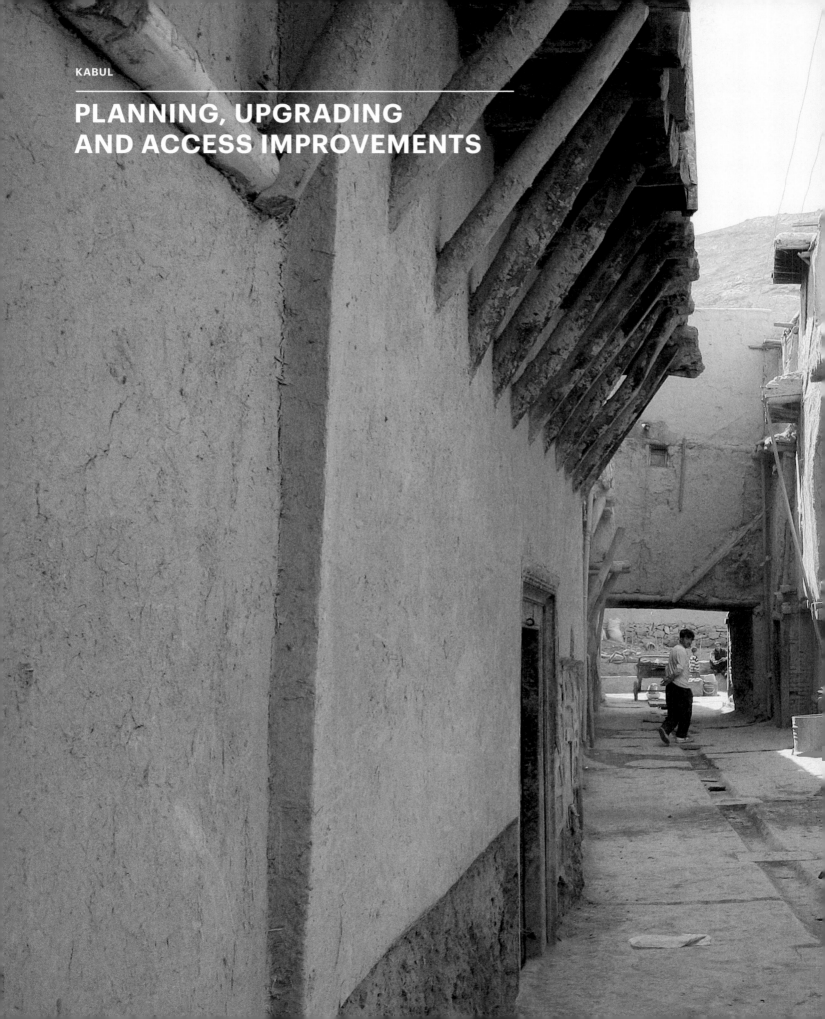

# PLANNING, UPGRADING AND ACCESS IMPROVEMENTS

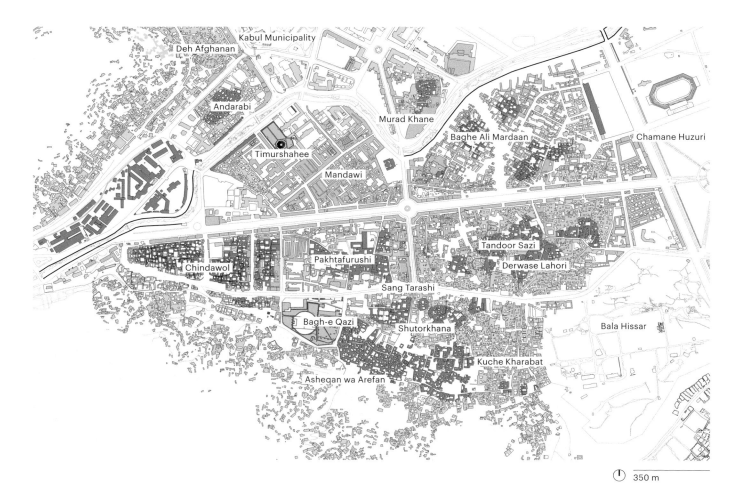

Deh Afghanan

Kabul Municipality

Andarabi

Murad Khane

Timurshahee

Baghe Ali Mardaan

Chamane Huzuri

Mandawi

Tandoor Sazi

Pakhtafurushi

Chindawol

Derwase Lahori

Sang Tarashi

Bagh-e Qazi

Shutorkhana

Bala Hissar

Kuche Kharabat

Asheqan wa Arefan

350 m

**Preceding pages, restoration of public spaces and streetscapes as part of AKTC's conservation programme in the Old City.**

**Above, mapping of historic areas and quarters, Kabul Old City.**

◼ Key surviving historic areas
▫ Traditional residential areas in rapid transformation
▫ High-density commerce in rapid transformation

**Below, poor and inadequate infrastructure is one of the main causes of health-related problems in the Old City.**

## PLANNING

The construction boom that Kabul has witnessed since 2003 continues to generate employment for those engaged in the many commercial construction sites in the city. In the Old City, however, four out of five residents are recent immigrants, many of whom rely on casual employment in the adjacent bazaars that, at best, provide meagre and insecure wages. The subdivided homes of the Old City are one of the few places in the centre where such immigrants can find affordable rooms to rent. Whereas the bulk of new migrants had in the past built basic homes for themselves in the informal settlements on vacant government land, this is now less accessible. Rising prices have forced families seeking affordable shelter to the outer margins of the city, where there has been negligible investment in public infrastructure and, with few opportunities for employment, many families now face impoverishment.

In the context of a process of urban recovery that since 2002 has been largely ad hoc and uncontrolled, AKTC works with Afghan institutions and residents to prepare neighbourhood plans to guide reconstruction and development within specific quarters, while ensuring that such initiatives are consistent with wider planning processes for the metropolitan area of Kabul. An important contribution to the planning process was made through the formulation in 2005 of a joint planning framework for the residential neighbourhood of Chindawol, which remains under intense pressure from commercial development in adjoining areas. Initial mapping of land use, infrastructure and services was followed by a series of intensive participatory planning exercises with municipal staff and representatives from Chindawol, leading to identification of development priorities over a five-year period, along with assignment of institutional responsibilities.

In order to address the issue of responsibilities for planning and urban management, an Old City Development Commission was formed in 2004, with a view to ensuring more effective collaboration between concerned institutions. With participation from ministerial and municipal staff, academics, professionals and community representatives, the Commission serves as a clearing house for information and provides a valuable platform for consultations between professionals and residents on critical development and technical issues. Its efforts to contribute to the process of planning, however, have been less successful, due both to a lack of professional capacity and persistent institutional rivalries.

As pressure on urban land and housing mounts, and uncontrolled 'development' encroaches on the surviving historic fabric, the future of the Old City requires action

Above, construction of hillside stairs as part of access improvement work around Babur's Garden.

Below, removal and disposal of accumulated waste from public drains in the historic areas in the Old City.

at a variety of levels: formulation of effective national policy on urban heritage; and the promotion of consultative processes of planning. Also needed is more effective urban management; the enhancement of professional and craft skills; technical support for families to repair or upgrade traditional homes; and the promotion of economic activity to enable residents to afford these.

The various initiatives being undertaken by AKTC in the Old City of Kabul require combined efforts on different levels: contributing to policy formulation in the ministerial domain; promoting effective urban governance among municipal staff; facilitating participatory area planning with all stakeholders; defining neighbourhood priorities with community representatives; identifying affordable ways of repairing or upgrading homes with individual owners; and training Afghan professionals and craftsmen in conservation and project management. In all of these discussions and negotiations, it remains important to maintain a balance between conservation and development, that is, basing interventions on a sound understanding of the past while allowing for new needs and opportunities to emerge, in response to the aspirations and resources of local residents.

Despite an official ban imposed in 2002 on new construction in the Old City, pending the formulation of a rehabilitation plan, commercial redevelopment has proceeded along Jade Maiwand and other main roads, while the reconstruction of traditional residential property has quietly continued inside many quarters and along the steep hillsides above the Old City. With property values rising throughout the city, pressure to lift the ban has mounted from owners and developers. While officials, who earlier advocated comprehensive redevelopment of the Old City, now accept the need for safeguarding key areas (which has been enshrined in the draft Afghan national urban strategy), their institutions have limited capacity to undertake the analysis and negotiation required in the formulation of a workable rehabilitation plan.

### UPGRADING AND ACCESS IMPROVEMENTS

A critical component of AKTC's Area Development Programme focuses on the upgrading of basic infrastructure and services in the Old City and around key historic sites such as Babur's Garden and Timur Shah's Mausoleum and park. Due to decades

**Above, joint planning exercise with government officials, professionals and community representatives.**

**Left, construction of storm-water drainage around Babur's Garden led to a significant reduction in the destruction of hillside settlements.**

**Right, construction of suitable drainage and alleyways and installation of potable water pumps have contributed to an improvement in living conditions for many in the Old City.**

of under-investment and neglect, as well as more recent conflict-related damage, much of the fragile stock of housing in these areas is subdivided and residents have access to only the most rudimentary services.

In order to address the abject living conditions facing the majority of residents in these areas, since 2002 AKTC has invested in repairs or construction of drains, paving of alleyways and streets, and provision of safer water supplies, benefiting nearly 25,000 inhabitants. These interventions have generated significant employment within the resident communities, which have also benefited from a range of measures aimed at promoting small-scale economic activity, especially among women. Together with the jobs created through conservation projects, these investments have contributed to the process of recovery across these quarters, where self-built repair and infill construction is on the increase.

As part of efforts to improve living conditions for the residents, nearly six kilometres of underground and surface drains have been repaired or rebuilt, while an area of more than 22,000 square metres of pedestrian alleyways and streets has been paved within the historic fabric of the Old City.

In the residential area surrounding Babur's Garden, where sustained conflict had caused widespread damage to the housing stock, more than 9.5 kilometres of stormwater drainage have been created and two kilometres of access improvements have been made, including the construction of hillside staircases that allow communities access to water and other services. Investments made by AKTC in upgrading and improving public infrastructure have encouraged homeowners to rebuild or improve their properties. With a significant rise in property prices in recent years, further affected by the proximity of residences to the restored Babur's Garden, the socio-economic status of communities living around the garden has greatly improved.

Meeting of the coordination group responsible for planning and upgrading activities around Babur's Garden.

# HERAT

# INTRODUCTION

Preceding pages, the Ikhtyaruddin Citadel as seen from the Mullah Rasoul Mosque in the Old City of Herat.

Herat Old City quarters.

1  Bar Durrani
2  Qutbe Chaq
3  Momandha
4  Abdullah Mesri

Old City of Herat: new constructions (2002–09).

Residential buildings
Public buildings

250 m

## HISTORY

From its origins as an outpost of the Achaemenid Empire, the repeated strengthening of the citadel of Qala Ikhtyaruddin, and the setting out of a walled settlement by the Ghaznavids, the city of Herat has had a turbulent history. Situated at the crossroads of regional trade, in the midst of rich irrigated agricultural land, the area has been a prize for successive invaders. The city became a centre for Islamic culture and learning during the reign of Timur, whose successors commissioned several monumental buildings, but it then fell into decline under the Mughals. Considered part of Persia during the Safavid era, in the eighteenth century, it was not until 1863 that Herat was incorporated into the emerging Afghan state.

The distinctive rectilinear layout of the city of Herat was delineated by massive earthen walls that protected the bazaars and residential quarters that lay within. This was the extent of the city until the middle of the twentieth century, when administrative buildings were constructed outside the walls to the north-east. In time, wealthier families moved away from the densely inhabited historic fabric into suburbs that spread across what had been gardens to the north. The historic quarters remained home to some 60,000 people by the time that unrest broke out in 1979, resulting in the depopulation of the western quarters, where traditional buildings soon fell into disrepair or collapsed and infrastructure was looted or damaged. It was not until 1992 that clearance of mines and unexploded ordnance began, enabling families to re-settle in the war-affected historic quarters and begin the process of rebuilding.

With a rapid increase in urban population since 2002, pressure on central residential neighbourhoods has intensified, even though the state of the infrastructure and the few public facilities result in poor living conditions for most inhabitants. In many cases, returning families who had become accustomed to modern dwellings while in exile have demolished their traditional homes and, in the absence of building controls, built incongruous concrete structures, dozens of which now rise above the skyline of the Old City. Residential areas that adjoin main roads are rapidly being commercialized, with the construction of multi-storey 'markets' that have a negative environmental and visual impact on the historic fabric.

In order to address these transformations, AKTC's programme in Herat has, since 2005, involved processes of documentation, building conservation and upgrading, in parallel with measures to strengthen the capacity of, and coordination between, key institutions.

Above, view of the Old City showing residential and commercial areas, with the Ikhtyaruddin Citadel (centre) and minarets (centre-left) seen in the distance, 1916–17.

Below, mid-19th-century sketch-plan of the Old City of Herat, measuring roughly 1.5 kilometres square, prepared by the Royal Engineers of the British Army.

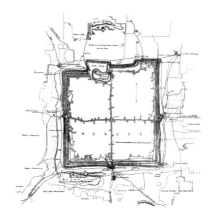

# PHYSICAL CONSERVATION
# AND RESTORATION

# HERAT OLD CITY

## HISTORY

Having largely survived periods of neglect and conflict, the Old City of Herat faces threats, as new-found prosperity drives a construction boom and uncontrolled 'development' spreads throughout the traditional historic fabric. In the face of this damaging process of transformation, AKTC established an Area Development Programme in early 2005 to document the surviving fabric, as a basis for initiating pilot conservation and upgrading measures in key neighbourhoods, while promoting more effective management of the urban environment. The challenge was to find a balance between addressing poor living conditions in key 'pressure points' in the Old City and to meet urgent conservation needs, while simultaneously strengthening institutional capacity. This has required work at a variety of levels: with central government to promote administrative reform and accountability; with local government to promote effective coordination and enhance professionalism; among the wider Afghan professional community to raise awareness and build partnerships; among donors and international organizations to draw attention to both the rehabilitation needs and continuing threats posed to the fragile historic fabric of the Old City of Herat. Given the pace of change, one of the first priorities was to map the historic fabric and establish systems for monitoring demolitions and new construction. A survey of more than 25,000 residential and commercial properties in the Old City yielded important information about the urban environment, which was mapped and linked to a database.

The prime focus of AKTC's conservation work has been on two clusters that are part of the historic fabric, extending across the Bar Durrani and Abdullah Mesri quarters, where investments have been made in the conservation of key public buildings — mosques, cisterns and bazaars — as well as historic houses. A system of small-scale grants and building advice was also established, aimed at enabling some fifty owners of traditional homes to undertake basic repairs, which has resulted in improved living conditions while protecting the integrity of the historic fabric. As well as safeguarding historic property, these projects have provided a platform for the training of craftsmen, while demonstrating the potential of conservation and adaptive reuse in a context where there is a growing tendency to demolish historic property and 'redevelop'.

At the centre of one such cluster lies the domed Chahar Suq Cistern, built in 1634; along with smaller cisterns, it remained the primary source of water for inhabitants of the Old City until the 1970s. The massive structure supports a brick dome that spans nearly twenty metres over a square reservoir that, at the time of initial surveys, was filled with domestic waste. Extensive repairs were carried out on the war-damaged

Preceding pages, the restored Chahar Suq Cistern and market complex as seen from the congested crossroads at the geographic centre of the Old City.

Opposite page, typical Herati courtyard houses, such as the ones seen here, are fast being replaced with modern concrete constructions.

Above, a general view of an alleyway within the dense fabric of the area, partially covered by a traditional vaulted *dalan*.

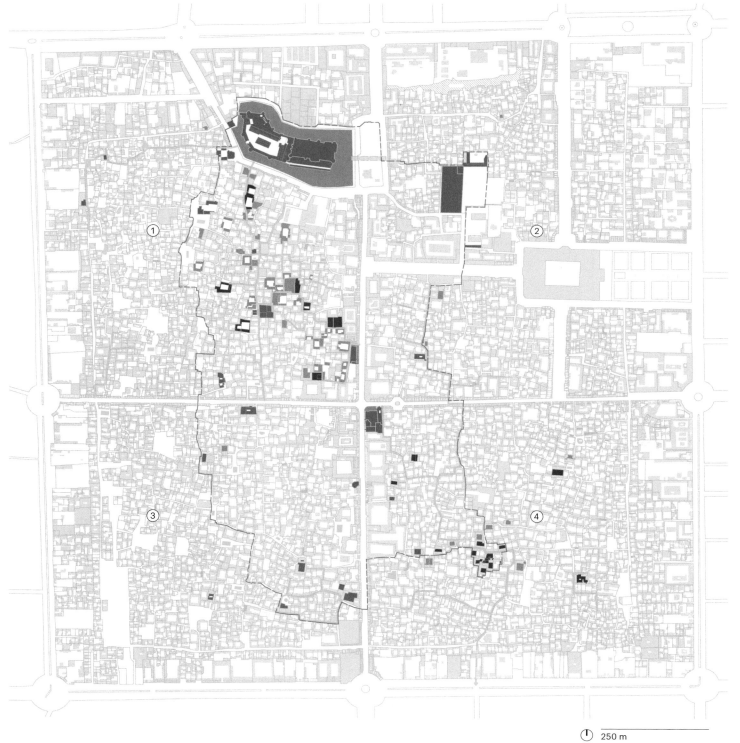

**Herat Old City quarters.**

1  Bar Durrani
2  Qutbe Chaq
3  Momandha
4  Abdullah Mesri

**AKTC interventions: Herat Old City (2005–11).**

Small-scale residential
Full-scale residential
Public buildings
Drainage and access
Landscaping
--- Core of intervention area

250 m

dome and the masonry substructure that had been weakened by encroachments from adjoining shops. An urban square has been created in front of the north entrance, after the relocation of shops that had encroached on this area. Since its conservation, the Chahar Suq Cistern has been in regular use for cultural events, including exhibitions and music recitals.

Of the other cisterns that have been conserved in the Old City, one is being used as an art gallery, another is being converted into a public library, while another serves as a study space for students of a madrasa. Among other initiatives aimed at promoting the adaptive reuse of historic buildings is the Karbasi House, now a school for traditional music and crafts, and the Yu Aw Synagogue that is now used as a kindergarten. Among the thirty other public buildings that have been conserved in the Old City are the historic mosques of Hazrat Ali and Khwaja Rokhband as well as several shrines, synagogues and a hammam or bathhouse. The single largest project undertaken in Herat by AKTC entailed the conservation of parts of the historic citadel of Qala Ikhtyaruddin, where work began in late 2008 and was completed at the end of 2011.

Together with conservation of historic homes, these initiatives have provided opportunities for training in traditional construction and decorative techniques. Among the most significant of these dwellings is the Attarbashi House, which dates from the early twentieth century and retains distinctive northern and southern groups of rooms (for use in summer and winter respectively), arranged around a courtyard. Traces of decorated plasterwork and intricate lattice *orosi* screens were found in a partially collapsed section of the house, which has been rebuilt, along with a small hammam for use by the family. To the south, in the Abdullah Mesri quarter, a very unusual painted mural was discovered in 2008 in the Ghulam Haider Posteendoz House. Once the home of a wealthy family, the complex was found to be in a poor state of repair, and conservation work is under way on the structure, following documentation and stabilization of the mural.

As much as building conservation, however, the upgrading of infrastructure is critical to the future of the Old City of Herat. In order to contribute to the improvement of living conditions, nearly five kilometres of underground and surface drains have been repaired or rebuilt, and more than 6000 square metres of pedestrian alleyways and streets paved to facilitate access through the historic fabric. Together with the building conservation work, this has generated more than 240,000 workdays of skilled and unskilled labour, largely drawn from residents of the Old City, since 2005. These investments have directly benefited at least half of the population of the Old City, prompting

An aerial image of the square plan of the Old City,
showing the main crossroads laid out according
to cardinal directions.

community-implemented improvements in some quarters that were not covered under AKTC's urban conservation programme.

Aside from the physical challenges facing the historic fabric and the need for additional investment to render the Old City more habitable, the issue of management of the urban environment is now more critical than ever. Despite assurances that new development will be rigorously controlled, and appropriate plans drawn up to ensure safeguarding of the unique fabric of the Old City, municipal officials seem unable or unwilling to act to halt demolitions or inappropriate 'redevelopment'. Given that many such officials lack the professional training or experience to effectively manage urban growth in this sensitive context, AKTC staff provide technical assistance to a Commission for the Safeguarding and Development of the Old City of Herat, comprising representatives from key institutions and professional bodies. While it has made limited progress on reform of systems of building permits and the monitoring of new construction or demolition, the Commission provides a platform for discussion between key stakeholders, and a clearing house for information. While some progress has been made in involving communities themselves in the safeguarding of historic property, the absence of effective leadership on the part of civil servants has often handicapped these initiatives.

**Below, left, speculative commercial development continues unabated, seen here encroaching upon the outer fortifications of the Old City.**

**Right, above, historic property being demolished and replaced with a modern construction.**

**Right, below, a historic mosque destroyed overnight, together with any archaeology that may have remained in the area, preparing the way for a new cast-concrete construction.**

**Masons lay traditional brick pavers at the
Khwaja Rokhband Shrine.**

Most of the key historic monuments in the Old City have now been formally registered
as part of an ongoing collaboration between AKTC and the Department of Historic
Monuments of the Ministry of Information and Culture. In order to build local professional capacity, students from Herat University have been engaged in on-the-job
education through the AKTC programme, which also supports site visits and lectures
about conservation, planning and urban management issues. It is hoped that this
cadre of young Afghan professionals will be in the vanguard of continued efforts to
safeguard and develop their city, and possibly other historic centres in Afghanistan.

Over the course of its seven-year conservation initiative in Herat, the AKTC programme prioritized projects that addressed the poor living conditions of inhabitants
of the Old City, while meeting urgent conservation needs through a balanced engagement with local communities and institutional partners. In the process, significant support was provided towards strengthening institutional capacity and promoting accountability, while outreach and awareness-raising programmes effectively
engaged the community as supporters and advocates of conservation initiatives.
Partnerships built under this programme with local professionals, donors, and international organizations have had a lasting impact as Afghan professionals and craftsmen trained by the AKTC continue to be engaged in conservation projects in the city.
While key challenges have been effectively addressed during the course of AKTC's
work, others persist, posing significant risk to the historic fabric of Herat and requiring concerted efforts to prevent further destruction to one of Afghanistan's most
important historic cities.

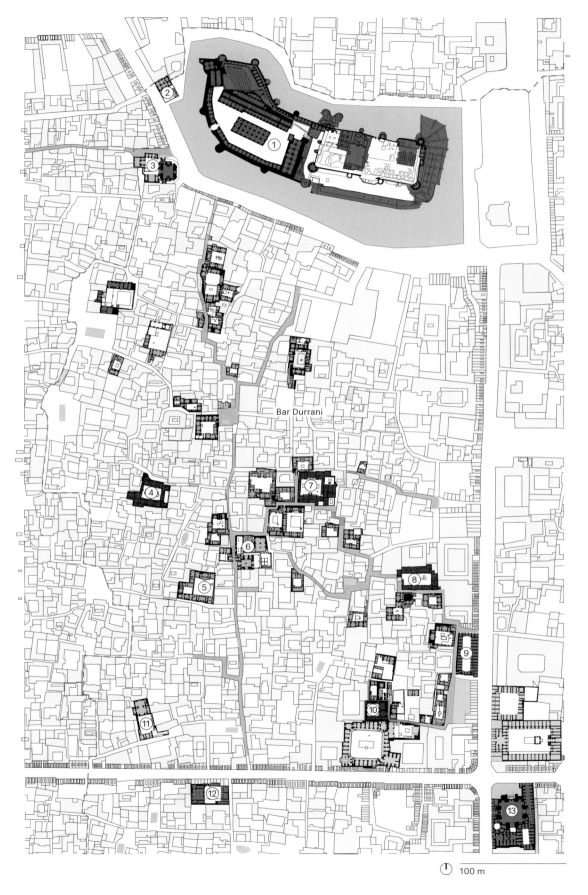

1 Ikhtyaruddin Citadel
2 Shash Nal Mosque
3 Malik Mosque and
  Cistern Complex
4 Attarbashi House
5 Qandahari House
6 Khwaja Rokhband
  Mosque and Cistern
  Complex
7 Karbasi House
8 Akhawan House
9 Arbabzadah Serai
10 Mukhtarzada House
11 Hazrat-e Bilal Mosque
12 Hariva School
13 Chahar Suq Cistern
  and Market Complex

Conservation of
religious buildings
Conservation of
public buildings
Full-scale residential
conservation
Small-scale
residential repairs
Public access and
infrastructure/
commercial
Other properties
documented
Open (green) space
rehabilitation

Bar Durrani

100 m

167

# Malik Mosque and Cistern Complex

Above, the Malik Mosque and Cistern complex prior to restoration.

Below, the water cistern was in a poor state of repair and used by traders and residents as a waste dump.

### HISTORY AND CHARACTERISTICS

The summer and winter mosques that adjoin the domed Malik Cistern are thought to have been built on the site of a Ghorid-era Sufi place of worship (*khanaqa*). The cistern was badly damaged in an earthquake in 1485 and was not repaired until the seventeenth century, under the Safavids. By the nineteenth century, both mosques had fallen into disrepair and inscriptions at both sites document that in 1857 repairs to the winter mosque were undertaken by Qorban Ali, while the summer mosque was repaired in 1865 by Faramarz Khan. The winter mosque follows the traditional form, with three semi-subterranean domed bays lit from above and accessed from the courtyard through a brick vault on the eastern side. Along with the variable quality of the brick masonry, traces of glazed bricks under modern plaster on this elevation confirm that it was extensively rebuilt. A range of lower study rooms along the north side of the courtyard may date from the original *khanaqa*. The high brick arch (*iwan*) that covers the prayer space in the summer mosque dominates the southern side of the courtyard, above which there is a raised platform flanked by two levels of study rooms. The brick-domed water cistern that forms the eastern side of the courtyard was the principal water source for the inhabitants of the Darb-e Malik neighbourhood until the 1970s and possibly also for the garrison in the adjoining citadel of Qala Ikhtyaruddin. Originally supplied by a channel that led water from outside the city to the north, the cistern had fallen into disrepair and was being used as a rubbish-tip when documentation began in 2005. The marble water outlet, carved in the shape of a lion, survives. The external brickwork of the cistern suggests that buildings that adjoined it to the south and east were demolished, probably at the time that a vehicular road was created through the northern gate of the Old City (Darwaza Malik) in the 1950s.

### WORK UNDERTAKEN

Restoration of the Malik Mosque and Cistern complex began in early 2005 with the clearance of waste from the interior of the redundant cistern and removal of a thick layer of accumulated earth from the dome. Following a thorough inspection of the brick-masonry vaults and squinches, supporting the brick dome spanning the semi-underground rectangular cistern, repairs were carried out with traditional fired bricks laid in lime mortar. The roof surface was then weatherproofed with lime mortar and finished with brick paving in order to provide a durable surface for maintenance. The waterproof plaster of the tank was then repaired, using a mix of lime, sand, wood

Top left, conservation work commenced with repairs to the dome of the cistern.

Top right, accumulated debris had to be removed from the roof of the cistern before structural consolidation and repair work (seen here) could begin.

Bottom left, masons working to repair brickwork at the entrance to the Malik Mosque.

Bottom right, brick paving laid in the courtyard of the mosque will enable additional areas for communal prayer.

Above, no longer suitable to contain water, the restored Malik Cistern is being used for cultural training activities.

Left, the courtyard of the restored Malik Mosque.

Right, the restored cistern with areas of repairs and repointing clearly distinguishable.

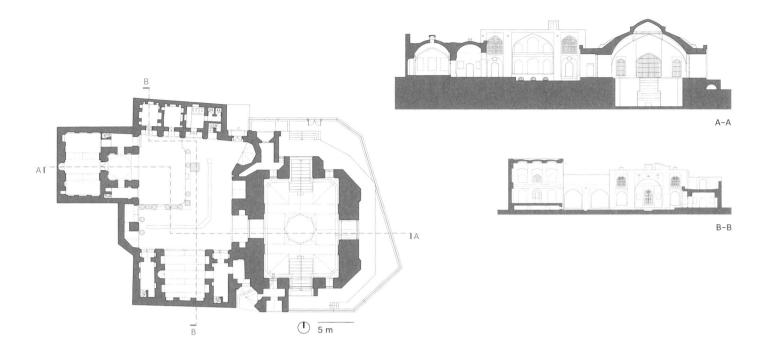

A–A

B–B

B

A

B

⊕ 5 m

ash, coal, plant fibres and brick powder prepared in the traditional manner. During the course of repairs to damaged walls to the east, traces were found of a plinth, which has been reconstructed in order to protect the building from traffic along the adjoining street. The bulk of the restoration work on the Malik Cistern was completed at the end of 2006.

Following detailed surveys, restoration work was initiated in early 2006 on the summer mosque. Using fired bricks applied with lime mortar, repairs were carried out to the *iwan* over the main prayer space, which had become separated from the southern back wall of the complex. Following the removal of a modern concrete floor in the prayer space, the substructure of parallel brick vaults was repaired and the area re-paved with fired bricks. Small prayer rooms on the upper level on each side of the main space were repaired and their traditional wooden screens (*orosi)* that give on to the courtyard were restored. Missing parts of the carved marble inscription that runs as a frieze around the main prayer space were located and refixed in place. Restoration work was completed by early 2007.

During the course of work in 2006, modern cement plaster and flooring were removed from the interior of the semi-underground winter mosque, which showed signs of extensive rising damp. The structure was left to dry out, before modern plaster on the east elevation was removed, revealing several sections of glazed brickwork around the modest *iwan*. The restoration of this elevation has entailed the reopening of the central arch to the courtyard and the installation of traditional *orosi* screens in the openings on the upper floor. The removal of the modern concrete floor and backfill material inside the winter mosque restored its original floor level, matching the raised prayer platform in the courtyard. A row of small vaulted study rooms along the north side of the courtyard, which had all but collapsed, were rebuilt using the original bricks applied with lime mortar. As part of efforts to improve access to basic services for the inhabitants of the area, the public water supply in the courtyard was upgraded, followed by the construction of drainage and a small ablution block and toilet.

The restoration project for the Malik complex (mosque and cistern) received an 'Award of Excellence' in the 2008 UNESCO Asia-Pacific Heritage Awards for Cultural Heritage Conservation and currently the cistern serves as an art gallery for painting and calligraphy.

**Above, ground-floor plan and sections.**

**Below, a public display of calligraphy and paintings produced inside the restored cistern.**

# Khwaja Rokhband Mosque and Cistern Complex

**Above, comprised of a water cistern, several spaces for prayer and a courtyard area for gathering, the Khwaja Rokhband Mosque was in a poor state of repair.**

**Below, the complex is one of the finest examples of religious monuments remaining in Herat.**

### HISTORY AND CHARACTERISTICS

The shrine of Khwaja Rokhband (literally the "master who covers his face"), located in the Bar Durrani quarter of the Old City, comprises three mosques and a water cistern grouped around a historic graveyard — shaded by several mature pistachio and pine trees. During conservation of historic graves in the courtyard of the complex, a dedication carved in the original marble headstone dating from AD 846 (AH 232) was discovered concealed beneath a modern marble panel surrounding the grave of Khwaja Rokhband. While the original shrine may have dated from the mid-ninth century, it was rebuilt in the seventeenth century by the Safavid rulers of Herat and later, in the later nineteenth century, repaired by a local merchant by the name of Attarbashi — whose house was also restored by AKTC in 2008. The water cistern and underground mosque was probably built during the Safavid reconstruction of the site, while the winter mosque is an early twentieth-century addition by the community.

### WORK UNDERTAKEN

Accessed from a small narrow covered passage (*dalan*), the Khwaja Rokhband Shrine was surveyed extensively in 2006, when it was discovered that the multiple buildings of the complex required extensive structural repair and weatherproofing. Conservation work began with stripping damp internal plaster from the walls of the semi-underground winter mosque, in order to assess the condition of the structural brick masonry, which was subsequently repaired and partially reconstructed. During the course of this work, a number of fired-clay vessels was found to have been built into the squinches of the brick vault, presumably to reduce the weight above arches and allow for ventilation of masonry.

Modern concrete was then removed from the internal floor of the winter mosque, which was re-paved with fired bricks. At this stage, it was possible to repair the roof surface of the mosque, which serves as a raised outdoor prayer area and a place for religious education. Small skylights were introduced in the fired-brick surface to provide light to the mosque below.

Work on the conservation of the cistern began with the removal of accumulated waste from inside the main water reservoir, followed by clearance of the mud-straw plaster (*kahgil*) finish from the surface of the brick-masonry dome that covers the centre of this building. Following repairs to sections of the fired-brick masonry, a layer of traditional weatherproof lime concrete was laid and finished with fired bricks, which provide a durable surface over the entire roof. During the course of the work,

Above, constructed on multiple levels, masons work to repair the masonry domes over the winter prayer space.

Left, roof-level opening that looks onto the courtyard after restoration.

Right, masons laying durable baked-brick pavers above a waterproof layer of lime concrete on the roof of the cistern.

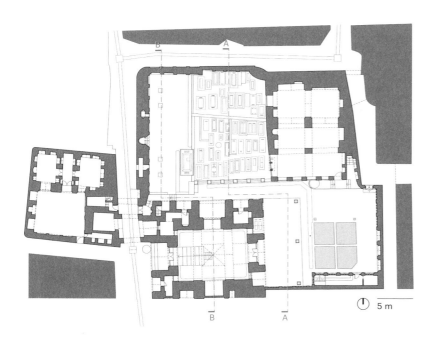

A–A

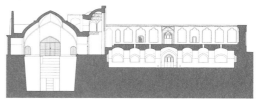

B–B

5 m

**Above, ground-floor plan and sections.**

**Below, left, view of restored *muqarnas* decoration above the main arch (*iwan*) of the cistern.**

**Right, inscriptions found on marble within the complex date to the mid-9th century.**

the brick arch on the east side of the cistern was found to be structurally unstable, and was therefore largely rebuilt using materials similar to the original ones. On the north side of the cistern, ribbed plaster decoration in the central arch was repaired, following the pattern of the original work. On the east side of the cistern, an area used for community prayers was re-paved with fired bricks.

The final stage of the work entailed stabilization of damaged sections of internal lime plaster, and the fixing of screens to the openings, to deter those intending to dispose of waste in the reservoir. A new ablution block was built in the south-east corner of the compound, and brick paving laid between the historic graves in the adjoining cemetery, which is an important part of the complex.

Left, the restored conical dome of the cistern against the backdrop of the Old City.

Below, the restored complex provides a space for relaxation and contemplation.

# Shash Nal Mosque

**The Shash Nal Mosque is located within a dense commercial area affected by road expansion work.**

### HISTORY AND CHARACTERISTICS

The restoration of the Shash Nal Mosque, a late-nineteenth-century structure located south of the Ikhtyaruddin Citadel and forming part of the historic Darb-e Malik (the northern gate to the walled city), has enabled the safeguarding of an important architectural ensemble regularly used for prayer and religious education. The mosque risked demolition under a road-widening scheme, which would also have incurred destroying other historic structures in its path. AKTC's restoration of this mosque prevented widespread damage.

Prior to restoration work, which started in early 2010, the whole complex was in a poor state of repair with the courtyard surfaced in modern concrete while the fired-brick perimeter walls were in a precarious condition. The mosque comprises six brick-domed bays, four of which make up the main prayer space, facing a walled court-yard to the south that is also used as an outdoor prayer area. As part of the restoration, a small ablution and toilet block was reconstructed in the south-east corner of the courtyard. The main south elevation facing the courtyard is articulated into seven bays of fired-brick masonry.

### WORK UNDERTAKEN

Conservation work commenced with the removal of accumulated earth material from the roof, allowing AKTC teams to inspect the condition of the brick-masonry dome underneath. It was found to be in poor condition, and repairs were carried out before backfilling with brick fragments and weatherproofing the roof with lime concrete. Flat fired-brick paving was used to finish the roof, providing a durable surface for mainte-nance. The main south-facing facade of the mosque was cleaned and exposed brick-work was repointed. Damaged sections of internal and external load-bearing brick walls and columns were repaired, followed by the paving of floors in the prayer space using flat fired bricks applied with damp-proof lime mortar.

Modern steel windows and doors were replaced with traditional cedar (*archa*) wood fenestration produced in AKTC's carpentry workshop. In the final stage of work, traditional fired-brick paving was laid in the courtyard, followed by the construction of a water well and ablution facilities. The mosque was handed back to the commu-nity in 2011 and has since been used for daily worship.

Above, one of the few historic structures remaining in an area otherwise transformed by speculative development, the mosque provides a glimpse of the architecture of the Old City in the late 19th century.

Left, view from the courtyard of the mosque towards the Iktyaruddin Citadel.

Right, worshippers praying within the restored mosque.

Below, ground-floor plan.

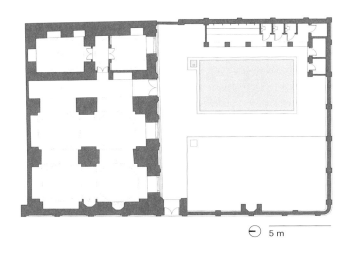

5 m

# Hazrat-e Bilal Mosque

Although the Hazrat-e Bilal Mosque was in use prior to restoration, it remained in a poor state of repair.

## HISTORY AND CHARACTERISTICS

Situated in the Bar Durrani quarter, the structure that is now used as the Hazrat-e Bilal Mosque was originally built as a synagogue in the early twentieth century. It was one of four principal synagogues in the Old City and was originally named the Gul Synagogue, having been built for the use of the sizeable Jewish community that lived in Herat at that time.

Most probably erected on the foundations of an earlier building, the main structure is built of mud and surfaced with fired bricks, comprising a large central dome surrounded by arched and vaulted spaces, with a smaller secondary dome to the north. A screened gallery on the first floor, which was possibly used by women, runs around the north and east sides of this main space. A brick-vaulted basement extends beneath the structure. It is accessed from the courtyard to the south by stairs leading to an open lobby that runs along the east side of the building. It is thought that this site began to be used as a mosque in the 1970s, after the departure of the Jewish community from Herat. At this time the raised platform (*bima*) in the central space was removed, a prayer niche (*mihrab*) created on one of the main piers of the structure, and the internal decoration on the soffit of the dome (part of which is still visible) painted over.

In the western wall, the space in which the Torah was kept has been retained, along with the original plaster decoration. The main elevation, which is made up of an arched panel within which lie three doors at the lower level and a central screened window flanked by smaller openings above, is similar to other synagogues in Herat. In the Hazrat-e Bilal Mosque, the brick-domed underground chamber (*mikveh*), which was originally used for ritual cleansing, also survives.

## WORK UNDERTAKEN

After discussions with community representatives, conservation work on the Hazrat-e Bilal Mosque started in 2009 with the removal of a concrete platform that had been added in the courtyard, which blocked access to the basement. This was followed by demolition of a recently constructed dividing wall in the courtyard directly above the dome of the underground *mikveh*, which was subsequently cleared of rubble and waste. The first stage of conservation of the main building entailed removal of earth from the domes, which were repaired before laying a weatherproof layer of lime concrete finished with fired bricks. Unstable parts of the upper gallery were rebuilt, along with the flanking walls in the courtyard. Modern steel windows and doors on the south elevation were replaced with traditional wooden ones.

Top left, above, masons work to reconstruct damaged sections of the mosque.

Middle left, a craftsman repairing plaster screens constructed to provide ventilation between internal spaces.

Above, courtyard areas were paved in order to prevent seepage of water into the foundations of the building.

Left, locally produced bricks enabled masons to reconstruct damage to masonry structures.

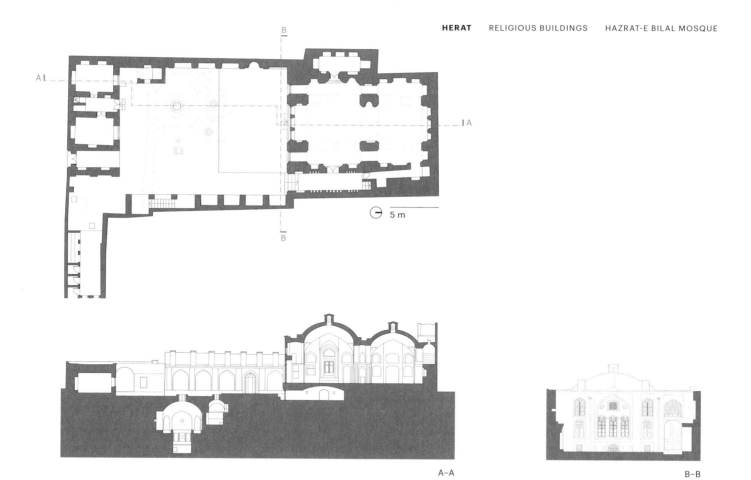

5 m

A–A

B–B

The final stage of the work entailed paving the courtyard and upgrading toilets and ablution facilities to the south-east of the complex. The conserved building is again in use as a mosque, and religious classes have resumed in the courtyard and rooms to south.

Opposite page, above, ground-floor plan and sections. Below, the restored building provides much-needed space for prayer and communal gatherings.

Above, paving laid to falls enables the redirection of water to gutters and off the roof of the building.

Below, interior view of the restored mosque.

# Mukhtarzadah House

**Above, a fine example of a large early 20th-century residential property, the Mukhtarzadah House had been abandoned during the conflict in the Old City.**

**Below, skilled labourers work to reconstruct a section of roofing.**

## HISTORY AND CHARACTERISTICS

Built by a well-known Herati merchant, whose name it bears, the Mukhtarzadah House represents an important part of the surviving traditional fabric in its area. Dating from the early twentieth century and built next to a commercial complex (*serai*) also owned by the family, the house is located in the historic Bar Durrani quarter of the Old City. The house was expanded over time to include two interconnected courtyard houses. The smaller of the two houses was the focus of a pilot conservation initiative undertaken by AKTC in early 2005. What makes the Mukhtarzadah House unique among comparable houses that survived the intense conflict in the Old City in the early 1990s is that part of it spans a covered public street (*dalan*). Once a common feature of the Old City that has mostly been destroyed, shaded *dalans* enabled the public to move through the Old City in relative comfort in warmer months and provided shelter from rain and snow.

The house is accessed through an arched gateway from the *dalan*, leading to a masonry domed octagonal vestibule (*hashti*), which retains fine brick decoration. This in turn provides access to a central courtyard, which originally formed a forecourt for a larger residence that survives to the north-west of this house. With one, large, brick-domed reception room on the ground floor, the bulk of the family quarters are on the upper level, and retain the distinctive glazed timber screens (*orosi*).

## WORK UNDERTAKEN

Following the reconstruction of the brick-domed reception room on the ground floor, where there had been infiltration of water, the flat roofs of both north and south ranges were repaired. The extensive wooden *orosi*, some of which retain panes of coloured glass at the upper levels of the house, were repaired or replaced. The final stage of the conservation work entailed repairs to the moulded brick decoration on the courtyard elevations and on the underside of the domed entrance. In parallel with the restoration work on the house, the brick-vaulted *dalan* was repaired, and drains were laid under the new stone paving.

One of the first historic houses restored by AKTC in the Old City, the project enabled technical teams to better understand brick-masonry architecture and to explore traditional conservation techniques, while providing local craftsmen an opportunity for on-the-job training. When completed, the house was used as a venue for awareness-raising events with community representatives, before being returned to its owners.

Above, left, a variety of building styles and techniques, displaying both local and regional architectural influences, were retained in the restored house.

Above, right, following its restoration, the house was handed back to owners who continue to occupy the residence.

Middle, left, restored internal space enclosed by a timber screen wall, which is uncommon to Herat, possibly inspired by the historic houses of Kabul.

Middle, right, the house is accessed through a ribbed dome space linked to a covered alleyway (*dalan*).

Below, first-floor plan and section.

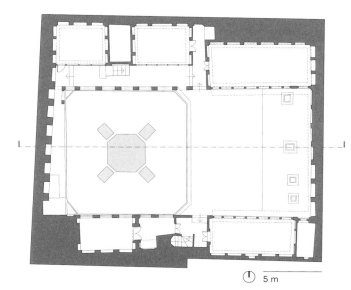

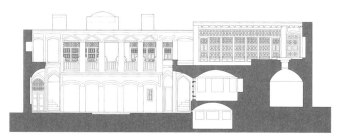

5 m

# Akhawan House

**Above, the Akhawan House prior to conservation.**

**Below, the courtyard of the house was paved in order to provide a durable finish.**

## HISTORY AND CHARACTERISTICS

The Akhawan House is an important example of the versatility of the traditional 'court-yard house' layout and local construction techniques, which have over time been adapted to the changing needs of their owners. Probably dating from the early twentieth century and possibly built on older foundations, the residential spaces of the Akhawan House are arranged in a conventional typology, with a single-storey northern and double-storey southern range of rooms. The latter range extends over the adjacent covered street (*dalan*), off which there is access via a long, vaulted corridor to the central paved courtyard of the house. There is a large pool in the centre of this courtyard and an unusually large family hammam is situated in a semi-basement area on the west side of the house. Both ranges of the house have brick-vaulted semi-basements, while the inhabited spaces on the ground and first floors have timber joist roofs. Access to rooms on the northern side is through an internal vaulted corridor that runs down the back of these spaces, separating private spaces used by the family from reception space for guests. On the southern side, there are two flights of stairs at the back of deep landings that serve as lobbies to these spaces.

## WORK UNDERTAKEN

Restoration of the Akhawan House entailed the removal of earth from most of the flat roof areas, enabling the repair of timber rafters that were close to collapse. The initial focus of conservation was on the western end of the complex, where the removal of an adjacent *dalan* had resulted in the partial subsidence of the building. Accumulated earth was removed from the semi-basements along the north side of the house, and the walls were stabilized where necessary using newly produced fired bricks and lime mortar. The roofs were stripped, damaged joists replaced, and a new protective layer of mud-straw plaster (*kahgil*) was applied. Internal plaster decoration was consolidated and repairs to damaged sections of decorative brickwork required the production of new bricks. Gypsum moulds were taken of original sections of embossed bricks and copies were made in a specially commissioned kiln, as part of AKTC's efforts to resuscitate traditional construction crafts, before being used in the conservation of the external brick facade.

Following repairs to the roofs on the southern range, modern steel windows were replaced with timber fenestration that is in keeping with the original. The paved courtyard was repaired, along with the central pool. The conservation of the Akhawan House was completed in late 2006, when it was reoccupied by the owner and his family.

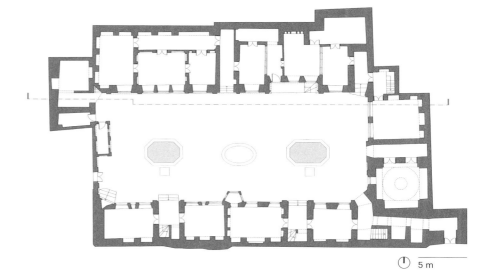

Above, stabilization work was carried out before conservation of external brick decoration could begin.

Right, ground-floor plan and section.

Below, in an environment where tourism in Herat is becoming possible, such homes may generate significant income as guesthouses or small hotels.

# Attarbashi House

**The Attarbashi House prior to conservation showing a large section of the southern range of two-storey rooms that had collapsed due to disrepair and neglect.**

## HISTORY AND CHARACTERISTICS

Located in the Bar Durrani quarter of the Old City of Herat, the Attarbashi (or Herbalists) House was built in the early twentieth century by a distinguished Herati physician and practitioner of herbal medicine. This sizeable residential complex, the various wings of which date from different periods or phases of expansion, had partially collapsed when documentation activities began in the spring of 2005.

The entrance to the house was originally from a covered street (*dalan*) over which several of its rooms stood, but which has since collapsed. The house retained characteristic features of large family homes of that era, including a northern (winter) and southern (summer) range of rooms built around a large central courtyard. Living spaces in the summer quarters were constructed with traditional wind scoops (*baadgir*), keeping spaces ventilated and cool during warmer months of the year. Upper floors on both wings are accessed via external colonnades of timber posts decorated with plaster, behind which are rooms with wooden screens (*orosi*). A collapsed, double-height, domed space retained traces of fine internal decorated plasterwork and intricate lattice screens.

As with other homes of this period, the Attarbashi House has a secondary service wing to the west, with a small octagonal courtyard giving on to a domed kitchen space with a large fireplace. In the eastern wing, close to the stables and street entrance, an unusual family bathhouse (hammam) was discovered. There is also a small shrine adjacent to the main entrance.

## WORK UNDERTAKEN

As part of AKTC's Area Development Programme in the Old City, a detailed survey of the house was undertaken, providing an opportunity to document a range of traditional construction techniques. Remains of decorated plasterwork and lattice screens excavated under the ruins of a double-height reception room in the southern range were carefully documented, and elements that could be repaired and reused in the conservation were relocated to a carpentry workshop established on the premises. Documentation of the house took place in parallel with emergency protection of vulnerable plaster decoration.

Elsewhere, most rooms of this large house had flat roofs with timber joists, which were found to be infested with termites. Accumulated earth was removed from above the roofs, following which damaged timber joists were replaced, new wooden boards were installed, and a protective layer of mud-straw plaster was applied.

Top left, rebuilding of a partially collapsed wall separating stables from a covered hammam or bathing area.

Top right, existing sections of decorated column capitals cleaned and repaired during conservation work.

Bottom left, timber columns are wrapped in straw rope before being finished with plaster.

Bottom right, large sections of decorated *orosi* windows and screens on the first-floor elevations of the house were restored and repaired, after which protective linseed oil was applied to prevent damage.

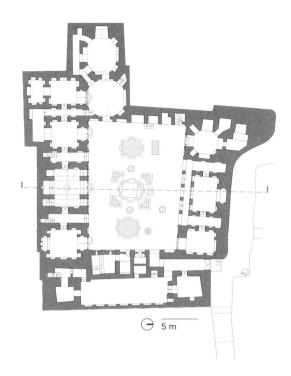

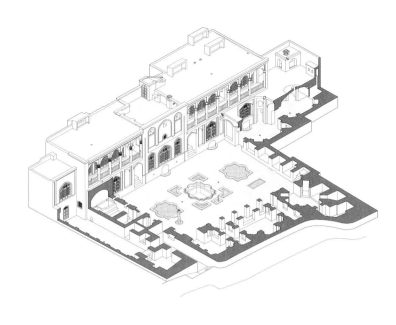

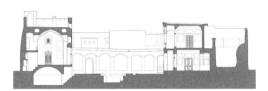

**Above, ground-floor plan, section and axonometric view.**

**Below, left, view of the upper colonnade following restoration.**

**Below, right, registered as a national monument, the restored house retains original characteristics that make it one of the finest residences in Herat.**

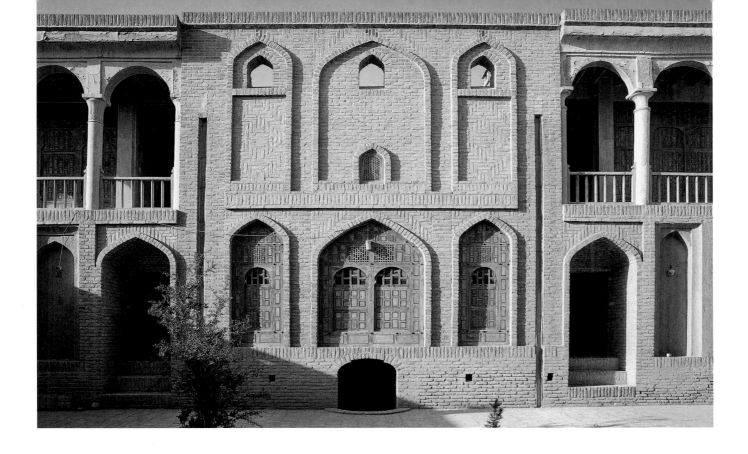

Reconstruction of the domed reception space in the southern range was undertaken, drawing on examples from similar homes in the area. External colonnades in the upper sections of both wings were restored, along with extensive repairs made to timber screens. The diversity of restoration work in the Attarbashi House has enabled the development of a range of skills among Herati craftsmen and contributed to efforts to raise awareness among community members and professionals in Herat.

Water again flows through a pool shaded by mature mulberry trees in the courtyard of the restored Attarbashi House, which is a testament to the quality of Herat's architectural heritage.

Above, view of the restored main elevation.

Left, restored living quarters on upper floors of the house.

Right, an arched internal niche on the first floor of the southern range of rooms enclosed by an *orosi* screen window.

Following pages, northern range of rooms following completion of conservation activities.

# Qandahari House

**Above, built in several phases, the Qandahari House was in a poor state of repair prior to restoration.**

**Below, damaged sections of masonry and colour-glazed tile decorations were carefully repaired.**

### HISTORY AND CHARACTERISTICS

While the Qandahari House is said to have originally been built in the third quarter of the nineteenth century, its present form may include building extensions from a later period. The house is an important example of how the courtyard layout, with separate summer and winter quarters, and traditional construction techniques came to be adapted in the early to mid-twentieth century.

Access to the house is via a small vaulted vestibule with doors to each of the two dwellings that make up the residential complex. To the east are the large family quarters, arranged in the manner of traditional Herati homes of this period: a double-storey range of rooms faces north for use in the summer, and a single-storey south-facing range on a single storey with an arcaded veranda for use in the winter months. The north-facing elevation of this house is decorated with extensive colour-glazed tile work, unusual for a residential property and more in the manner of a religious building. All rooms in the dwelling face on to a large courtyard, which is paved with brick and has a central planted area. The adjoining single-storey dwelling, which was used to entertain and for house guests, is more modest in scale and decoration.

### WORK UNDERTAKEN

Based on the physical documentation and a condition assessment prepared in 2006, conservation work on the Qandahari House has entailed focusing on structural repairs to the northern wing of the property and the replacement of large sections of the roof that had been at risk of collapse. The lower sections of load-bearing brick walls facing the courtyard, which had been damaged by water penetration, were replaced with newly produced fired bricks and repointed using lime mortar.

Areas of exposed brick arches in the main elevations had to be consolidated *in situ*, with newly produced colour-glazed tiles used to replace missing sections of external decoration. Subsequent to repairs of the brick paving of the courtyard, the house was returned to its owners in 2009.

Left, unique in Herat for its extensive use of colour-glazed tile decoration, the house displays a variety of architectural design influences.

Right, double-height decorated niches on a boundary wall help unify the architectural vocabulary on the courtyard elevations of the house.

Bottom, first-floor plan and section.

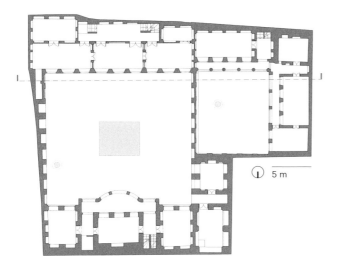

5 m

# Karbasi House

**Above, the Karbasi House was named after its owner, a merchant of linen cloth, and required extensive repair.**

**Below, sections of the original woodwork were salvaged and reused in the restoration of the house.**

### HISTORY AND CHARACTERISTICS

The Karbasi House, situated in a dense residential neighbourhood in the Bar Durrani quarter, was built on the foundations of an older traditional house in 1915 and the south range was extensively remodelled in 1959. The residential complex is on the scale of several other Old City homes of wealthy trading families, most of which have been subdivided and fallen into disrepair. The house comprises twenty rooms, partially laid out on two floors, arranged around four independent courtyards, which would originally have provided an important focus for the domestic life of the occupants.

As in other homes, the customary separation between the family quarters and guests is ingeniously ensured by the built form. With external walls of earth and straw plaster over traditional mud bricks, it is only when entering the courtyards that visitors become aware how elements of contemporary architectural styles are incorporated in the internal elevations and the fenestration. The newer south range incorporates a traditional semi-basement, used for storage or for sleeping in summer, while the north range is on a single level and retains elaborate decorative moulded brickwork around the windows.

### WORK UNDERTAKEN

Work on the Karbasi House began in mid-2006 in response to a need for suitable premises for a school of traditional music. Conservation work entailed extensive repairs to the traditional roofs, stabilization of sections of structural masonry in the north-western corner and the restoration of brick flooring, along with covered vaults that were found to exist inside the northern range. Damaged sections of decorated brickwork on the northern courtyard elevation were restored, reusing the original fired bricks where possible. The final stage of restoration entailed the removal of concrete from the courtyards and re-paving using traditional fired bricks, and landscaping. Now used as a school for traditional music run by the Aga Khan Music Initiative (AKMI; see pp. 360–369) and previously as a workshop for traditional crafts, including glass-blowing and production of decorated bricks, the complex also demonstrates the potential for adaptive reuse for contemporary needs.

The Karbasi House, together with the Malik complex (mosque and cistern) and the Abresham Bazaar, received the Award of Excellence in the 2008 UNESCO Asia-Pacific Heritage Awards for Cultural Heritage Conservation.

Above, teams working to clear debris and repair masonry brickwork.

Left, perimeter wall foundations were repaired and stabilized in sections using coarse stone masonry.

Right, *ustads* and students practicing traditional music in the courtyard of the restored house as part of the Aga Khan Music Initiative.

Below, ground-floor plan and section.

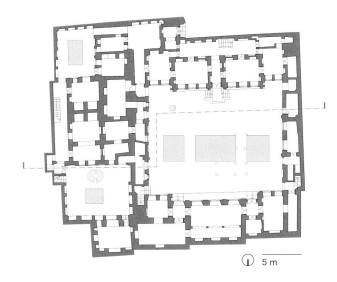

5 m

# Posteendoz House

**Above, in a poor state of repair, the Posteendoz House is one of the most important houses restored by AKTC in Herat.**

**Opposite page, craftsmen worked simultaneously to repair structural damage and consolidate existing decorative elements.**

### HISTORY AND CHARACTERISTICS

Located in the Abdullah Mesri quarter of the Old City, the Posteendoz House (named after its owner who was a furrier) is one of the most important examples of residential property to be recorded as part of AKTC's surveys in the Old City.

With highly unusual figurative painted decoration as well as fine timber fenestration and internal plasterwork, the large, two-storey courtyard house is believed to have been built at the end of the nineteenth century. At the time of AKTC's initial survey in 2008, the house had been extensively damaged, with sections of the northern range having collapsed. Additional destruction to the south-eastern corner of the courtyard had occurred after this part of the house had been sold off and redeveloped by its new owners. In addition to the size and fine architectural features of the house, what distinguished this property from others surveyed by AKTC was the discovery of an extraordinary mural painted on a plastered dome in one of the lower rooms of the western range.

Stylistically, this mural resembles the folk art of the coffee house (*qahva khanah*), popular in Iran in the late-nineteenth-century Qajar period. These paintings usually provided a backdrop for storytelling and religious rituals, particularly during Muharram, but it is not clear how this small domestic space might have been used. While some traditional houses in Herat have floral or geometric painted decoration, a figurative painting on this scale is very unusual.

### WORK UNDERTAKEN

Full-scale conservation work began in late 2009 and entailed the reconstruction of collapsed sections of structural brick masonry as well as repairs to the roofs, the colonnaded veranda, and the distinctive moulded brickwork on the courtyard elevations of the house. The external timber screens, containing sections of coloured glass, along the upper northern colonnade were repaired and conserved. Surviving areas of internal decorative painted plaster were carefully cleaned and consolidated. New timber screens and doors were produced, following traditional designs and using cedar wood, and installed in areas where the previous fenestration had been missing or destroyed. Following the completion of building conservation, the courtyard was paved using fired bricks and measures were taken to improve drainage in the wider area in order to reduce the risk of future flooding of this low-lying property.

Teams of restorers were engaged and trained in the preservation of the figurative mural decorating the internal surface of a dome in the western range. Using specialist

Above, an exquisite figurative mural, located in one of the lower rooms, was carefully restored.

Below, decorated niches in living quarters were cleaned and missing sections replaced.

Right, a carpenter working to repair damage to timber screens.

materials, detached sections of plaster were reattached to the masonry dome and missing areas were consolidated using gypsum plaster, preventing further damage to original sections of the mural. The painted surface of the mural was conserved in order to prevent damage from moisture or dust, making it possible to clean and maintain the painting in the future.

The project has also provided opportunities for on-the-job training of Afghan professionals and craftsmen in the conservation of painted decoration and carved plaster.

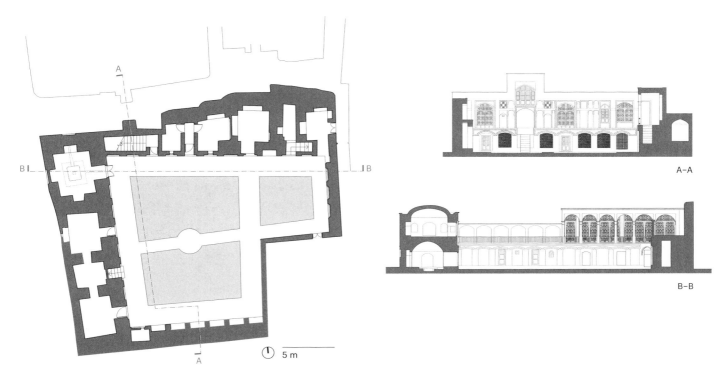

Above, ground-floor plan and sections.

Below, landscaping work was carried out and the restored house handed back to its owners.

# Entezari House

**Above, resembling historic homes in Kabul due to its extensive use of timber screens, the Entezari House was in a poor state of repair prior to restoration.**

**Below, the timber screens of the house were affected by water damage.**

### HISTORY AND CHARACTERISTICS

The Entezari House is located in the Abdullah Mesri quarter of the Old City and is believed to have been built at the end of the nineteenth century by the grandfather of the current owner. A large family house was expanded during successive generations. The property is built around two courtyards: a smaller western courtyard, which is intended for entertaining guests (*saracha*), and a larger inner courtyard around which the residential quarters are arranged.

Consisting of one- and two-storey levels, with a basement on three sides of the residential area, the house is accessed through a covered street (*dalan*) leading to the smaller western courtyard, from which an octagonal domed space (*hashti*) provides access to the private family area.

With separate areas for stables, a kitchen and storage areas, and a family hammam, the most architecturally significant space is a second-floor reception hall containing decorated niches (*chini khana*), folding timber screens (*pataii*), and a decorated wooden ceiling. The existence of wind scoops (*baadgir*) in this room means that the hall would have been occupied in the summer, making use of Herat's famous 120 days of summer winds (*baad-hae sad-o-bist rouza*), and providing the family with much-needed respite from hot summer months.

With distinctive spaces intended for separate use in summer and winter months, by guests and family members, and others allocated for services and storage, the layouts of this and other traditional Herati houses are both functional and rich in architectural variation.

### WORK UNDERTAKEN

As part of AKTC's conservation initiative in the Old City, restoration work began in mid-2007 with the removal of accumulated debris from above the roofs of the various wings of the house, followed by repairs to the timber joists and re-roofing of the building using traditional methods and materials. Once the house was protected from rain and snow, internal work included repairs and conservation of *pataii* screens, the plastering of internal spaces surrounding the eastern courtyard, and laying appropriate floor finishes. Additional work included the repair and restoration of the outer facades, including the installation of glazed tiles and decorative brickwork. Following the laying of fired-brick paving in the courtyard, the house was returned to its owners in early 2008.

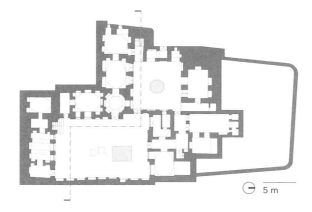

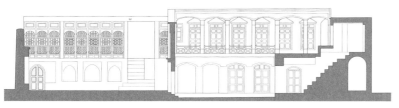

Top left, carpenters working to repair and replace sections of decorative screens.

Top right, additional work was carried out to reconstruct large areas of the roof using traditional techniques.

Above, the restored house serves as an excellent example of the cross-fertilization of architectural forms and materials between different regions of the country.

Left, ground-floor plan and section.

5 m

5 m

# Ikhtyaruddin Citadel

**Above, the Ikhtyaruddin Citadel — seen in this early 20th-century image — continued to be used as a military garrison until 2006, when it was transferred to the custodianship of the Ministry of Information and Culture.**

**Below, painted decoration within the royal residences located in the upper citadel.**

### HISTORY AND CHARACTERISTICS

As one of the most iconic landmarks in Herat, Qala Ikhtyaruddin is central to the turbulent history of the city and is an impressive example of surviving citadels in the region. Alexander the Great besieged Herat in 300 BC during his campaign against the Achaemenids. Known at the time as Artacoana (the ancient capital of Aria), Herat was rebuilt and called Alexandria of Aria. It is believed that a citadel was first established on its current site during this period. Incorporated into the northern perimeter of a square walled city by the Ghaznavids, the *qala* stood witness to the changing fortunes of successive empires before being laid waste by Genghis Khan in 1222. Rebuilt by the Kart dynasty that occupied the city in 1245, Herat was again destroyed by Timur in 1381. His son Shah Rukh transformed the citadel of Qala Ikhtyaruddin after 1415, when the fortifications were entirely rebuilt with fired bricks and new buildings were erected inside its walls. Shah Rukh located his royal residences within the citadel and the city flourished as a centre for Islamic culture and learning, with the poet Jami and the painter Behzad part of the royal court.

After falling into decline under the Mughals, Herat was the centre of a struggle for territorial control between the Persians, Uzbeks and Afghans. Critical to British strategy during the "Great Game", its forces assisted Afghans in defending Herat against a joint Russian-Persian assault in 1837. Their fortified positions were located within the citadel, before the city was formally designated as part of the emerging Afghan state in 1857. While Qala Ikhtyaruddin continued at times to play an important defensive role, its earth and fired-brick structure fell into disrepair. Fortifications were in such a poor state that the commander of the Herat garrison began to demolish them and cart off the materials for reuse in new military facilities elsewhere. This prompted the central government to intervene and to initiate a joint programme of consolidation and preservation with UNESCO in 1976.

Many of the buildings inside the upper and lower enclosures were of mud brick and largely in ruins when restoration work began in 1976. The remains of the treasury in the north-east corner of the upper citadel and the barracks and stable blocks in the lower area were stabilized or rebuilt using fired bricks in lime mortar — or gypsum for domes or vaults. A number of residential structures arranged around paved courtyards, some retaining fragments of painted plaster decoration, were also found in the upper enclosure during these investigations. Archaeological excavations along the north side of the fortifications at that time revealed a paved slope, or glacis, of large sandstone slabs laid in horizontal layers over the man-made embankment from which

20 m

# Chahar Suq Cistern and Market Complex

**Above, view of one of the last instances where the Chahar Suq Cistern was used to store and distribute water in the Old City, 1976.**

**Below, the Chahar Suq Cistern was in a poor state of repair prior to conservation work.**

### HISTORY AND CHARACTERISTICS

Built in 1634 by the Safavid governor of Herat, the Chahar Suq Cistern is located at the central crossroads of the square Old City of Herat and directly adjacent to a historic covered bazaar demolished during the British occupation of the city in 1840–42. Its name refers to the intersection of four bazaars (*chahar suq*). The structure functioned as a vital source of water for the inhabitants of the Old City until the 1970s. The brick dome of the cistern is the largest in Afghanistan, with a clear internal span of twenty metres and height of sixteen metres, capped by a large 'lantern' skylight. Built on a massive square supporting structure, the ribbed dome is covered with a sixteen-facetted infill brick-masonry surface. Open on four sides through arched portals (*iwan*), the structure is accessible from the north and west through flights of high stairs used for collecting water and cleaning the cistern. The northern main *iwan* is built with geometric ribbed brickwork, decorated with a spare use of colour-glazed tiles.

The Chahar Suq Cistern, capable of storing more than 2400 cubic metres of water, is the largest of seventeen known cisterns in an ingenious potable water network that provided water to inhabitants of the city. Water from the Harirud River was re-directed more than eighteen kilometres through the Enjil Canal into Herat and entered the cistern through an inlet on the north-eastern wall. During water shortages, water remained in the cistern where it would have been used by the public. When water was plentiful, the cistern would have been filled and an outlet on the southern wall allowed water to flow directly to houses in the Abdullah Mesri quarters of the Old City.

The Abresham Bazaar was built in the second quarter of the nineteenth century, directly adjacent to the southern elevation of the cistern. Probably sited on an earlier structure, this bazaar was built by Haji Musa, a rich merchant who also dedicated a fine mosque in the northern Qutbe Chaq quarter, where he is buried. The bazaar has been a centre for trade in silk thread since its construction, and producers from the outlying village bring silk thread for sale in the bazaar to this day, where woven woollen products are also sold.

One of only two traditional covered commercial complexes left in the Old City, the spine of the bazaar is a vaulted double-height space that leads directly from the street, and is flanked on both sides by two-storey, small, brick-domed workshops and stores.

On the upper level, these spaces retain distinctive wooden screens (*orosi*) opening on to the central space, which is lit from above by 'lantern' skylights. The structure of the bazaar is of traditional fired brick which, in the wing that adjoins the Chahar Suq Cistern, shows signs of extensive alterations and repairs. The Abresham Bazaar extends

Above, modern encroachments had been built upon the open public space at the main entrance to the cistern.

Below, accumulated debris had to be removed before structural consolidation and repair work could commence on the roofs of the complex.

**With repair work completed, brick pavers were laid on top of the dome of the cistern.**

to the east where a later addition to the market (*serai*) is arranged around an open rectangular courtyard, while another smaller complex (*qaisariah*) grouped around a tiny hexagonal courtyard lies to the north-west. This ensemble demonstrates the ingenuity of traditional builders in maximizing the use of space, while creating a series of micro-environments to address seasonal extremes. The covered Qannaad Bazaar was built at the end of the nineteenth century, replacing an earlier construction on the north-eastern side of the Chahar Suq Cistern. Together with the Abresham and Qaisariah Bazaars, these constructions have permanently transformed the external elevations of the Chahar Suq Cistern.

Having undergone a range of attempts at repair over the years, surveys conducted by AKTC in 2005 revealed significant settlement in parts of the superstructure of the cistern, caused in part by excavations carried out to construct the adjoining bazaars and as a result of damage sustained during conflict. Sections of the roofs of the Abresham and Qannaad Bazaars had suffered significant damage, with internal partition walls and timber screens in an advanced state of disrepair.

## WORK UNDERTAKEN

Conservation of the Chahar Suq complex was implemented in phases, with work commencing on the cistern in 2005. Conservation of the cistern entailed the removal of more than a metre of accumulated earth from the roof, to enable the examination of the state of brick masonry. Large sections of the dome, damaged by artillery fire, required complex structural consolidation and repair before the roof surface was finished with durable brick paving laid on lime concrete.

An outbreak of cholera in 1978 forced authorities to seal open-water cisterns and construct a piped water network for the Old City, resulting in the slow deterioration of these structures, which remained unused. Subsequent interior work included removal of accumulated waste and debris from within the cistern, before repairs could be carried out on deformed brick relieving arches under the dome. Temporary partition walls built by shop owners at entrances to the *iwans* were removed, restoring natural light and ventilation for the internal space. The walls of the water reservoir, once containing thousands of cubic metres of water, were plastered using a traditional waterproof plaster (*saru*). A mixture of hydrated lime, wood ash, natural plant fibres and animal fat, the *saru* plaster retains the black colour of coal powder used in the mix.

Restoration of the Abresham Bazaar commenced at the end of 2006, in parallel with the completion of work on the dome of the cistern. The relatively fragile state of the structure, parts of which were close to collapse, was revealed when earth was removed from the roof of the adjoining Chahar Suq Cistern, exposing ad hoc alterations to the massive brick structure that abuts the more recently built bazaar. It was also found that a double-height storage space to the south of the cistern had in fact been an open courtyard, through which water from the cistern had previously overflowed. The removal of the modern roof and a dividing wall also revealed a finely patterned brick dome over the area where water had in the past been collected by those working in or visiting the surrounding bazaars.

Above, masonry domes, vaults and arches were repaired and weatherproofed.

Below, a mason replacing missing sections of brickwork.

Left, ribbed plaster decorations (*karbandi*) were reconstructed according to designs found on original sections of the building.

With the physical link between the cistern and the Abresham Bazaar re-established, work began on phased repairs to structural masonry along the west side of the vaulted central space, where a number of the small domes over workshop areas were found to have collapsed. Several brick arches and vaults needed to be completely rebuilt, using traditional fired bricks laid in lime mortar. A series of domed workshop spaces along the south side were restored, along with the vaulted corridor by which they are accessed. With the supporting structure stabilized on both sides, the earth layer was removed from the six principal domes over the central spine of the bazaar. This enabled repairs to be made to the domes and the series of brick arches supporting them.

Matching the work that had been carried out on the adjoining Chahar Suq Cistern, the domes and the areas of flat roof over the Abresham Bazaar were finished with fired-brick paving, and brick-masonry 'lantern' skylights were rebuilt over all six domes. The underside of the entire central brick-masonry structure was then repointed with lime mortar, once access had been negotiated with the shopkeepers. A dozen traditional wooden screens were removed from the upper workshops, repaired and refixed, while several additional screens were introduced in spaces where traces of frames indicated that they had originally existed. The final stage of the work entailed the replacement of modern concrete flooring throughout with traditional fired-brick

Opposite page, the restored Sayed Mohammad Khan Bazaar being used for the sale of household goods.

Top left, with the restoration of the masonry structure and woodwork complete, workers lay brick paving in the Abresham Bazaar.

Top right, teams of carpenters work to repair and restore the timber screen of the Abresham Bazaar.

Above, individual shop units in the bazaars were repaired and made usable.

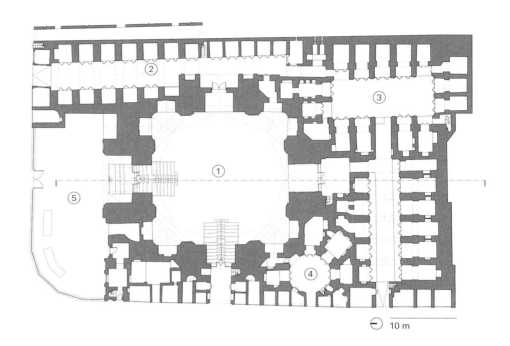

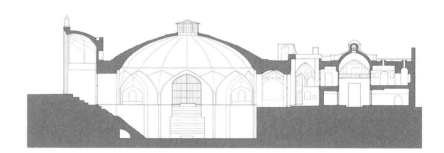

⊖ 10 m

**Right, ground-floor plan and section.**

1 Chahar Suq Cistern
2 Sayed Mohammad Khan Bazaar
3 Abresham Bazaar
4 Qaysareya Bazaar
5 Courtyard access to cistern

**Below, left,** the single-shell dome of the cistern is the largest of its kind in Afghanistan with a span of twenty metres.

**Centre,** a view of one of the restored staircases leading to the roof of the complex.

**Right,** intermittently used for public cultural functions, the restored complex provides a glimpse into the ingenuity of its builders.

paving. This also allowed for the introduction of improved underground drainage between the bazaar and neighbouring buildings. Although only part of the building was used when the restoration work started, the Abresham Bazaar has since largely reverted to its original wholesale/retail function.

Since the completion of major restoration work in 2008, the cistern has been used for public and cultural functions on an ad hoc basis. Following extensive discussions with relevant authorities and owners of commercial facilities, ad hoc encroachments to the front of the cistern were removed and an urban public plaza was restored. In addition to the main cistern space, the newly repaired roof of the cistern and adjacent bazaars provide a large recreational area, with views over the rooftops of the Old City to the east and north. The restoration of the Abresham Bazaar has enhanced the businesses of those currently leasing shops and workshops in the complex, many of whom continue traditional trade in raw silk and also sell products woven inside the market.

The restored cistern and market complex occupies a key location at the geographical centre of the Old City.

# Wazir Cistern

**Encroached upon by more recent construction, the Wazir Cistern was being used by residents of the surrounding area as a dumping ground for household waste. Below, an internal view of the cistern showing extensive damage caused by water penetration from the roof.**

## HISTORY AND CHARACTERISTICS

One of the few remaining covered water cisterns in the Old City, the Wazir Cistern is located in the Momandha quarter, 200 metres to the south of the Chahar Suq Cistern. A dedication above the main eastern arch (*iwan*) states that the cistern was built by the Safavid governor of Herat in the seventeenth century. Originally part of a larger historic fabric of bazaars and covered passages (*dalan*), the cistern is now embedded within a range of commercial premises located on the main north-south access into the Old City.

The masonry structure covering the cistern is composed of two main arches spanning approximately nine metres on a rectangular base, intersecting two sub-arches filled with half-domes and a small dome at its centre capped by an octagonal 'lantern' skylight. Having remained functional up to 1979 (when an outbreak of cholera forced its closure), at the time of surveys conducted by AKTC in 2005 the cistern was filled with waste deposited by shop owners and posed an environmental concern for residents.

## WORK UNDERTAKEN

Conservation work began in 2006 with the removal of waste and accumulated debris from within the cistern. Access to the building was provided following the removal of a temporary construction blocking its main entrance. Work on the roof of the structure required the removal of accumulated earth and repair of one of the main arches, which had deformed when penetrating water had softened its mud mortar. Following structural consolidation, the roof was backfilled using lightweight brick fragments before a weatherproof layer of lime concrete was applied and paved with fired brick.

Drainage from adjoining properties, which had until then been channelled into the cistern, was redirected to main drains and internal masonry walls allowed to dry out. Internal exposed brick elevations were cleaned and repointed, before waterproof plaster (*saru*) was applied to lower sections of the reservoir. External load-bearing walls and sections of the main *iwan* were repaired and repointed. Following completion of restoration, the property was registered as a national monument and returned to the local Department of Historic Monuments, which uses it occasionally for public events or tourist purposes.

Left, following repairs to the structure, the internal brick elevations of the restored cistern were cleaned and repointed using lime mortar.

Above, light filters through an oculus at the apex of the dome.

Below, in addition to repairing the domes and masonry arches of the cistern, new brick paving was laid on its roof and internal spaces.

Bottom, ground-floor plan and section.

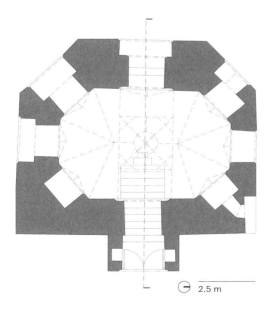

2.5 m

# Hariva School

**Above, students at the Hariva School studied in donated tents prior to conservation work.**

**Below, in a poor state of repair, the school was unsafe for use by children from the local community.**

## HISTORY AND CHARACTERISTICS

Situated in the Momandha quarter of the Old City of Herat, the structure that has been used since the 1980s as the Hariva Primary School was originally built as a synagogue in the late nineteenth century. One of four principal synagogues in the Old City, the Shamawel (or Samuel) Synagogue was built by the sizeable Jewish community that lived in Herat at that time. Probably built on the foundations of an earlier building, the present structure follows the established form, with nine brick-domed bays forming the main prayer space, at the centre of which stands a raised platform bound by four supporting piers. Along the west wall of this space are a series of small rooms that were used for religious rituals, and where the Torah was kept. The east elevation, which faces a large courtyard, makes use of both classical and vernacular elements, including traditional glazed tile work. In the courtyard lies a brick-domed underground chamber (*mikveh*) that was used for ritual cleansing. Additional buildings along the west side of the complex were in ruins at the time of surveys in 2006.

## WORK UNDERTAKEN

After protracted negotiation with the Departments of Education and Historic Monuments in Herat, it was agreed that the historic part of the synagogue would be restored and that new classrooms would be constructed to the east, on the site of the ruined outbuildings. Work began on site in 2009 with the propping of unstable parts of the structure and dismantling of those parts that were to be replaced. This was followed by the construction of the new classrooms, which follow the footprint of the original building and have been designed to respect the roofline of surrounding buildings in the Old City. Toilets and washing facilities have also been incorporated into the new building.

During the later stages of this construction, restoration work was initiated on the historic synagogue, which was re-roofed and internal plasterwork repaired, along with damaged parts of the east elevation. The completed building was handed back for use as a primary school, improving access to education for the estimated 15,000 school-age children in the Old City.

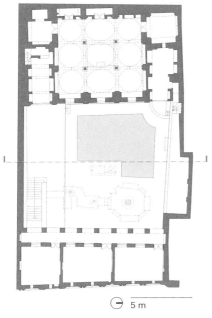

5 m

Left, first-floor plan and section.

Above, the restored school provides much-needed space for primary education in one of the densest residential areas in Herat.

Below, built originally as a synagogue, the historic parts of the building currently serve as classrooms.

# Yu Aw (Synagogue)

**Above, built by a sizeable Jewish community, the Yu Aw Synagogue was in a poor state of repair, with areas of the building having collapsed.**

**Below, the ruined sites had been vacated and served as a playground for children from the community.**

### HISTORY AND CHARACTERISTICS

Abandoned when the Jewish community left Herat in the 1970s, the Yu Aw Synagogue seems to have fallen into disrepair by the time that significant damage was inflicted on western parts of the city during the 1978 upraising and during the years of conflict that followed. Located in the Momandha quarter of the Old City, photographs from the 1990s already showed the extent of this damage with fine internal plaster decoration extensively impaired. By the time that surveys were undertaken by AKTC in 2006, the structural integrity of the complex was compromised (sizeable sections of the brick-masonry side vaults had collapsed) affecting the stability of other parts of the building.

Dating from the turn of the twentieth century, this building follows a pattern seen in other synagogues in Herat, with a large domed central space, in the centre of which stands a raised platform (*bima*).

### WORK UNDERTAKEN

Technical support was provided by AKTC to the Department of Historic Monuments towards the conservation of the synagogue in 2007. Clearance work focused on the removal of significant amounts of earth material from the ground floor of the synagogue complex (under the main prayer area), following which the structure was left for several weeks to allow the waterlogged brick-masonry walls to dry. This enabled inspection of the condition of the foundations of the main part of the complex which, it was found, took the form of a series of parallel barrel vaults running in an east-west direction.

Initial stabilization activities focused on repairs to the interior skin of the brick-masonry walling in the basement area and reconstruction of two damaged barrel vaults at the north end of the structure. At the same time, the west wall of the synagogue was propped from the outside and new brickwork inserted in areas where the brick masonry had crumbled as a result of rising damp from the adjoining street.

Following the stabilization of the basement of the synagogue, timber props were inserted into the main first-floor prayer area, whose masonry arches showed signs of structural failure. Although the entire structure was fragile, this propping enabled a thorough inspection of the surface of the brick-masonry domes, after the removal of a small section of the earth covering. Further analysis of the stability of the structure resulted in the repair of two brick arches that flanked the main prayer area, enabling the reconstruction of the two narrow brick vaults, using bricks of the same dimensions as those found in the original.

Having removed the earth over the entire upper surface of the main dome, it was found that the original brick masonry could be repaired by filling smaller cracks with gypsum, while using lime mortar in sections of new brickwork. The cavity between the upper surfaces of the dome and (original and new) vaults was therefore filled with brick masonry in lime mortar, in order to provide the necessary mass to stabilize the structure. In order to weatherproof the roof and enable redirection of rainwater, brick paving was laid to falls above a layer of lime concrete. All exposed areas were then finished with lime concrete, over which a surface of fired bricks was laid.

Having secured the roof of the main wing of the building, areas of decorated plaster that had become detached from the brick walling were stabilized by injecting gypsum into cavities behind the plaster. In certain areas, it was also necessary to fill deep cracks in the structural brickwork with the same gypsum mix. At the same time, remaining sections of the distinctive plaster latticework on the main facade

**The first stage of restoration work focused on stabilizing existing sections of the building and consolidating the painted plaster decorations.**

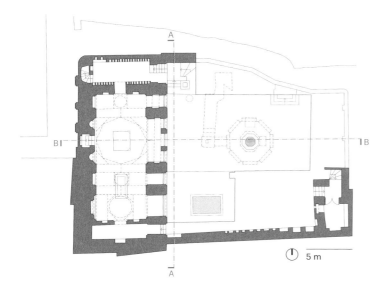

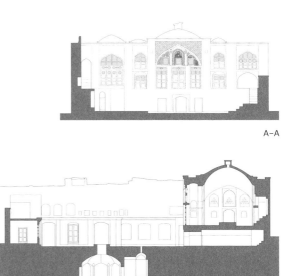

A–A

B–B

5 m

Above, first-floor plan and sections.

Below, the restored building serves as a
testament to the quality of its construction
and painted decoration.

were stabilized with gypsum, while the small windows (seen on photos of the building taken in the 1970s) have been restored. Elsewhere on this facade, conventional casement windows have been reinstalled.

During the course of surveys, mention was made by local residents of a stairway that led to an underground well, which had served as a source of water for the surrounding community. While laying brick paving in the synagogue courtyard, the oculus of a small domed space was revealed, and this led to the discovery of a narrow stair (blocked by earth after partial collapse) that gave access to this octagonal underground space (*mikveh*) in the centre of which there is a pool. This highly unusual structure, which might have served both practical and ritual functions, has now been cleared and repaired. Given the instability of the range of rooms on the eastern side of the courtyard of the complex, two new rooms were built on stone foundations providing a small latrine for future users of the complex. The perimeter wall along the north side of the courtyard was also rebuilt before the building was handed back to the Department of Historic Monuments in 2009.

An important component of the social history and built heritage of Herat, the restored synagogue is now used as an educational and cultural centre for women and children from the surrounding neighbourhood. As well as contributing to the development of skills among Afghan professionals and craftsmen, this project has helped to promote awareness of the richness of traditional construction and decorative techniques in the Old City.

**Above, the restored site is being used as a kindergarten for children from the surrounding community.**

**Below, timber woodwork and plaster screens were carefully restored.**

225

# Arbabzadah Serai

**The Arbabzadah Serai is an example of mid-20th-century commercial construction in the Old City.**

### HISTORY AND CHARACTERISTICS

In late 2008, work began on the reconstruction of the roof of the Arbabzadah Serai (built in the 1940s) as part of efforts to promote economic recovery in what was once the commercial heart of the Old City. The building comprises two floors of split-level shops and workshops arranged around a central courtyard, spanned by a lightweight arched timber structure in the form of a large barrel vault. An ingenious reinterpretation of the traditional masonry vaults that covered the historic bazaars in the Old City and for which Herat was known regionally, the structure was found to be in a precarious state of repair during an initial assessment. The shops within the *serai* were largely abandoned at the time of surveys and the courtyard was being used as a car park and storage space.

### WORK UNDERTAKEN

Following detailed documentation, designs were prepared for a system of laminated timber beams matching the curve of the original vault. After testing various techniques of fixings, twenty-six laminated beams were manufactured in the AKTC carpentry workshop and then erected along the ten-metre-length of the central space of the bazaar. Timber boarding was then fixed between the beams and covered with galvanized sheeting, as was the case in the original building. A series of timber 'lantern' skylights along the ridge of the roof were reconstructed, as was the ingenious system of openings at either end of the building that enabled cross-ventilation of the central space, which remains usable even during the fierce heat of the summer months in Herat.

Building on the experience of conservation of the nearby Abresham Bazaar, where silk traders and weavers have now re-established their businesses, work on the Arbabzadah Serai enabled the safeguarding of a distinctive structure and will contribute to economic recovery of the Old City. In a context where historic structures are being demolished and replaced with speculative concrete-frame constructions, the rehabilitation of the Arbabzadah Serai established an important precedent for the reuse of existing historic structures for commercial purposes.

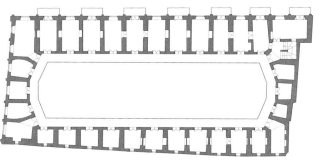

5 m

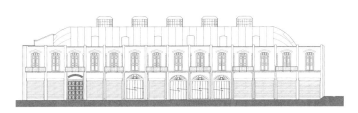

Top, after conservation, the *serai* continues to be used as commercial premises and a wholesale warehouse.

Middle, first-floor plan and east elevation.

Bottom, left, sections of curved timber rafters were constructed in an off-site carpentry workshop and assembled *in situ*.

Right, pavers were laid at the main entrance from the street, preventing the parking of vehicles within the market.

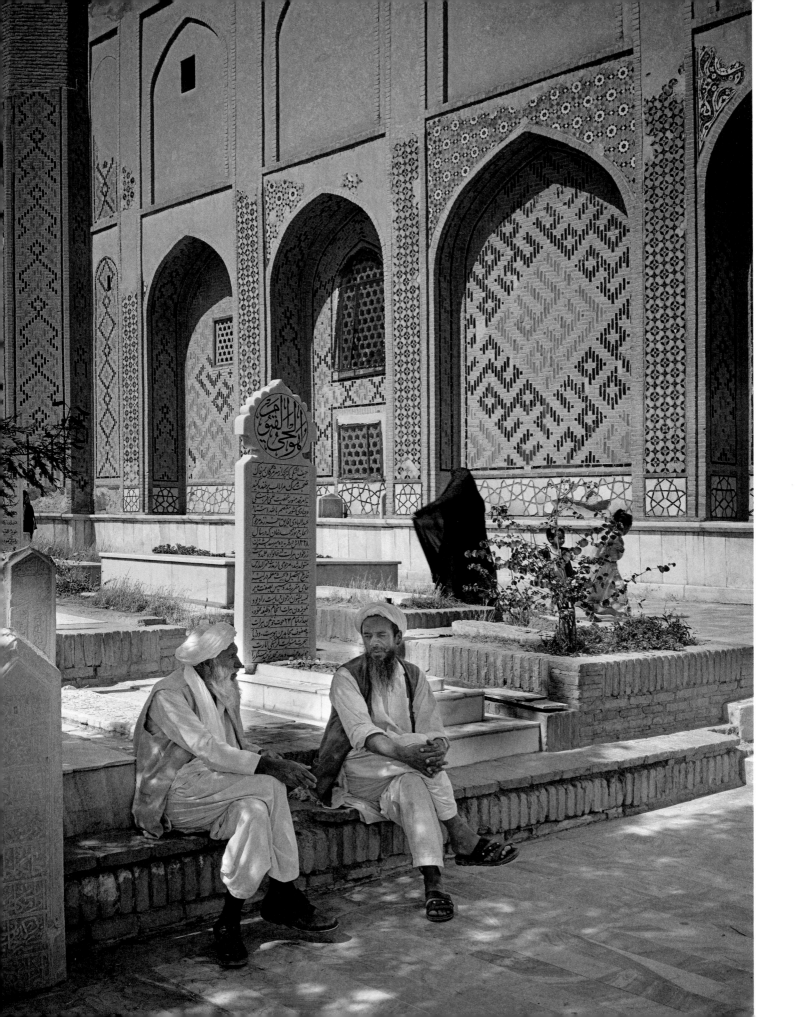

# GAZURGAH VILLAGE

The internal courtyard elevations of the
shrine were originally decorated with fine
glazed tiles.

# Abdullah Ansari Shrine

**Above, seen here in an early 20th-century image, Gazurgah village is located approximately six kilometres to the north-east of the Old City of Herat, 1916–17.**

**Below, a worshipper resting against a marble grave within the shrine, 1959–61.**

## HISTORY AND CHARACTERISTICS

The shrine complex of Khwaja Abdullah Ansari in Gazurgah, north-east of Herat, is both an important example of Timurid architecture and a popular place of pilgrimage. Having spent a life of contemplation and writing in and around the village, Ansari was buried here in 1089. Records suggest that a madrasa was established in Gazurgah in the late twelfth century, and this was probably the complex reconstructed by Shah Rukh in 1425 and which now makes up the shrine complex.

The large courtyard of the tomb (*hazira*) of Abdullah Ansari, with its arched *iwans* on the main axis and rows of study rooms between, takes a form that is more commonly associated with a madrasa. The main entrance is flanked by two symmetric mosques the dome of which is decorated with plaster *muqarnas*. Both the main entrance arch and the high *iwan* that rises above Ansari's grave retain sections of fine colour-glazed tile epigraphy and areas of geometric decoration. Worked in a mosaic technique (*moarraq*), the designs combine glazed and unglazed tiles (in instances worked with pristine white marble) in a manner that includes large sections of intricate perforated screens (*jali*) in front of openings. Some of the finest extant Timurid decoration in the region, this has been documented as part of AKTC's limited intervention in the complex. In a manner befitting the recycling of architectural objects from one historic site to another, the lower section of Ansari's grave enclosure is decorated with fine carved marble relocated from the base of minarets in the Musalla complex.

Over time the courtyard of the shrine has become a cemetery containing the graves of some of the best-known figures in the region, including the Afghan king Amir Dost Muhammad Khan and Abdullah Ansari's two sons. The graves of six close relatives of Timurid sultan Husayn Bayqara are also located within the courtyard on a raised platform referred to as the Timurid Platform (Takht-e Timuri).

Of the range of rooms to the north of the courtyard, the most important houses the grave of Sultan Husayn Bayqara's son Gharib Mirza, an intricately decorated grey soapstone cenotaph known widely as the *sang-e haft qalam* (stone worked with seven chisels).

## WORK UNDERTAKEN

From 2005, repairs were carried out on all roofs of the shrine, which had been poorly maintained and risked damage to the fragile internal plaster decoration in parts of the complex. Roofs were structurally stabilized and repaired using traditional methods

before a durable layer of brick paving was applied to falls in order to ensure greater resilience against extreme weather and a lack of maintenance.

During the course of this work, evidence emerged of alterations that had been made over time to the eastern *iwan*, which rises more than eighteen metres above the surrounding village. The removal of modern concrete that dated from the 1970s enabled a detailed structural analysis to take place, on which basis a series of brick buttresses were built on the eastern side. These buttresses included four, low, one-storey structures and two flying buttresses, providing structural support for the main

**Above, left, the twenty-seven-metre-high *iwan* arch of the shrine required structural retrofitting entailing the construction of steel supports and brick-masonry buttresses.**

**Right, waterproofing and re-paving areas repaired during conservation work.**

**Below, site plan.**

1  Abdullah Ansari Shrine
2  Zarnegar Khanaqa
3  Zamzam Cistern
4  Namakdan Pavilion
5  Bagh-e Naw

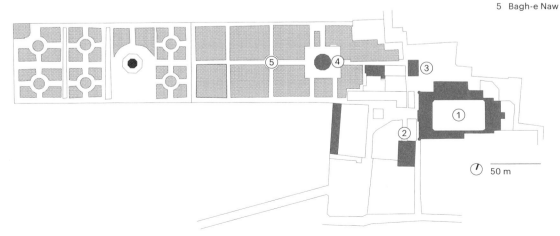

50 m

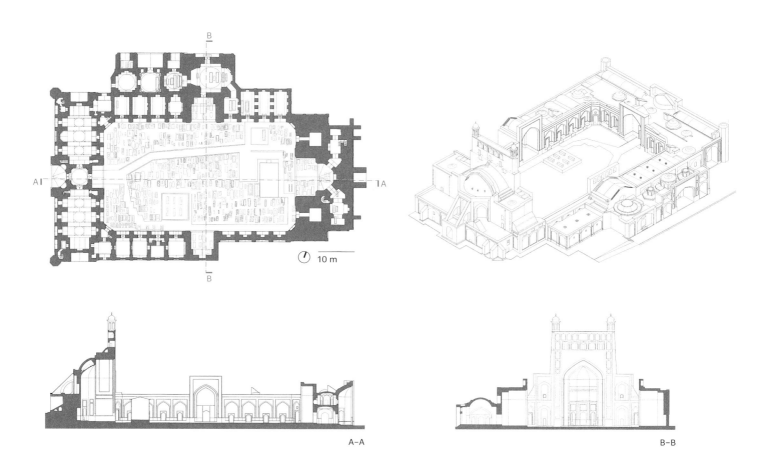

10 m

A–A

B–B

*iwan*, which was discovered to have been leaning due to unequal settlement beneath its foundations. At the same time, three vaulted rooms in the north-east corner of the complex, which were found to be unstable, were rebuilt on the same footprint as the original, using traditional materials.

In order to facilitate the visits of pilgrims, original sections of marble paving were relaid at the main entrance, whose incongruous aluminium doors were replaced with traditional wood, along with other doors leading on to the courtyard. The historic gravestones that now fill this courtyard were documented, prior to repairs and consolidation of the most vulnerable graves. This documentation formed the basis of an extensive publication by AKTC on the epigraphy of gravestones found within the courtyard of the building.

Brick paving was also laid in key areas, to enable access and discourage the removal of historic stones when new graves are dug within the courtyard. A surface drainage channel was incorporated into the new paving in order to redirect rainwater away from the building and cemetery. Additional fired-brick and stone paving was laid around the entire external perimeter of the shrine in order to divert water away from the vulnerable foundations of the building. Discreet external lighting was also installed around the courtyard, which is regularly used at night for religious ceremonies.

Opposite page, above, ground-floor plan, sections and axonometric view. Below, worshippers pushing a nail into a wooden post adjacent to the grave of Abdullah Ansari.

Above, left, the restored Abdullah Ansari Shrine as seen from Gazurgah village.

Right, the restored roofs of the shrine used during Friday prayers.

5 m

Above, west elevation.

Left, a pilgrim at the Gazurgah Shrine.

Right, several graves have been erected beneath the main *iwan* (arch) of the shrine.

Opposite page, restoration of the shrine included the paving of walkways to enable worshippers better access to the site.

# Namakdan Pavilion

**The late-15th-century Namakdan Pavilion had been extensively transformed through a series of interventions.**

## HISTORY AND CHARACTERISTICS

Built between 1490 and 1494 by Amir Ali Sher Nawai (Minister to Sultan Husayn Bayqara) after he retired from the court and became custodian of the Abdullah Ansari Shrine, the Namakdan Pavilion was laid out as part of a formal garden adjoining the shrine complex. Referred to as Bagh-e Naw, the garden became one of several formal gardens established by members of the Timurid court north of the city of Herat. Within the garden, Nawai had two identical pavilions built on a sloping east-west axis, the lower of which has been destroyed.

The Namakdan Pavilion, apparently named after its resemblance to a saltcellar, is a twelve-sided, two-storey structure with a dome spanning a central double-height octagonal space covered by a ribbed dome. Around this internal space — on the first floor — a gallery gives access to a series of twelve niche-like external spaces that overlook the surrounding garden. The ingenious geometric design enables a flawless transition of a twelve-sided pavilion to an octagonal internal space arranged around a marble water tank. Variations in the design of the upper niches alternate from open pentagonal balconies to square spaces enclosed by arched openings. Ribbed arches (*karbandi*) above these spaces are made with gypsum plaster, decorated with colour-glazed tiles above four of the square spaces.

During the 1950s, significant alterations were made to the pavilion that, while saving the building from collapse, radically changed its historic character.

## WORK UNDERTAKEN

In 2005, detailed surveys were undertaken to assess the structural condition of the Namakdan Pavilion, which until then had been used as a guesthouse by the custodian of the Abdullah Ansari Shrine. Conservation work that followed entailed the removal of accumulated earth from above the roof that had caused significant damage to the masonry domes of the pavilion by placing additional weight on the fragile structure. Simultaneously, temporary structures built within the pavilion were removed and the original elevations were exposed for documentation and repair. Structural damage caused by settlement in the perimeter of the pavilion had resulted in large sections of the main elevation becoming broken and deformed in places. Compounded by the loss of original wooden tensile elements that had been destroyed by termites, the pavilion was at substantial risk of structural failure. Urgent work began on repairing the fragile central brick dome, after which a system of steel ring beams and ties was introduced on multiple levels around and through the supporting brick masonry.

These metal ties were reinserted into voids left by the original timber reinforcement. Subsequently, brick-masonry footings were strengthened, using lime mortar — as used in the original structure. In the course of this work, traces of *karbandi* ribbed plaster decoration were found, along with coloured Timurid tile work on two of the elevations. These areas were stabilized and, where possible, restored according to established conservation practices.

During the course of removal of modern additions, an octagonal water tank was rediscovered, along with traces of a water cascade and channel, all of which were subsequently restored, and new brick paving was laid within the building. Water flowing from the Zamzam Cistern, located east of the pavilion, was redirected into an open surface channel and into the octagonal water tank at the centre of the building. From there water flows down a cascade and into the Bagh-e Naw where it serves to irrigate the garden.

After more than four years of painstaking conservation, the Namakdan Pavilion again resembles the structure that its Timurid builders intended. An important monument has thus been safeguarded for future generations.

Above, modern layers of paint and plaster had to be removed before structural consolidation work could commence.

Below, left, with significant deformation caused by settlement in the masonry walls, retrofitting measures were used to stabilize the Timurid-era structure.

Centre, a mason preparing a marble slab to be used in restoring a water channel.

Right, discovered beneath later interventions, the original octagonal water tank was restored.

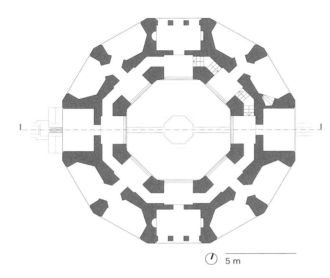

Opposite page, water flows again through the restored pavilion.

Above, first-floor plan and section.

Below, constructed within the Bagh-e Naw (garden), the restored pavilion enables visitors to appreciate the austere beauty of its architecture.

5 m

# Zarnegar Khanaqa

**An early 20th-century photograph showing the fine painted decoration of the Zarnegar Khanaqa (place of Sufi worship), 1910–19.**

## HISTORY AND CHARACTERISTICS

The Zarnegar Khanaqa, built at the end of the fifteenth century, is located to the south-west of the Abdullah Ansari Shrine. Intended for use by Sufi dervishes as a hospice and centre for the propagation of Sufism, the building takes its name from the rich turquoise and gold painted decoration on the underside of its low brick dome. A rectangular building, composed of a large square central space, covered by a single-shell dome resting on a square base, it is accessed from the north via a deep-set vestibule *iwan*. The original Timurid construction was encapsulated by a late-nineteenth-century masonry shell, believed to have been built to counter significant structural damage to the original building, which also blocked separate entrances to the central space of the *khanaqa*.

Located directly opposite the Zarnegar Khanaqa, across from the entrance to the Abdullah Ansari Shrine, the Zamzam Cistern was built on Timurid ruler Shah Rukh's orders and was allegedly filled with sacred water sourced from the Zamzam well in Mecca. The *khanaqa*, together with the Abdullah Ansari Shrine, Namakdan Pavilion, Zamzam Cistern and an underground mosque, forms an ensemble of historic structures on the western perimeter of Gazurgah village.

## WORK UNDERTAKEN

Conservation of the *khanaqa* started in 2006 with a structural intervention entailing the removal of reinforced-concrete slabs from above all areas of the roof. While traditional materials such as brick and lime tend to be porous and enable structures affected by damp to evaporate and easily dry out, concrete on the other hand retains moisture, resulting over time in the deterioration of brick and lime. Extensive damp areas beneath the concrete slabs were allowed to dry out before the consolidation of the masonry dome and arches began. A section of the vault above the southern *iwan* was found to be structurally incapable of carrying the load of the roof above. As a result, three smaller arches were built above the vault in order to redistribute the weight of the roof onto adjacent brick piers. Once complete, the entire roof surface was weatherproofed with the application of a layer of lime concrete protected with durable brick paving.

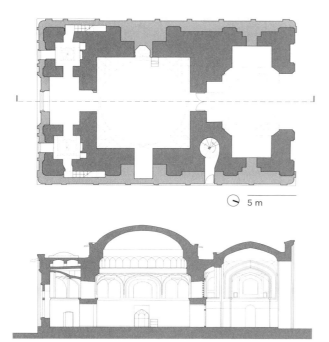

Above, restoration work on the *khanaqa* entailed the removal of accumulated debris and repairs to its masonry domes and walls, before timber joinery was prepared and installed.

Left, ground-floor plan and section.

█ Original period
█ Additions (1880)

5 m

# PLANNING, UPGRADING AND ACCESS IMPROVEMENTS

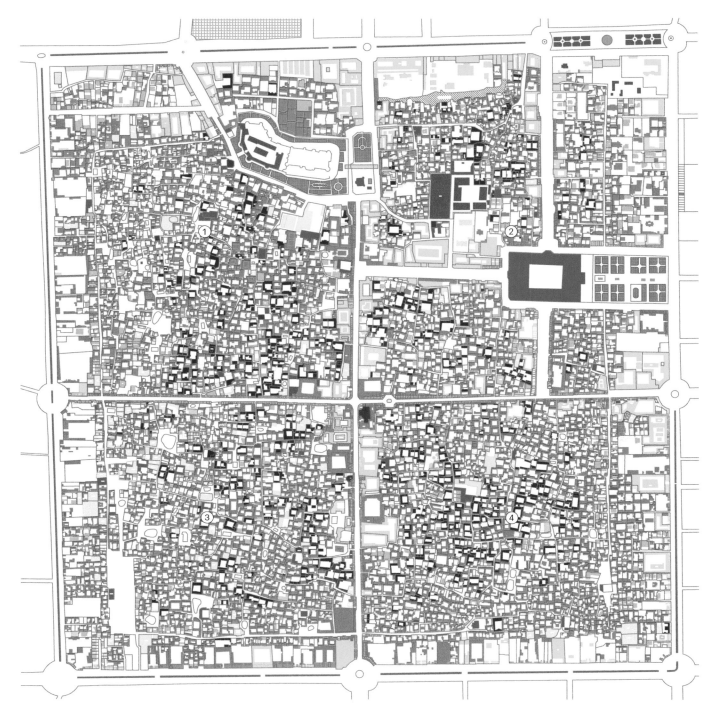

Preceding pages, community members
gather to discuss documentation activities
in the **Old City of Herat.**

**Herat Old City: property use survey** (* less than 10 years old).

RESIDENTIAL
  Modern*
  Traditional
  Historic
  Ruins

COMMERCIAL
  Modern
  Historic

RELIGIOUS
  Modern
  Historic

SCHOOLS/
MADRASAS
  Modern
  Historic

OTHERS
  Cisterns
  Hammams
  Public buildings

**Herat Old City quarters.**

1  Bar Durrani
2  Qutbe Chaq
3  Momandha
4  Abdullah Mesri

ⓘ _____
   250 m

## PLANNING

Given the pace of change and the absence of documentation for the Old City of Herat, one of the first priorities for AKTC was to map the physical environment and establish an appropriate system for monitoring ongoing transformations. A preliminary survey of historic residential property during early 2005 provided a basis on which to identify specific clusters in which to initiate pilot repairs and upgrading work. A team of fifteen AKTC surveyors, ten of whom were women, subsequently undertook a more detailed property survey of 25,000 residential and commercial premises, in 2005–06. This has yielded useful information on location, occupancy and use, key construction or architectural characteristics, age and date of alterations, state of repair, availability of services and level of vulnerability of the property. This information served as a valuable resource for planning initiatives and for ongoing upgrading and conservation work. The results of the property survey illustrate the diversity of the various quarters, due to the combined impact of the conflict and redevelopment. Surveys revealed that the bulk of houses in the Old City were traditional in form and construction, yet two out of ten homes were modern, compared to one in ten homes that were considered to be of social or historic importance. Furthermore, one in five homes in the Old City was occupied by more than one family, with indications that densities were gradually increasing in some neighbourhoods.

In comparison, three quarters of commercial premises were modern, with more than 170 new shops or markets recorded as having been built from 2002–07, often on the site of illegally demolished homes. The alarming trend in the destruction of heritage properties, replaced by modern infill, reflected a significant increase in the wealth of those investing in residential reconstruction and speculative commercial development in the Old City. In addition to the importance of individual heritage sites, the significance of the Old City of Herat lies in its unique urban pattern, which is constituted by a 'fabric' of passageways, covered streets and public spaces defining an interlinking of historic streetscapes. These transformations threaten to irreversibly change the intrinsic nature and character of the Old City, one of the last remaining traditional fabrics in the region.

While appropriate forms of redevelopment, using traditional materials and building typologies addressing Herat's unique built heritage, could have enabled communities to reconstruct their homes and businesses, local authorities lacked clear mechanisms and controls to manage this process. In response to the rapid and uncontrolled destruction of the historic fabric, AKTC provided technical assistance

Inadequate public infrastructure results in poor environmental conditions in the Old City.

Above, reconstruction of a *dalan* (covered alleyway) in the Bar Durrani quarter.

Below, the repair of open sumps (*khandaqs*) and rainwater drains, combined with the upgrading of public access, greatly improved environmental conditions in the Old City.

Right, more than 5.5 kilometres of underground and surface drains were repaired and restored in the Old City.

to a newly established Commission for the Safeguarding and Development of the Old City of Herat, comprising representatives from key institutions and professional bodies. The Commission provided a platform for discussion between key stakeholders and established temporary measures by which new construction would be evaluated, following which recommendations would be made on the suitability of the project to local authorities. While the Commission was effective in limiting the pace of destruction and involving communities in safeguarding historic properties, the absence of leadership on the part of civil servants became a significant obstacle to establishing long-term conservation policies, reform of systems of building permits and monitoring of new construction or illegal demolitions. As part of its activity, AKTC supported local and international organizations working to improve urban policy or heritage management, including initial steps in the process of potentially inscribing Herat on the World Heritage List.

In order to address the lack of technical and management capacity, students and professionals were engaged in on-the-job training through the AKTC programme, which also supported site visits and lectures about conservation, planning and urban management issues. It is hoped that this cadre of young Afghan professionals will be in the vanguard of continued efforts to safeguard and develop their city. In the absence of effective policies to safeguard Herat's built heritage, further legal protection was provided by inscribing key historic monuments in the Old City on a register developed by the Department of Historic Monuments. This provided a level of legal protection under Afghanistan's heritage laws and enabled limited oversight by the Ministry of Information and Culture.

## UPGRADING AND ACCESS IMPROVEMENTS

One of the key challenges in convincing owners to value historic and traditional homes in the Old City remains the fact that living conditions are generally poor, due to high rates of unemployment, degraded infrastructure and non-existent services. The principal problem facing many households is the lack of adequate drainage, due to the failure of the underground network that served many historic quarters, as well as the fact that the growing population has rendered the long-established system of open sumps (*khandaqs*) inadequate. The resulting water logging has damaged many traditional mud-brick structures in the Old City, while also affecting the health of the inhabitants, particularly children. The fact that most streets and alleyways through the historic fabric were unpaved added to these problems. In order to address some of the most immediate needs, support was provided under the AKTC programme to community groups to organize the evacuation of liquid waste from fifty *khandaqs* in residential areas. Further coordination with Herat Municipality on the preparation of long-term waste-management plans, which mobilized local communities in establishing collection points and enforcing appropriate practices, directly benefited most of the 63,000 residents of the Old City.

Given the density of settlement, many pedestrian alleyways have had rooms or terraces built over them. Constructed of fired or mud bricks, these vaulted passages (*dalan*) provide safe, covered access to adjacent homes, but many of these fell into disrepair, while others were demolished in recent years as part of residential redevelopment activities. Support has been provided by AKTC for the repair and paving of one of the longest surviving vaulted *dalan* in the Bar Durrani quarter, among others, as a demonstration of the potential of access improvements.

In order to contribute to the improvement of living conditions, more than five kilometres of the existing system of underground drains have been repaired or rebuilt, and more than 6000 square metres of streets and pedestrian alleyways in specific residential clusters have been paved. These activities have directly benefited a further 30,000 people, or nearly half of the resident population of the Old City. In a context where unemployment is a major preoccupation, upgrading activities have generated more than 240,000 workdays of skilled and unskilled labour, largely drawn from residents of the Old City.

**Left, upgrading activities have promoted small-scale local investments in retail and residential areas.**

**Centre, a restored *dalan* in the Bar Durrani quarter of the Old City of Herat.**

**Right, an alleyway in the Old City paved with stone, which enables access for both pedestrians and vehicles.**

# BALKH

# INTRODUCTION

Preceding pages, view of the Noh Gunbad Mosque, believed to have been built between the late 8th and early 9th century, 1959–61.

Top, excavations being conducted by the French Archaeological mission at the base of the historic fortifications of Balkh.

Middle, the Bala Hissar (citadel) of Balkh covers a one-square-kilometre area and contains one of the earliest settlements in the region – dating back to the 2nd millennia BC.

Bottom, a match of Buzkashi played above the archaeological ruins of the citadel, with its walls visible in the distance.

## INTRODUCTION

Located in the fertile pastureland descending from the steppes of Central Asia, south of the Oxus River, Balkh (ancient Bactra) is the largest city in an area referred to by ancient Greek historians as a "land of a thousand cities". Regarded by scholars as one of the oldest cities in the world and by Arab conquerors as "Umm Al-Bilad" (Mother of Cities), recorded settlements in the region date back to the Bronze Age and continued throughout the subsequent Iron Age civilizations. Archaeological excavations in and around Balkh have revealed multiple Zoroastrian sites, including a large 'fire-temple' in Chashmae Shafa, reinforcing the belief that the Zoroaster lived in the vicinity of Balkh in 900 BC.

The city was also the most northerly base for Alexander of Macedonia (Alexander the Great) in 329–327 BC, from where he led several attempts to expand his territories across the Oxus River to the north. Under the Kushans, when Buddhism was practiced across Afghanistan, Balkh was the location of an expansive complex of Buddhist temples and monasteries. At the burial site of a Kushan prince near Balkh, at Tella Tappa (Mound of Gold), in 1970 archaeologists discovered approximately 20,000 fine gold objects depicting animals, mythical birds and warriors.

Arab conquerors spread the influence of Islam throughout the region. Recent research would seem to indicate that one of the earliest mosques (Noh Gunbad) in Balkh and possibly in the wider region was built between the late eighth and early ninth centuries with the support of the influential Barmakid family. Originally hereditary priests from the great Buddhist temple of Naw Bahar in Balkh, the Barmakids embraced Islam and became powerful ministers (*wazirs*) at the Abbasid court in Baghdad. In the centuries that followed, Balkh was one of the main centres of Islamic culture and trade (a key town on the Silk Road), and home to some of the most renowned thinkers and writers of the Persian language, including Rabia Balkhi — the first woman to compose Persian poetry in the Islamic period — and the birthplace of Nasir Khusrau and Jalal al-Din Muhammad Balkhi (known widely as Rumi).

As important as it became for the cultural development of the wider region, the centre of Balkh was razed at the beginning of the thirteenth century when Genghis Khan led his army of 10,000 Mongol invaders through the city, massacring its inhabitants. Regardless of this and subsequent devastation caused by Timur in the fourteenth century, Marco Polo described Balkh as "a noble city and a great seat of learning". Instead, Ibn Battuta visited the city in 1333 and described it as a city still "in ruins". While further destruction to the citadel of Balkh was caused by Timur in 1389,

Above, the Imam Sahib Shrine in Balkh dates back to the 12th century, 1959.

Below, an internal view of the Takhta Pul Mosque being used to store cotton, 1959.

Above, traditional indigenous settlements on the outskirts of Balkh.

Below, aerial view of Balkh showing the circular Bala Hissar (centre top) and the adjacent radial streets of an early 20th-century planning intervention.

under the enlightened rule of Shah Rukh and his queen, Gowharshad (based in Herat), the citadel was rebuilt in 1407.

With the rise of Uzbek khanates, the city changed hands briefly in 1511, when Babur — the future founder of the Mughal Empire — held Balkh for a year. The city changed hands multiple times over the next three and a half centuries until it was finally conquered by Amir Dost Muhammad Khan in 1850 and incorporated into the modern state of Afghanistan. In 1866, the city was abandoned due to chronic outbreaks of malaria and cholera and the administrative capital of Balkh province was relocated to Mazar-e Sharif. Balkh remained a small town until the 1930s when modernization schemes resulted in further destruction of the once magnificent city.

Experts nonetheless believe Balkh to be one of the most intact and unspoiled archaeological landscapes in the world. While few of its magnificent structures remain, the site was inscribed on UNESCO's World Heritage tentative list in 2009. Since 2002, a significant increase in unregulated development has threatened to further transform the character of historic Balkh and to destroy archaeological evidence that could further enlighten the world about the history of this important region.

In the context of AKTC's ongoing conservation programmes, work commenced in Balkh in 2011 with a multi-year project to stabilize the remains of the early ninth-century Noh Gunbad Mosque. One of the most important early Islamic-era buildings in the region, the project entailed complex structural consolidation of remains of the building without damaging the unique stucco decorations adorning its arches and columns. While a second phase of conservation continues on this extraordinary monument, the project enabled AKTC's technical teams to undertake wider surveys in the Balkh region and build partnerships with local authorities and professionals. In response to requests for wider assistance and recognizing the urgent need for additional conservation programmes in Balkh, AKTC commenced a multi-year Area Development Programme in 2012 that prioritized documentation, conservation, socio-economic training and upgrading activities.

In order to identify suitable conservation projects, physical surveys and documentation were prepared using three-dimensional laser-scanning technology. Pioneered by AKTC in Afghanistan, this technology enabled a small team of Afghan professionals to carry out physical surveys in a fraction of the time and cost required by more conventional methods. The information collected through this process provided the basis on which conservation projects were designed and implemented. Recognizing the importance of documenting Balkh's fragile historic sites, survey activities have collected detailed information about more than twenty-five individual sites and monuments. Historic structures that remain in Balkh consist mainly of mosques, shrines and madrasas, reflecting the deeply religious nature of these communities and the sustained religious donations (*zakat*) that are made towards the maintenance of these structures. In addition to worship and religious education, such communal spaces are often used by the residents of the area to hold council, discuss community matters and at times for large gatherings aimed at finding resolutions to shared problems. As such they represent important spaces of prayer, teaching and communal and social interaction.

One of the first projects undertaken was the restoration of the early sixteenth-century Khwaja Parsa Shrine located in central Balkh within a circular public park that was developed as part of modernization programmes in the 1930s. A well-known proponent of the Naqshbandi order of Sufi Islam, Khwaja Abu Nasr Parsa is believed to be buried near an unmarked tombstone in front of the monument. Originally a late Timurid-era structure, which had been expanded and reconstructed on at least two

occasions, parts of the external elevations retain large sections of fine colour-glazed tile work. The building is flanked by the remains of two circular minarets with cork-screw columns and the central prayer space is covered by a tiled ribbed dome resembling those seen in Gawharshad's mausoleum in Herat. Work commenced with the demolition of inappropriate reinforced-concrete structures built abutting the monument, followed by the reconstruction of a domed masonry mosque on the remains of a nineteenth-century structure that served to provide structural support to both minarets. Conservation of the historic structure entailed structural reinforcement of the weakened masonry dome and the reapplication of newly produced colour-glazed tiles before large sections of the original sixteenth-century tile work on the elevations of the shrine were stabilized. This work was carried out simultaneously with land-scaping and paving activities in and around the 3.5-hectare public park, which served as an open market on a regular basis. The park also contained the remains of the main *iwan* of the late-sixteenth-century Subhan Qoli Madrasa Gate, which, together with the mausoleum of Rabia Balki — the first woman poet in the Persian language — was also restored as part of this project. In the subsequent four-year period, a number of other historic monuments and public sites were restored in and around the old town of Balkh, including small shrines, mosques and a tenth-century flood-protection structure.

As part of a comprehensive approach to conservation, aimed at extending its benefits to the wider community, physical upgrading and vocational training pro-grammes were established in consultation with local authorities and residents. On the basis of a socio-economic survey of 475 (one in seven) households in the old town of Balkh, drainage, access improvement and training programmes focused on providing support to those most in need. Ongoing programmes have provided more than 110 young students with training in the production of glazed tiles, carpentry and masonry. Investments in upgrading public infrastructure have resulted in the construction of approximately 3.5 kilometres of drainage and more than 1400 square metres of access improvements.

In order to undertake conservation and upgrading initiatives, AKTC teams en-gaged local authorities and community groups in sustained discussions on appropri-ate forms of planning and development in a historic context. While residents and civil servants recognized the historic importance of Balkh, they were less aware of the value and method of preserving its sites and monuments. The dialogue has enabled better awareness and conservation projects implemented by AKTC to continue to receive widespread support. Further consultation on the establishment of vocational training programmes and focus of upgrading activities has placed the responsibility of directing investment with local communities.

# PHYSICAL CONSERVATION AND RESTORATION

# BALKH OLD TOWN

Preceding pages, restorers work to apply
a protective layer to the gypsum decorations
of the Noh Gunbad Mosque.

Left, the Khwaja Parsa Mosque, restored
as part of AKTC's conservation programme
in Balkh.

# Noh Gunbad Mosque

Above, the outer walls of the Noh Gunbad Mosque were built using a combination of compacted- and rammed-earth construction, supported at intervals by fired-brick columns, 1959–61.

Below, detailed view of the Abassid-era gypsum decoration of the mosque. Similar decoration has been discovered by archaeologists on two other known sites, including the Palace of the Caliph in Samarra, Iraq, 1959–61.

## HISTORY AND CHARACTERISTICS

The Noh Gunbad Mosque is believed by many historians and archaeologists to be one of the earliest standing Islamic-era religious structures in Afghanistan and possibly in the wider region. While scholarly opinion differs on the exact date of construction, there is general consensus that the mosque was built during the Abbasid era between the late eighth and early ninth century AD. Historian Lisa Golombek, who wrote an article on the mosque in 1969 following a visit to the site three years earlier, is widely credited with making the monument known to the outside world.

Located approximately four kilometres south of the centre of the old town of Balkh, the mosque and its remaining stucco decoration is a highly important and exquisite example of early Islamic-era architecture. Measuring approximately twenty metres by twenty metres in plan, the square mosque is located on a flat site near a large shallow water reservoir flanked by a number of mature plane trees. The name Noh Gunbad (nine domes) is derived from the number of masonry domes that once covered the mosque. Significantly, the internal walls, columns and arches are decorated with exquisite stucco motifs, including highly articulated geometric and floral patters that bear resemblance to other Abassid-era buildings in Samarra, Iraq. Originally resting on sixteen columns — of which six were free-standing and the remaining embedded within outer enclosure walls — all of its nine decorated domes have since collapsed, covering the original floor with rubble containing important remains of plaster decoration.

Other remains of this 1200-year-old mosque include large sections of the outer enclosure walls within which three of the four free-standing circular columns, measuring approximately 1.5 metres in diameter, are connected by two perpendicular arches spanning more than four metres. The building was exposed to the natural elements for centuries, resulting in severe erosion of the structure and damage to the fine stucco decoration. It was not until 1972 that a large protective metal hanger was erected above the site.

The building is known locally as the "Mosque of Hajj-e Pyada", named after a small inconspicuous shrine built outside its northern wall. Translated, the name means "[those who] ... perform the Hajj on foot" and it refers to the story of two companions who travelled from Balkh to Mecca for the ritual Hajj. The story chronicles how the two friends shared a camel along the journey. Each friend offered his companion the chance to ride the camel while the other walked. But being close friends each refused the offer in turn and both ended up walking all the way to Mecca and back. The story

Complex conservation work was undertaken by AKTC beneath a protective structure built over the site in the 1970s.

has been passed down through generations and has been used to underscore the bond between friends and pilgrims.

Recognized as one of Afghanistan's most important yet least understood sites, and built at a time that marked the passing of its centuries-old Buddhist traditions and the arrival of Islam, the Noh Gunbad Mosque has been described as an architectural 'Rosetta stone' — containing within its form and decorative elements the secrets of a lost transitional period of coexistence and cross-fertilization between diverse cultures and traditions. Preserving what remains of this building and enabling a better understanding of the site and its architecture is critical to understanding the history of the region and further establishing its significance as a place of great knowledge and cultural diversity, a crossroads of civilizations.

## WORK UNDERTAKEN

The genesis of the conservation project aimed at safeguarding the Noh Gunbad Mosque, which was in a state of significant deterioration and near collapse, saw the light in 2008 with a visit to the site by AKTC personnel at the request of the Afghan authorities. As part of AKTC's collaboration with the Afghan Government, providing advisory assistance to the Ministry of Information and Culture (MoIC), the visit paved the way for further engagement in the conservation of the monument. While temporary measures implemented in the past had averted the collapse of key sections of the Noh Gunbad Mosque, the convergence of key project management and technical capacity — led by AKTC's experienced conservation teams — and support from partners, including the French Archaeological Delegation in Afghanistan (DAFA), the

Right, expert restorers work together with Afghan craftsmen to clean the plaster decoration.

Middle, protective facing paper being applied to prevent movement and fracture of decorative elements ahead of structural consolidation work.

Bottom, glass-fibre mesh being applied with plaster to reinforce sections of decoration.

World Monuments Fund (WMF), and the Associazione Giovanni Secco Suardo (AGSS), provided a unique opportunity to address the structural deterioration of the building.

Over the course of the six years that followed the initial site visit, expert teams of international conservation architects, structural and materials engineers, and gypsum plaster conservators were engaged by AKTC and worked hand-in-hand with their Afghan counterparts to design and implement one of the most challenging structural consolidation and conservation projects ever attempted in Afghanistan. The challenge of the project was to implement complex structural stabilization measures without affecting the architecture or decoration of the monument.

Due to the condition and fragility of the mosque, the project entailed the construction of a full-scale replica of the damaged sections of the mosque in order to test structural consolidation measures before they could be implemented on the monument. Testing of material composition and analysis of structural consolidation techniques were carried out at the laboratories of the Department of Architecture at Florence University.

Before consolidation work could commence, a network of temporary stabilization measures was constructed beneath arches and adjacent to free-standing columns. Backfill areas of mud-brick masonry were removed from spaces above the broken arches, followed by the cleaning of its external surface. In order to stabilize deflections in the arches, designs called for the insertion of reinforced glass-fibre mesh between alternating rows of brick masonry, replacing weakened sections of the original mud mortar with specially prepared plaster slurry. Exposed lengths of the glass-fibre mesh were embedded into a composite lime mortar, before lengths of uni-direction carbon-fibre reinforced-polymer (CFRP) were applied with epoxy above the extrados of both remaining arches. Additional stabilization measures included the construction of supporting "Franelli" arches and stainless-steel box trusses, embedded above the arch and anchored to free-standing columns.

Left, survey drawing.

Below, top left, repair work to the broken arches of the mosque entailed application of reinforced-carbon fibre above the consolidated structure.

Top right, work to strengthen internal arches at the springing line.

Bottom left, located in an earthquake zone, the installation of stainless-steel box trusses within the masonry of the arches greatly improved their structural performance.

Bottom right, in areas where previous arches had collapsed, carbon-fibre rods were used to structurally stitch loose masonry.

2.5 m

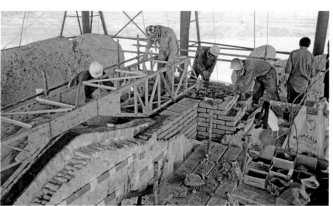

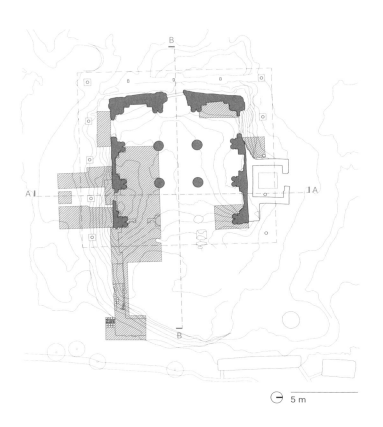

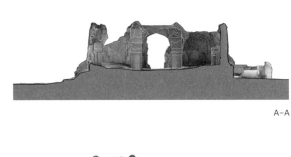

A–A

B–B

5 m

In order to ensure that the structural consolidation of the mosque would not damage large sections of stucco decoration lining the internal surfaces of the building, French conservators carried out extensive consolidation work prior to the structural intervention and then again afterwards, further cleaning and restoring the decorative elements. Logistic challenges required that project consultants and technical experts should conduct their work with specialist materials, supplies and equipment that had to be procured outside Afghanistan and delivered on site.

The innovative and groundbreaking techniques used in this project have been implemented by conservation teams with more than a decade of experience in Afghanistan, employing local technicians and craftsmen. For AKTC, the project also paved the way for the establishment of a wider Area Development Programme in Balkh, which has resulted in the conservation of key historic monuments and landscapes, employing and training hundreds of local labourers, while providing upgrading, access and infrastructure improvements that benefited communities living around these sites.

At the time of this publication, a second phase of conservation and archaeological work is being undertaken by AKTC technical teams and project partners with a focus on the consolidation of the external load-bearing walls of the Noh Gunbad Mosque. When complete, this work will further protect the building and enable extensive archaeological excavations within and around the mosque. Preliminary investigations on site have thus far revealed traces of a larger complex of buildings attached to the mosque, some with the same decorated stucco reliefs as those found within the mosque. Those who consider that this small, largely ruined mosque stood in isolation in the agricultural fields of Balkh for more than a millennium will be excited to learn that there is still more to be revealed by exploring this extraordinary monument.

Opposite page, above, ground-floor plan, showing areas of recent archaeological excavations in light grey, latitudinal and longitudinal sections. Left, conservation of the broken arches concluded with the cleaning and restoration of gypsum decoration located on the face and soffits of the arches and at the top of columns. Right, believed to be one of Afghanistan's most important monuments, the restoration of the mosque brought together experts from the region and across Europe.

Above, with the conservation of the freestanding columns and arches complete, the next phase of work will entail the consolidation of the perimeter wall and the restoration of large sections of gypsum decoration currently hidden beneath rubble.

# Khwaja Parsa Mosque and Park

Above, the twenty-seven-metre-high ribbed tile dome of the Khwaja Parsa Mosque can be seen behind an 18th-century addition, 1959.

Below, road work undertaken prior to conservation had caused damage to the structure of the mosque.

Opposite page, work to point brick pavers laid above a reconstruction of the 18th-century mosque.

## HISTORY AND CHARACTERISTICS

The Khwaja Parsa Mosque is named after Khwaja Abu Nasr Parsa (d. 1460), a respected spiritual leader of the Naqshbandi Sufi order and a well-known theologian in Balkh, who is believed to be buried in an unmarked grave on a raised platform opposite the main arched portal (*iwan*) of the monument.

Late fifteenth-century texts repeatedly refer to Khwaja Parsa as a great mediator of peace and the foremost representative of the population of historic Balkh. While little is known about the cause of his death and the exact location of his grave, the mosque bearing his name was commissioned by Mir Mazid Arghun in 1467. A prominent Timurid politician and military leader, Arghun is believed to have chosen Khwaja Parsa's burial site as the location for his family mausoleum. With the construction of several madrasas near the building in the sixteenth and seventeenth centuries, including the expansive Subhan Qoli Madrasa, the district around the mosque became renowned for its impressive religious structures.

Little is known of developments with the building until travellers to Balkh in the nineteenth and early twentieth centuries, including the British travel writer Robert Byron, documented the site in a state of ruin. Historical texts refer to a massive earthquake at the end of the nineteenth century, which may have caused the partial collapse of the mosque's dome and minarets. Large-scale modernization work in the centre of Balkh in the 1930s resulted in the construction of a 'radial plan' for the town, at the centre of which the Khwaja Parsa Mosque was left surrounded by a public park. Since then, sections of the mosque have been repaired, renovated and reconstructed on at least three occasions, the most recent carried out in the 1970s by the Archaeological Survey of India (ASI), which partially reconstructed its masonry dome. In the 1980s two single-storey, concrete-frame buildings were built on remains of earlier structures flanking the historic mosque in order to provide additional space for prayer.

The original late Timurid-era mosque is an octagonal masonry structure, with a square internal space topped by a double-skin 'ribbed dome' with clerestory windows decorated with gypsum latticework located at the base of the external drum. The lower octagonal 'plinth' has alternating openings of different sizes on each of its faces, culminating in a double-height *iwan* on its eastern elevation. The *iwan* retains large areas of elaborate colour-glazed tiling and is flanked by two corkscrew pillars rising from bulbous vase-like shapes at its base. Together with a pair of circular minarets erected behind the *iwan*, decorated with panels of 'Kufic' religious scripts, these

Right, tile masons work to lay out a geometric pattern used to consolidate missing sections of tile work.

Middle, timber windows being installed in a reconstructed section of the mosque.

Bottom, brick paving was used to replace large sections of concrete, which had caused extensive damage to the mosque by raising the level of damp in the ground surrounding the monument.

features are highly unusual for a Timurid-era construction in Afghanistan. Furthermore, the intricate external dome, containing fifty-two semicircular ribs supported by elaborate corbels decorated with glazed-tile *muqarnas*, resembles the dome of Gawharshad's mausoleum in Herat — the only other building in Afghanistan in this architectural style.

Remnants of domes and arches discovered within external niches to the south and north of the mosque suggest that the building had previously been adjoined by two separate constructions. Having collapsed or been demolished, these were replaced more recently by two one-storey concrete mosques. In addition to encroaching on a heritage site, the construction of the concrete additions had caused the build-up of moisture beneath the brick foundations of the shrine, resulting in subsidence of the minarets and the formation of large cracks in masonry areas behind the *iwan*.

As well as being the main congregational mosque in Balkh, the site is regularly visited by pilgrims and tourists from Balkh and the wider region. At the request of local authorities and community representatives, the Khwaja Parsa Mosque and a complex of historic structures located in the public park were prioritized as requiring urgent conservation and consolidation work.

**WORK UNDERTAKEN**

Survey and documentation activities on site were undertaken in parallel with building archaeology and desk-based research aimed at learning more about the mosque. Historic photographs and descriptions helped establish the sequence and scale of transformations that had occurred in the past, enabling the conservation team to differentiate between the original sections of the building and later interventions. In order to protect the historic mosque and render it safe for use, it became evident that the dilapidated concrete additions had to be dismantled. As suitable space was required for prayer, it was decided, together with local authorities and members of the community, that the traditional structure that had previously occupied the site would be reconstructed. In addition to enabling the community to continue to use the mosque for prayer, the reconstruction would provide a suitable opportunity to strengthen and stabilize remains of the historic mosque. The demolition of these concrete interventions was led by the community and phased, so as to enable the transfer of furnishings and use of the reconstructed wings, before further demolition could proceed.

Once the first concrete building and its footings had been removed, a team of archaeologists conducted excavations in order to identify the foundations of the older structure. Archaeological evidence and photographic information provided the basis for an accurate reconstruction of the traditional masonry structure that had once occupied the site next to the historic mosque. Once the southern wing was reconstructed and rendered usable by the community, the concrete structure to the north of the mosque was dismantled and an infill building was constructed using traditional techniques and materials. The reconstruction enabled the use of materials compatible with those of the mosque and provided structural support by buttressing weakened areas of the subsiding minarets. With the historic mosque protected against further damage, the focus of work turned to the consolidation and conservation of the ribbed dome.

Scaffolding was erected above the ribbed dome to enable a closer inspection of the glazed turquoise tiles applied to its surface as part of a recent retiling project. A combination of newly produced commercial tiles had been used together with recycled older tiles from the 1970s. The area was found to be in a dilapidated state

**Laser-scan survey drawing, showing the cross-section of the mosque (centre) and new extensions built to replace modern concrete constructions.**

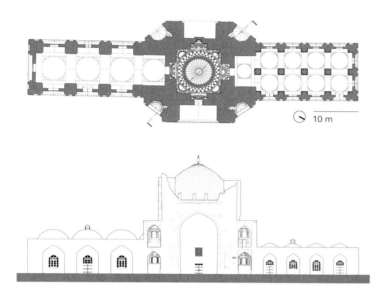

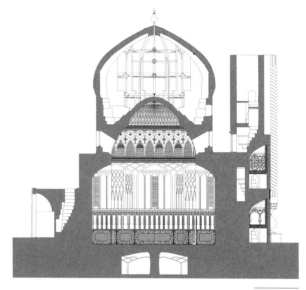

**Above, ground-floor plan, east elevation and section.**

**Below, the dome of the mosque was consolidated and strengthened prior to application of glazed tiles.**

of repair. A combination of inferior materials and poor craftsmanship had resulted in large sections of tiles becoming detached and broken. As a result, water penetration risked damaging key areas of the reconstructed external dome. Site investigations had revealed that the external dome of the mosque had been further weakened by the removal of structural timber elements, originally built in the void between the inner and outer domes of the double-skin dome. Based on this information and evidence of severe fracturing in the outer dome, it was decided to remove sections of the outer tiled ribs in order to assess the condition of the masonry structure. Soon it became evident that the ribbing of the external tiled surface had been constructed using loose rubble backfill, which explained why newly laid sections of tiling were so easily dismantled. Of more concern was the discovery that the thickness of the external dome had been extensively 'cut back' so as to enable easier tiling of the curved surface. As a result, in some areas where only fifteen to twenty centimetres of brick masonry remained, fractures had formed that were large enough to insert an arm up to the elbow. It was decided to remove the external surface of ribbed tiles and carry out urgent structural repairs to the dome; if left unaddressed, it would result in its total collapse. As it was no longer possible to dismantle and properly reconstruct the dome, it was decided to reconstruct internal timber supports — between the double-skin dome — as a first step to carrying out more extensive structural consolidation work. AKTC technical teams devised an ingenious solution for replacing the structural mass cut back during previous retiling work. The solution rested in constructing structural masonry ribs — much like fingers — stitched onto the outside of the external dome. These ribs would provide both the structural support required to stabilize the dome and a suitable substructure for the reapplication of colour-glazed tiles. The fifty-two individual ribs were constructed with square fired bricks, laid in lime mortar and reinforced using glass-fibre mesh.

Retiling the dome entailed the construction of a traditional kiln, operated by master tile makers knowledgeable in indigenous techniques and glaze mixes. Large plaster forms were prepared according to the measurements of ribbed sections of tiles required for the dome. Newly produced, high-quality turquoise tiles were laid within the formwork and reinforced using glass-fibre threading. Composite gypsum plaster was poured behind the tile pieces to create curved sections of tile panels. These panels were numbered and lifted to the level of the dome, where they were sequentially installed onto masonry ribbing and fixed in place with plaster slurry. With the retiling of the dome complete, focus turned to the consolidation of original sections of its corbels, made with intricate *muqarnas* decoration. Further repairs were carried out on large sections of decorated glazed tiling on the drum, minarets and main elevations of the shrine. Remaining areas of historic tiling were cleaned and consolidated, while areas where the tiles had fallen off were cleared of debris and refilled using a lime-based plaster. This prevented driving rain and the build-up of ice from damaging nearby areas of historic tiles in the future.

Within the mosque, decorative elements consisted of large sections of painted geometric and floral patterns on the walls and beneath the dome. A low band of floral designs made using coloured mosaic tiles (*moarraq*) at the base of internal walls, leads to a significant area of glazed *muqarnas* around the prayer niche (*mihrab*). An inability to reproduce missing sections of the original tile work in the course of previous interventions had resulted in repairs with crudely painted plaster infill. As part of restoration work carried out within the mosque, original tile and painted surfaces were cleaned and consolidated.

While rehabilitation work continued in the public park surrounding the mosque, the restored monument was handed back to its custodians in 2014 and has since been used for prayer and communal gatherings.

**Conservation included work on the ribbed dome and main *iwan* arch, as well as the painted and original glazed-tile decoration.**

Preceding pages, the restored mosque stands opposite a platform containing a series of graves, including that of Khwaja Abu Nasr Parsa.

Above, the Persian language poetess Rabia Balkhi is buried beneath this small shrine, reconstructed by AKTC to replace a dilapidated modern concrete structure.

### Rabia Balki Shrine

The shrine of the tenth-century poetess Rabia Balkhi, thought to be the first woman to compose poetry in the Persian language, is located near the Khawaja Parsa Mosque. It is said that the shrine was constructed at the site where she died and that she composed her last poem in her own blood. The partially subterranean grave had been covered by a dilapidated modern concrete structure, which was carefully dismantled by AKTC and replaced with a modest, traditional, masonry building befitting the memory of one of the finest poets in the Persian language.

### Khwaja Parsa Park

Landscaping work within the 3.5-hectare public park, within which these historic structures are located, focused on the removal of invasive species of plants and the dismantling of ad hoc constructions within the park — followed by the provision of irrigation and fired-brick paving in order to improve visitor access. More than 1200 species of indigenous trees and flowers were planted, followed by the construction of a mechanical irrigation network to support new planting in areas lacking surface channels. Additional investments were made for the provision of visitor facilities, including the repair of public toilets and an ablutions area near the mosque, followed by the construction of public seating areas. The perimeter enclosure was reconstructed, followed by the installation of security lighting at key intersections of pedestrian circulation and at the entrances to the park.

Left, residents of Balkh and the surrounding villages frequent the public park around the Khwaja Parsa Mosque, where produce and handicrafts markets are held weekly.

Below, top left, invasive species were replaced with indigenous plane trees.

Top right, public areas previously covered by concrete slabs were re-paved using bricks.

Bottom left, pedestrian walkways in the park were upgraded, enabling safe access for visitors.

Bottom right, landscaping work included the creation of flower beds planted with local roses, which are very popular with Afghans.

# Subhan Qoli Madrasa Gate

**The remains of the Subhan Qoli Madrasa Gate
are the last vestiges of a once magnificent
building located opposite the Khwaja Parsa
Mosque.**

### HISTORY AND CHARACTERISTICS

The remains of the Subhan Qoli Madrasa Gate date from the third quarter of the
seventeenth century. Subhan Qoli, a son of Balkh's Uzbek ruler Nazr Muhammad,
commissioned its construction from proceeds of trade on the Silk Route. Description
of the building from its endowment (*waqfiya*) states that "it comprises lofty arches
and vaulted niches, a majestic portal, a central courtyard and two large domed
rooms, one of which is intended as a lecture hall … the madrasa also has 150 chambers (*hojras*) on two floors". Built opposite the Khwaja Parsa Shrine, the madrasa is
believed to have been intended to mirror and surpass the architectural significance
of the shrine.

When the building fell into disrepair in the nineteenth century, remains of the
madrasa were demolished in order to construct a circular road around the park in the
1930s as part of wider modernization plans for Balkh.

### WORK UNDERTAKEN

Physical surveys of the gate confirmed a need for extensive structural work and
showed that pillars flanking the *iwan* had been reduced in thickness (as part of previous road construction work) resulting in the formation of large cracks in the brick
masonry. Consolidation designs entailed the construction of new sections of masonry
supports 'stitched' to remaining areas of original brickwork. Retaining only a fraction of the vibrant colour-glazed tiles that once decorated the elevations of the *iwan*,
conservation work commenced with the repair and consolidation of the honeycomb
masonry substructure, followed by the stabilization of fragile sections of the remaining tile work.

A protective lightweight roof was constructed above the gate, using curved
wooden rafters clad in galvanized metal sheeting, in order to weatherpoof the monument and provide shelter for visitors to the park. As it had been detached from its
surrounds and isolated as a stand-alone structure for more than six decades, paving
work focused on connecting the building to the circulation network of the park —
allowing future visitors to appreciate its fine architecture.

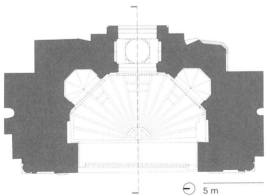

⊖ 5 m

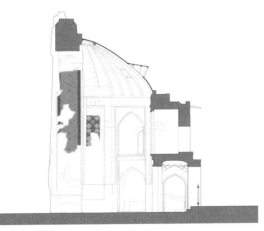

Top, mirroring its previous function, the restored structure is now a gateway into the Khwaja Parsa public park.

Left, ground-floor plan and section.

Centre, teams of masons and carpenters worked to consolidate the remains of the gate and to construct a lightweight roof, which prevented future damage to the structure.

Right, the restored gate showing an area of the original brick and glazed tile work beneath a lightweight timber roof.

# Dehdadi Mosque

Above, the Dehdadi Mosque had been
expanded over a two-hundred-year period
and was in a poor state of repair prior to
conservation.

Below, internal elevations of the mosque
damaged by rising damp were stripped
of plaster and the space ventilated, allowing
masonry walls to dry, before conservation
measures could be implemented.

### HISTORY AND CHARACTERISTICS
The Dehdadi Mosque is believed to have been built in two distinct periods, with an
early eighteenth-century wooden veranda decorated with intricate plaster reliefs and
later nineteenth-century additions replacing sections of the earlier construction with
a range of masonry domed rooms to the east. The original mosque and Sufi prayer
space (*khanaqa*) was built by Mirza Mohammad Yousuf, a Naqshbandi Sufi mystic
who distinguished himself as a scholar and poet. Mirza travelled to perform the Hajj
pilgrimage to Mecca, but fell ill on the way and died in Kuwait, where his disciples
built a tomb bearing his name. Internally, the Dehdadi Mosque contains finely carved
cedar doors and painted stucco decoration on the upper parts of the arches, domes
and prayer niche (*mihrab*), resembling similar religious buildings in Bukhara from
the eighteenth and nineteenth centuries. In the oldest section of the mosque, wooden
pillars stand on unique cylindrical bases, and its main walls are covered in plaster
floral motifs resembling the 'tree of life'.

The religious complex includes a large elliptical pool used for ablutions and
potable water by the community and an open-plan madrasa used for religious education and mass prayer. The structure was in a dilapidated condition, with structural
damage caused by weathering. An initial survey of the site was conducted in 2011.

### WORK UNDERTAKEN
Initial excavations revealed that the original masonry domes of the mosque were built
using adobe (mud brick), resulting in extensive damage caused by water penetration
over time. The first stage of structural consolidation work focused on carrying out
repairs to adobe brick-masonry domes, followed by the construction of a protective
secondary fired-brick dome (above the original structure) in order to prevent water
penetration and provide natural ventilation. Rising damp in the main eastern facade of
the mosque had resulted in settlement of load-bearing masonry walls, which required
the provision of a water barrier below ground and the construction of supporting
arches beneath existing openings. An external raised platform, which had been constructed above loose backfill, was reconstructed in order to provide additional space
for congregational prayers.

In order to provide safe access to a suitable water supply for worshippers and the
surrounding community, the large elliptical pool was drained and its embankments
were stabilized with brick-masonry retaining walls. The restored mosque and site was
handed back to local custodians following the completion of conservation work.

Top, the highly decorated mud-brick domes of the mosque were extensively damaged by water seepage, requiring the construction of a secondary protective masonry shell above the original domes.

Middle, partially responsible for the damage to the mosque from rising damp, an open-water reservoir adjacent to the building was emptied and reconstructed using brick masonry applied to a waterproof membrane.

Bottom, layers of modern plaster and paint were removed from the main elevations, before secondary arches were constructed beneath existing broken arches.

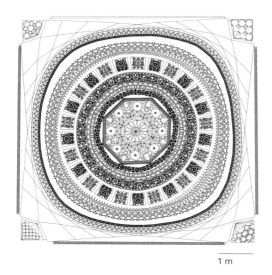

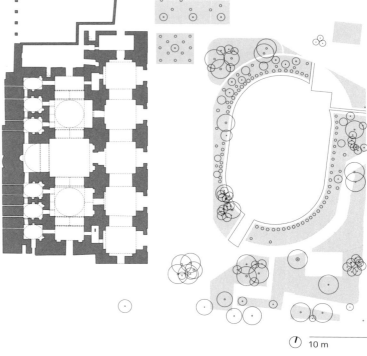

1 m

10 m

Above, reflective ceiling plan, site plan, east elevation.

Below, left, internal painted elevations and geometric plaster decorations were cleaned and consolidated.

Right, composed of interlinking domed spaces, the quality of decorations found within the mosque are some of the finest among those that remain in Balkh from this period.

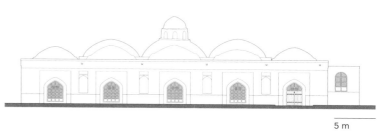

5 m

Above, small openings have been allowed for ventilating spaces between the double-dome structure.

Below, the restored shrine with additional outside space for communal prayer.

# Khwaja Nizamuddin Shrine

Above, the Khwaja Nizamuddin Shrine is a small, finely constructed, early 17th-century mausoleum in Balkh — seen here prior to restoration.

Below, laser-scan survey drawing.

### HISTORY AND CHARACTERISTICS

Located adjacent to a small cemetery in Balkh, this small eighteenth-century structure is believed to be the burial place of Hazrat Khwaja Nizamuddin, a Sufi religious scholar also known locally as Pir Baba (Eldest of Sufis) for his religious teaching in Balkh. Born in India, Khwaja Nizamuddin was the religious leader (*Shaikh-ul Islam*) in Mughal emperor Akbar's court in Delhi, before being exiled and living out his life in Balkh — where he is believed to have died in the early seventeenth century and buried within this shrine bearing his name. An octagonal masonry building with a single-shell elongated dome, Nizamuddin's grave is located at the centre of a square room and surrounded by a low decorated wooden enclosure. Accessed through an entrance to the south, the grave is oriented in a north-south direction as prescribed by Islamic law. Unlike other shrines containing a grave, a small prayer niche (*mihrab*) located within an arched recess indicates that this small shrine may have been used on occasion for prayer.

The building was found to be in urgent need of repair, and a survey of the shrine conducted in 2014 revealed large cracks in the masonry dome, which had resulted in the seepage of rainwater inside the structure and extensive discoloration of internal plaster.

### WORK UNDERTAKEN

Structural consolidation work entailed the removal of accumulated debris from the roof of the shrine, which had been repeatedly plastered with mud-straw in order to prevent leakage. Damaged sections of the dome and external arches were cleaned, repaired and treated with waterproof lime mortar before being resurfaced with fired-brick paving. An unusual plaster-screen 'lantern' skylight at the apex of the dome was clad using fired bricks in order to prevent damage to its fragile structure. A new brick parapet was designed and constructed above the load-bearing walls, between segments of elongated decorative pilasters that were fully restored using lime mortar.

Previously plastered elevations of the building were cleaned, with missing sections of brickwork repaired and repointed using lime mortar. Internal elevations of the shrine had been covered with gypsum and in places with cement plaster; this was carefully removed and the original brickwork was then restored. New timber doors were produced and installed beneath a remaining section of the original decorated carved timber doors that had been looted in the 1980s.

Conservation work was followed by the construction of a paved pathway around the shrine, preventing seepage of water into brick foundations, and the planting of local species of trees around the site.

Above, the restored shrine is both a place of worship and an excellent example of the austere building tradition of the region.

Left, interior view of the shrine with the grave of Khwaja Nizamuddin encased within a decorated wooden structure.

Right, structural repairs were carried out, followed by the re-roofing of the shrine and paving of external spaces.

Below, ground-floor plan and section.

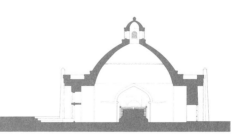

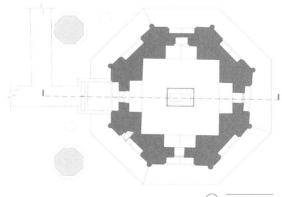

5 m

# Mir Ruzadar Shrine

**Above, the Mir Ruzadar Shrine is a late-15th-century building, one of the largest mausoleums remaining in Balkh.**

**Below, laser-scan survey drawing.**

## HISTORY AND CHARACTERISTICS

Rebuilt on the foundations of an earlier building on the orders of the Timurid king Shah Rukh, who visited the site shortly before his death, the Mir Ruzadar Shrine consists of an octagonal single-shell dome preceded by a rectangular vestibule entrance flanked by a pair of symmetric staircases leading to the roof. Mir Ruzadar was a Sufi mystic who, according to local legend, refused to suckle his mother's breast as a child, thus being called "Ruzadar" (one who fasts). The underside of the dome above his grave is decorated in stucco, reflecting a geometric combination of stars and polygons, finished with hand-painted floral patterns. The external elevations of the building are a combination of flat relief arches and recessed niches rising to a total height of 6.5 metres.

## WORK UNDERTAKEN

Conservation work commenced in 2014 with the removal of accumulated earth and the dismantling of ad hoc repairs followed by the consolidation of building foundations, including measures aimed at preventing rising damp and water penetration. Damage to the masonry walls of the building, caused by differential settlement, was consolidated with injections of lime grout and the construction of new brick foundations. A reinforced-steel ring beam was retrofitted at the intersection between the dome and the drum where large cracks had formed as a result of deformation in the masonry walls. In order to protect internal decoration, a secondary brick-masonry shell was constructed above the original dome with sufficient space between the structures to allow for ventilation. Precast gypsum screens were created and installed in existing openings at the base of the drum in order to prevent pigeons from entering the shrine. The roof of the shrine was finished with a layer of lime concrete and paved with durable fired bricks. The main elevations of the shrine were cleaned and damaged sections were repaired using techniques that distinguished new work from the original brickwork.

Internal work focused on the careful removal of lime-wash paint inappropriately applied to decorative sections of the dome. Gypsum panels that had become detached from the dome were consolidated and anchored to the masonry structure using bamboo and stainless-steel anchor bolts. Visible cracks were structurally stitched and filled with gypsum slurry, before a final layer of gypsum plaster was applied to large areas of internal walls.

In addition to the conservation of the shrine, a complex of tombs located adjacent to the shrine were consolidated and decorative colour-glazed tile panels located on its walls were conserved.

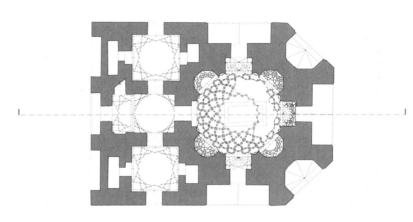

5 m

Top, areas of plaster and painted decoration that had become detached from the masonry structure were consolidated.

Above, masons work to repair brick foundations of the shrine.

Right, ground-floor plan and section.

Below, the restored shrine is set within a garden containing mature mulberry trees.

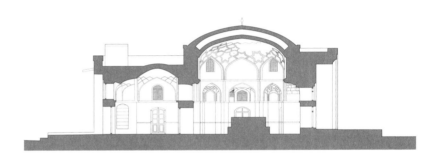

# Sultan Ahmad Khezraviah Shrine

**Above, the Sultan Ahmad Khezraviah Shrine is located on the perimeter of the main cemetery in Balkh.**

**Below, along with a second building, containing the remains of his wife, both buildings required structural repairs and conservation.**

### HISTORY AND CHARACTERISTICS

Located within the main cemetery of Balkh, along the outer perimeter of the Kushan-era city walls, the graves of Ahmad Khezraviah and his wife Fatima Balkhi are contained within two small single-storey shrines. Reference is made to Ahmad Khezraviah, a famous Sufi scholar living in Balkh in the ninth century, in the masterpiece by Jalal al-Din Muhammad Balkhi (commonly known as Rumi), *The Masnavi*. Rumi recounts a story about Ahmad Khezraviah and a young *halva* (sweetmeats) seller. The child weeps when Ahmad Khezraviah cannot pay him for sweets the scholar has purchased from him to placate his creditors. When a sum of money miraculously appears, including the small amount that Khezraviah owes the boy, Rumi reveals that the boy's sincere cries were needed to provoke God's mercy and proclaims, "until the halva-selling child has not cried, withheld is the sea of mercy's churning".

A well-respected Sufi in her own right, Fatima Balkhi's grave is frequented to this day by women who pray for the resolution of family problems.

### WORK UNDERTAKEN

Surveys conducted in 2014 revealed the extent of deterioration to both shrines, which were on the verge of collapse. Due to the critical state of the buildings and before consolidation and conservation work could commence, extensive temporary supports were built beneath the domes and adjacent to load-bearing walls. Once they were stabilized, large quantities of earth materials were removed from the roofs of the structures and from the exterior adjacent to its masonry walls. The brick-masonry domes were repaired using specially fabricated square bricks and lime-based mortar, applied in a stitching technique to damaged sections of the structure. External and internal elevations of the building were cleaned, repaired and repointed. A new brick parapet was designed and constructed above the load-bearing walls and new doors were produced and installed at the entrances to both shrines. As a final measure, the decorative wall of a grave located adjacent to Balkhi's Shrine was treated and protected against further damage, followed by improvements to public access entailing the construction of surface drains and paved pathways.

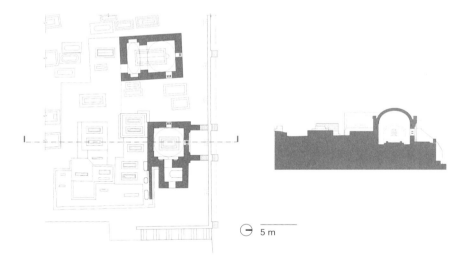

Above, the restored shrine and surrounding graves set against the backdrop of the Kushan-era fortifications of Balkh.

Middle, site plan and section.

Below, left, masons work to replace sections of damaged brickwork.

Centre, the single-span dome of the shrine was stabilized temporarily while consolidation work was undertaken.

Right, the intervention also entailed the upgrading of access to the shrine and repair of the adjacent grave site.

5 m

287

# Chahar Gunbad Shrine

**The Chahar Gunbad Shrine is believed to have been part of a much larger complex of religious structures destroyed during the Mongol sacking of Balkh in the early 13th century and later restored during the Timurid era.**

## HISTORY AND CHARACTERISTICS

Believed to have originally been built during the late Samanid period (819–999) as part of a larger complex, the Chahar Gunbad Shrine is recorded as having been restored during Timurid rule in the early fifteenth century. Prior to its restoration, the building and adjacent structures may have been used as a Sufi *khanaqa*. While little is known about the history of the site or who is buried there, records refer to the great reverence with which Balkh's rulers visited the building. Constructed with thick load-bearing masonry walls almost two metres in width, the building contains a large square internal space with irregular relief arches below the springing of the dome. With a single-shell masonry dome spanning more than eight metres and a height of ten metres above ground, the shrine is one of the largest remaining structures in Balkh.

Used as a fortified base by armed groups opposing the Soviet occupation, the site was extensively damaged by artillery fire during the 1980s.

## WORK UNDERTAKEN

Surveys of the building and the remains of surrounding structures were prepared in 2014 before emergency consolidation activities focused on repairs to sections of the building that were at high risk of collapse, using bricks collected during removal of debris. With the existing structure stabilized, the focus on consolidation work turned to strengthening the foundations of the shrine and sections of the building damaged by looters. Based on the dilapidated condition of the structure and further damage certain to result from exposure to rain and snow and following consultation with local authorities, it was decided that the best manner to protect this monument was to reconstruct its dome according to its original designs. In order to differentiate work being carried out by AKTC and the original architecture of the building, priority was given to applying methods prescribed by international charters on the conservation of historic sites. This included the use of different sized fired bricks and set-back techniques for the ongoing intervention.

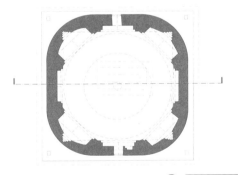

⊖ 5 m

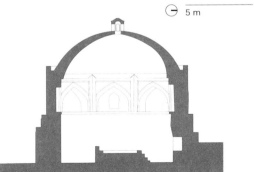

Above, detailed surveys of the building enabled an accurate reconstruction of the dome, which prevented further damage to the shrine.

Left, first-floor plan and section.

Below, remains of the original structure were conserved, before further work could be undertaken.

# Khwaja Bajgahi Shrine

Sections of the early 16th-century Khwaja Bajgahi Shrine had collapsed as recently as 2015 and the building was in urgent need of repair.

### HISTORY AND CHARACTERISTICS

Little is known about the Khwaja Bajgahi Shrine other than that it was built in the late Timurid period in a historic quarter of Balkh known for the residence of a state tax collector (*bajgahi*). There are indications that the building may have originally been built as a mausoleum, which over time was transformed into a shrine. Unlike other shrines or religious structures, which were expanded or restored in various historic periods, the Khwaja Bajgahi Shrine remains today as it was built and retains its spiritual value. It is frequented by locals who seek remedies for illnesses.

Built with fired-brick masonry applied with mud mortar, which may explain the extent of damage caused by exposure to rain and snow, the octagonal main space of the shrine (*hazira*) was covered with a plastered ribbed dome (*karbandi*) and accessed through a rectangular vaulted vestibule. A combination of weathering, settlement and damage inflicted during the conflict resulted in the collapse of its main dome and subsidence of the arched *iwan*. As it remained in a dilapidated condition for the past decade, local residents removed bricks from the site for use in the construction of their homes.

### WORK UNDERTAKEN

Based on requests from the local community, for whom the shrine represents an important religious site, remains of the building were surveyed in 2013. It was assessed to be in a critical state of disrepair, and the necessary structural consolidation work started with the construction of two masonry buttresses flanking the broken *iwan*. In order to avoid further damage resulting from exposure to rain and snow, following consultation with local authorities, it was decided that the best manner to protect this monument was to reconstruct its ribbed dome according to the original design. This work commenced with the stabilization of existing sections of the dome and the erection of reinforced-gypsum ribs (*karbandi*), followed by the laying of fired-brick infill providing a circular base for the construction of the dome. Once completed, the dome will be weatherproofed with lime mortar before the application of durable fired-brick paving. The last stage of the project will entail the provision of internal paving and external landscaping aimed at providing safe access and diverting rainwater away from the foundations of the monument.

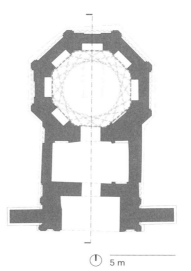

Top left, metal formwork being prepared for the construction of supporting arches.

Top right, conservation of original sections of the monument preceded the reconstruction of its masonry dome.

Above, based on detailed surveys of the existing structure, reconstructed areas of the shrine will be distinguishable from the original building, providing long-term protection for the monument.

Left, ground-floor plan and section.

5 m

# Takhta Pul Mosque

**Above, built as part of wider projects undertaken in the early 18th century, Takhta Pul Mosque was constructed by the builders of the Dehdadi Mosque, also restored by AKTC.**

**Below, laser-scan survey.**

## HISTORY AND CHARACTERISTICS

One of the best-preserved monuments in Balkh, the Takhta Pul Mosque and *khanaqa* was built in the early eighteenth century as part of a larger fort complex (*qala*) intended to house the governor of Balkh. The building is composed of two double-shell domed spaces, flanking a central square room with a higher single-shell dome capped by a 'lantern' skylight. In addition to being an expression of architectural form and embellishment, recessed niches within these spaces enabled builders to reduce the overall mass and thickness of walls. A row of smaller double-storey rooms to the west were used for spiritual meditation (*chila khana*). Internal elevations of the mosque are decorated with painted geometric and floral patterns, which were in various states of conservation at the time of documentation by AKTC. The mosque also contains two prayer niches (*mihrab*), with the external *mihrab* linked to a raised platform used for outdoor prayer. At the time of initial surveys of the monument, the building was assessed to require structural consolidation and preventative measures against future deterioration.

## WORK UNDERTAKEN

As with other monuments in Balkh, conservation work commenced with structural repairs entailing the stabilization of external load-bearing walls through the construction of low masonry buttresses. Ad hoc repairs, carried out previously to the roof of the building using cement mortar, were found to have compounded existing structural damage in the domes. These interventions were carefully dismantled, followed by the construction of low masonry walls in order to support the lateral thrust of domes. Arched masonry openings were built into support walls, enabling the natural ventilation of the internal decorative dome. Exposed surfaces of the roof were weatherproofed using lime concrete and finished with durable fired-brick paving.

Internal restoration work focused on the stabilization of key sections of plaster reliefs that had become detached from the masonry structure, followed by careful cleaning of painted decoration. Painted surfaces were conserved in order to prevent damage from moisture or dust, making it possible to clean and maintain the spaces in the future. External landscaping work included the construction of a large prayer platform to the east, followed by paving the perimeter of the building in order to prevent penetration of water into its foundations. The addition of new cedar doors and windows rendered the mosque functional, and it is currently being used by students of an agricultural institute nearby and travellers on the road to Balkh.

Above, repairs to the roof included stabilization of existing domes and the construction of low masonry buttresses in order to prevent further damage.

Left, internal plaster and painted decoration was repaired and consolidated.

Right, wider landscaping improvements around the building enable better access for worshippers.

Below, ground-floor plan and section.

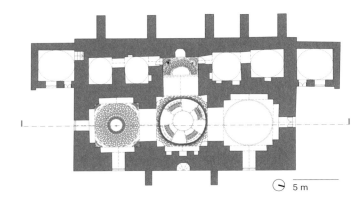

5 m

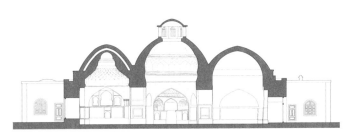

# Tanga-e Shadian

Believed to have been constructed for the dual purpose of defensive fortification and flood barrier, the structure at Tanga-e Shadian (seen here from the south) required urgent consolidation and partial reconstruction.

### HISTORY AND CHARACTERISTICS

The monumental arched brick-masonry structure at Tanga-e Shadian in Balkh, believed to have been built at the beginning of the eleventh century, has been at the centre of a local debate concerning its intended function. Located at the entrance to the Shadian pass, which leads to mountain villages north of Mazar-e Sharif, the structure spans between opposing cliffs of the Alborz Mountains. The pass serves both as a transportation route, with a single-lane public road passing beneath the arches of the structure, and the entry point of seasonal flooding areas in the plains north of the city. Based on this, it is believed that the historic structure at its entrance is either a defensive fortification gate or a protective structure, or possibly both.

Built using fired-brick masonry with an infill of broken stones set in lime mortar, the structure reaches sixteen metres in height and spans twenty-five metres at its widest point. Due to a slight shift in direction at the centre of the structure, the original masonry arch was built on multiple axes. Two small chambers at the top of the southern elevation of the structure are accessed by a narrow steep staircase on the internal face of the arch. At the time of surveys conducted by ATKC, the structure was found to have been damaged by vibration caused by passing traffic and extensively eroded by flooding, which often surpasses seven to ten metres in height, at its narrowest point beneath the broken arch of the monument.

### WORK UNDERTAKEN

The first stage of structural consolidation activity centred on separating the foundations of the historic structure from those of the cast-concrete road in order to reduce vibration caused by large trucks. Trenches were dug at the base of the arch, cutting back more than two metres of reinforced concrete, after which rubber dampers were installed and stone foundations rebuilt. The next stage of work entailed the protection of exposed areas of the arch against damage from flash floods, which tend to contain large stone boulders. Reinforced stone aprons were constructed at the base of the structure and stitched into the cliff face using stainless-steel anchor rods. Once the base of the structure had been secured, consolidation activity focused on replacing large areas of damaged brick walls, followed by the full-scale reconstruction of the nine-metre-high masonry arch on multiple axes using specially constructed formwork. In order to prevent further damage from weathering, the upper areas of the structure were reconstructed and protected with lime concrete and a durable

layer of fired-brick paving. While the stabilization of the structure has not resolved the debate on its intended function, its restoration means that successive generations will be afforded the opportunity to continue the discussion.

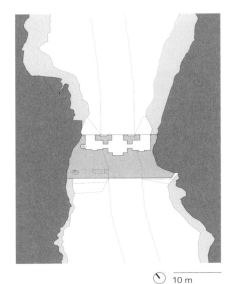

10 m

Top, the restored structure (seen here from the north) will provide a measure of protection from floodwaters that often reach more than twelve metres in height.

Above, the large masonry arch of the structure, which had collapsed causing erosion of backfill material, was reconstructed.

Left, floor plan and north elevation.

# PLANNING, UPGRADING AND ACCESS IMPROVEMENTS

⊕ ____ 500 m

**Preceding pages, surveyors preparing a socio-economic survey in residential areas in central Balkh.**

**Building use survey, Balkh old town.**

| | | | | |
|---|---|---|---|---|
| Public buildings | Commercial premises | Cemetery | Historic city walls / citadel |
| Residential area | Open space | | Water channel |

## PLANNING

In order to consolidate achievements involving physical conservation, upgrading and vocational training activities, planning support initiatives carried out under the Balkh Area Development Programme focused on providing support for local coordination, advocacy and governance structures. While the focus of recent large-scale urban development and construction projects remains in Mazar-e Sharif, the capital and administrative centre of Balkh province, an increase in modern infill construction has gradually transformed the historic landscape around the old town of Balkh.

In order to address this concern, in 2012 AKTC prioritized the establishment of a formal coordination mechanism with Balkh Municipality and the district governor's office aimed at supporting local planners, in an effort to balance sustainable urban development with the preservation of historic fabric in the old town. This was done in the context of AKTC's ongoing conservation programme, which established defined parameters for the preservation of built heritage, and enabled local residents to engage civil servants in decision-making exercises aimed at building a sustainable relationship between communities and state institutions. Through this forum, local residents and religious representatives became advocates for conservation activities aimed at protecting and rehabilitating communal structures and shared public spaces.

As part of planning activities, in 2013 a physical survey of residential and commercial properties was carried out in the old town and in areas surrounding historic sites restored under AKTC's conservation programme, yielding useful information on occupancy and use, architectural characteristics, availability of services, state of repair and level of vulnerability of the property. Surveys revealed that the bulk of houses in the historic old town were traditional in form and construction, yet one out of ten homes was modern. Furthermore, one in six homes in the old town was occupied by more than one family, with indications of a gradual increase in density. In comparison, more than three quarters of commercial premises were modern, with more than 200 new shops or markets recorded as having been built from 2002–13, often on the site of demolished early to mid-twentieth-century shops. The trend in the destruction of heritage properties, replaced by modern infill constructions, reflected a significant increase in the wealth of those investing in speculative commercial development in the historic old town.

In addition to facilitating the identification of priority areas requiring upgrading and access improvements, the physical survey enabled the establishment of key 'conservation zones' where development activities would be regulated and closely

Above, members of the community and civil servants receive an update on the conservation of the Khwaja Parsa Mosque.

Below, surveyors preparing a socio-economic survey in residential areas in central Balkh.

monitored. The documentation further enabled the preparation of a baseline socio-economic survey for 470 households, conducted in 2013 by a group of local female surveyors. The mapping of key socio-economic information on livelihoods and living conditions, correlated with data collected through physical surveys, enabled AKTC to prioritize investments in upgrading and access improvements in areas most in need of physical improvement and where the impact of these activities on living conditions would be highest.

Support for technical and management capacity was provided through opportunities for on-the-job training for students and professionals and in the context of an active engagement of civil servants on project sites. In the absence of formal policies to safeguard Balkh's built heritage, further legal protection was provided by AKTC towards the preparation of inscription dossiers for key historic monuments in the old town on a register developed by the Department of Historic Monuments.

## UPGRADING AND ACCESS IMPROVEMENT

Since 2012, AKTC's programmes in the old town of Balkh have helped communities living and working around historic sites benefit from focused investments in enhancing their environments. Physical upgrading and access work have improved living conditions for populations in areas surrounding historic sites, mitigating wider development pressures that often lead to historic areas being demolished and

Top left, construction of a covered irrigation channel near the Noh Gunbad Mosque.

Top right, upgrading of public drains opposite the Khwaja Parsa Park.

Bottom left, survey of the drainage network.

Bottom right, access improvements in residential areas in central Balkh.

redeveloped. In the residential quarters near the historic citadel of Balkh, residents suffered from chronic blockages in drainage of water along the Bandar-e Bala Hissar road — resulting in the flooding of adjacent residential streets and houses. In order to address the problem, damaged sections of underground drains (beneath the road) were excavated, reconstructed and covered with culverts that would enable access for future maintenance. Irrigated by the Balkh River some fourteen kilometres to the south of the historic old town, open drains provide an important source of water for agriculture and household irrigation. Damaged sections of irrigation channels in the centre of the town, along the Bandar-e Baghragh road near the Khwaja Parsa Mosque, were demolished and rebuilt so as to enable a better flow of water in the gravity-fed irrigation system. Additional drainage upgrading work carried out on the periphery of the Khwaja Parsa Park prevented flooding of roads and damage to monuments located within the park. In addition to the fact that they were poorly designed and constructed, chronic problems with the irrigation and drainage network were also due to deficiencies in the management of waste that resulted in blockages in the system. Support was provided for Balkh Municipality and local councils for improving the waste-management system for the centre of the historic old town, entailing identification of collection points and the regular disposal of waste. In coordination with local authorities and community councils, traders responsible in large part for the production and inappropriate disposal of waste were consulted and made aware of provisions for waste management.

Since 2012, more than 3.5 kilometres of covered drains have been repaired or ungraded by AKTC in the historic old town of Balkh, and more than 1200 square metres of pedestrian alleyways have been paved. These activities have directly benefited 10,000 people, or more than half of the resident population of the historic old town, generating approximately 12,000 workdays of skilled and unskilled labour, which has mainly been drawn from local residents.

Above, encroachment of residential development adjacent to the fortifications of the Bala Hissar (citadel).

Below, there is a significant increase in new development in commercial and residential areas of Balkh.

# BADAKHSHAN

Preceding pages, Badakhshan province in northern Afghanistan is located at the convergence of the Hindu Kush and Pamir mountain ranges, with the previous district centre Baharak (seen here) placed at the crossroads of smaller valleys headed towards Tajikistan, China and Pakistan.

Above, informal hillside settlements constructed above Faizabad, the current district capital of Badakhshan.

Right, the Kokcha River runs along a valley linking Baharak with districts in southern Badakshan, including Jurm and Yumgan.

## INTRODUCTION

The mountainous north-eastern Afghan province of Badakshan shares its borders with Tajikistan, northern Pakistan and China. Originally part of the historic greater 'Badakhshan Region', comprising areas of modern Tajikistan and northern Pakistan, the region was an important centre for trade in lapis lazuli as early as the fourth millennium BC and later during the active period of the Silk Road. Marco Polo wrote of its extraordinary rubies, part of the vast mineral wealth in the region, while travelling through the area towards the end of the thirteenth century. Ruled for centuries by kings (*mirs*) self-proclaimed to be descendants of Alexander of Macedonia (Alexander the Great), the last of whom was deposed during the Timurid dynasty in the fifteenth century, the region was fought over by the Mughal Empire and its rivals, the Uzbek khanates centred in Balkh. Although the region was gifted to Ahmad Shah Durrani (the founder of the modern state of Afghanistan) in 1750 by the amir of Bukhara, the province was officially conceded to the amir of Kabul and its boundaries established by a joint Anglo-Russian Boundary Commission only in 1888. Political motivations behind the demarcation of borders resulted in a thin strip of land, known as the Wakhan Corridor, being included in the Badakhshan province of Afghanistan in order to provide a buffer between Russian Central Asia and British India.

Badakhshan is the most seismically active region in Afghanistan, with frequent earthquakes measuring 6+ in magnitude on the Richter scale. The unavailability of traditional building materials, such as clay for making fired bricks, lime and wood, has meant that earthquakes have historically caused widespread damage to buildings constructed with stone. This may be one of the reasons why very few historic sites of significance remain in good condition in comparison with other regions with historic settlements. Building on AKTC's broad conservation experience in Afghanistan, documentation activities in Badakhshan commenced in 2007 with a series of field surveys in the Wakhan Corridor as part of the Wakhan Heritage Inventory, which comprises one hundred sites of historic or social significance in the area. In 2008, research was carried out on local folklore, which was subsequently presented in the *Tales of the Wakhan,* a booklet co-produced jointly with the Aga Khan Foundation that combines local legends passed on in oral history with material from the Wakhan Heritage Inventory and maps of the area.

Initial research and documentation efforts led to a 2010 agreement of cooperation with the Ministry of Information and Culture for the comprehensive restoration of the Nasir Khusrau Shrine in the Yamgan district of southern Badakhshan. Constructed

The Wakhan Corridor (seen here near Sahad-e Broghil) extends Afghanistan's borders with Tajikistan and Pakistan, while providing a seventy-six-kilometre border with China to the east.

**Above, traditional timber-front shops along the main road in the old town of Faizabad have been largely demolished as part of road-widening work.**

**Below, children bathing in a stream diverted from the Kokcha River for irrigation of agri-cultural fields near the old town of Faizabad.**

on the final resting place of the eleventh-century Ismaili scholar, philosopher and poet Nasir Khusrau, who came to Yamgan by way of Balkh and Faizabad in AD 1060, the shrine is located in a narrow valley on the eastern bank of the Kokcha River above the village of Hazrat-e Sayyed. The conservation project entailed structural consolidation of a loose conglomerate outcrop that the shrine was built on and the conservation of its unique internal decoration, including handwritten verses from the Qur'an painted on wooded rafters (in Thulth calligraphy) above the grave area (*mazar*). The first project carried out by AKTC in a remote rural setting, conservation work was carried out in tandem with training and upgrading activities and implemented jointly with local authorities and the small community of Hazrat-e Sayyed village.

Simultaneous to conservation activities in southern Badakhshan, AKTC undertook a systematic physical survey in areas of remaining historic fabric in the old town of Faizabad, the provincial capital of Badakhshan. The original settlement of Faizabad probably grew as a result of trade, given its location on the route between Taloqan and Kunduz (to the west) and Baharak, from where ancient trade routes access China through the Wakhan Corridor and the Indian subcontinent to the south. An account by John Wood in 1872 describes seven forts, probably built to protect trade routes, in the immediate vicinity of a settlement in the region. All that remains today, however, is scattered rubble or traces of foundations at Kuri. The name Faizabad is thought to refer to the act of bringing the cloak of the Prophet Muhammad to the town. This cloak was taken in the late nineteenth century by Amir Abdur Rahman Khan to Kandahar, where it remains to this day.

Little more than an extended village until two decades ago, and now the fast-growing administrative centre of Badakhshan province home to some 65,000 inhabi-tants, most of the traditional built heritage of Faizabad has been lost to recent mod-ernization programmes. Further to a series of preliminary documentation exercises in 2009, AKTC carried out an extensive socio-economic Quality of Life Assessment survey in 2011 with a sample size of approximately eight hundred households, or 15% of the population in the town. The findings of the Faizabad socio-economic survey provided important baseline information on the livelihood and living conditions of the population and enabled the planning and implementation of a multi-year conserva-tion and vocational training programme.

One of the first projects carried out by AKTC in Faizabad reflected a priority identified in the socio-economic survey for a suitable public space and recreational park. As in other regions, historic mausoleums were often constructed within open communal spaces. One such site was the shrine of Mir Yar Beg, in the Chatta district of the town, believed to contain the grave of an early nineteenth-century king of Badakhshan who lived in Faizabad. The small (one-room), domed, masonry structure was built at the highest point of a sloping site of almost half a hectare, south of the Kokcha River. In a dilapidated condition, the site provided an opportunity to restore an important monument and upgrade its landscape into a public park. In 2014, AKTC carried out conservation and landscaping work in parallel, resulting in the structural consolidation of the domed shrine and the terracing, planting and construction of a gravity-fed irrigation system in the surrounding park.

Physical surveys conducted in the old town of Faizabad identified an unused historic public bath (hammam), which was in urgent need of repair, located in an area where respondents to AKTC's survey had prioritized the need for hygienic bathing facilities. Following detailed documentation of the site, teams of craftsmen and labourers cleared the building of debris, before repairing and consolidating its masonry structure along with ancillary spaces around the central domed chambers.

On completion of the external building work, the hypocaust flooring, chimneys and vents were rebuilt and the hammam was made operational. Regular use of the historic hammam has sustainably revived a local business, while providing a much-needed service for the surrounding community.

Engaged with the local community and state institutions for conservation and vocational training programmes aimed at benefiting local populations, AKTC's on-going Area Development Programme in Badakhshan will continue to invest in safe-guarding historic areas, supporting the long-term process of building capacity, and promoting the institutional reform sought by most Afghans.

**Modern constructions interspersed with traditional settlements along the river in Faizabad.**

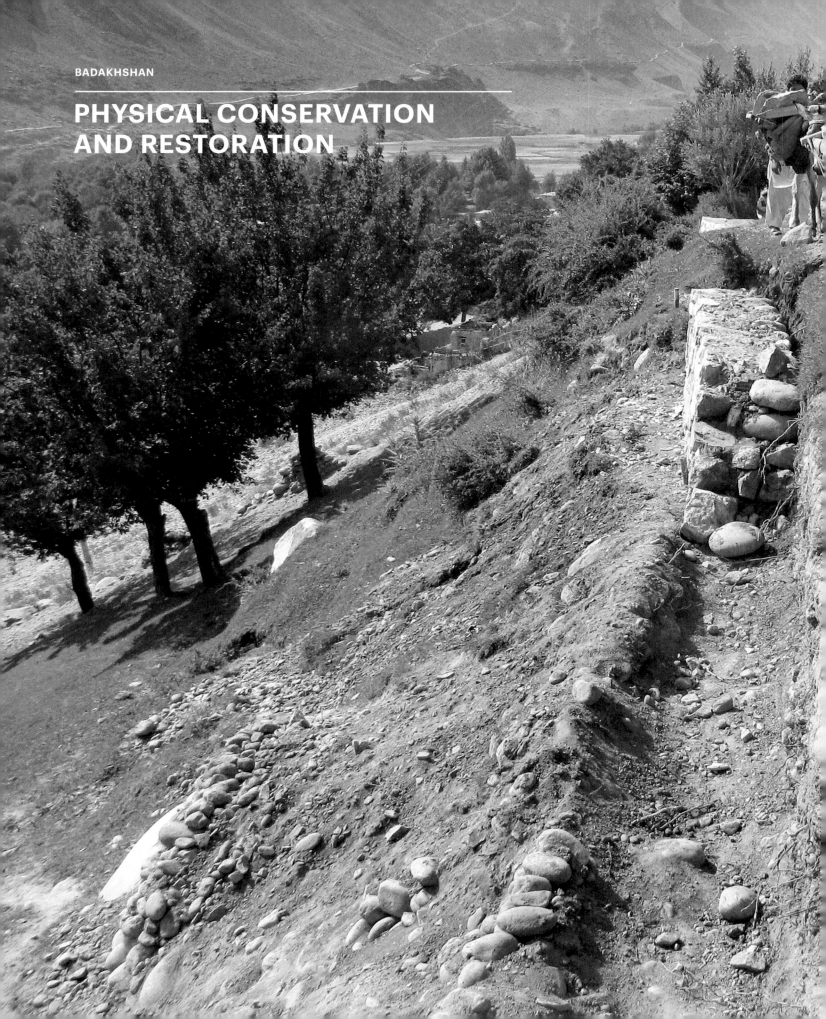

# PHYSICAL CONSERVATION AND RESTORATION

# Nasir Khusrau Shrine

Preceding pages, materials required for the conservation of the Nasir Khusrau Shrine in Yumgan were transported to the steep hillside site using pack animals.

Above, the Nasir Khusrau Shrine is located on a stone outcrop, above the village of Hazart-e Sayyed in Yumgan district, and contains the grave of the early 11th-century scholar and philosopher.

## HISTORY AND CHARACTERISTICS

As it stands today, the Nasir Khusrau Shrine, or *ziyarat*, is both a funerary structure, marking the grave of the great Persian writer and philosopher, and a place of prayer and pilgrimage. A fine example of vernacular construction, containing extraordinary decorative elements, the shrine is also a registered historic monument and protected under laws regarding the preservation and safeguarding of Afghanistan's heritage.

The shrine was constructed on the final resting place of Nasir Khusrau, the eleventh-century Ismaili scholar, philosopher and poet, who came to Yamgan after his stay in Fatimid Cairo by way of Balkh and Faizabad in 1060. The village of Hazrat-e Sayyed is located in a narrow valley on the eastern bank of the Kokcha River in southern Badakhshan. Located in a remote area, the village is a seven-hour drive on unpaved roads from Faizabad, with major settlements at Baharak and Jurm along the route. The precarious route south from Jurm winds through precipitous valleys and the area is often inaccessible during the winter.

The shrine is situated on a steep slope, on top of a fifteen-metre-high exposed conglomerate stone outcrop, fifty metres above the village of Hazrat-e Sayyed at an elevation of 2100 metres above sea level. The site is accessed by a narrow winding path from the south, leading to a large flat terrace paved with flat river stones. A stone-lined pool used for ablutions is filled with water from a stream that runs through the village. The terrace and the pool lie beneath the branches of a majestic plane tree at the entrance to the shrine. Directly to the south-east lie the ruins of a small mosque, which is said to have been rebuilt in the 1920s. To the north, there is a ruined kitchen (*langar khana*), where food was prepared during religious festivals. A small terraced garden for pilgrims, divided by stone retaining walls, has been laid out to the north-east of the shrine.

The fine inscriptions, found carved in timber in the grave chamber (*mazar*), indicate that the building was repaired and transformed in 1697. Repairs were again made during the reign of King Abdur Rahman Khan in the late nineteenth century, when a small mosque was built on an adjacent terrace. While the site has been in continuous use by Ismaili and Sunni Muslim communities, the shrine was damaged indirectly by aerial bombardment during the Soviet occupation of Afghanistan.

In comparison to the historic significance of Nasir Khusrau, this modest shrine contains four small spaces composed of two enclosed rooms, each preceded by separate vestibules. Listed in terms of architectural significance, the centrepiece of the shrine is Nasir Khusrau's *mazar* accessed from the east through a large open vestibule

lined with six decorated timber pillars and intricately carved wooden rafters. To the south, a more austere smaller vestibule leads to an unembellished mosque. Confined by the limited space on top of the outcrop on which it rests, the shrine occupies the entire surface of the stone conglomerate leaving only a narrow pathway around the perimeter of the building. With largely blank elevations on three sides and flat roofs of varying heights, the volumetric composition of the building places the highest importance on the elevated vestibule leading to the *mazar*, which is closed by a wooden screen and a low carved door. Three graves located in the large vestibule are said to contain the remains of hereditary custodians of the site.

While some historic sources indicate that the *mazar* chamber of the shrine may have originally been Nasir Khusrau's dwelling, the room measures approximately twenty square metres (4×5 metres) with a low ceiling height of just over 2.5 metres. Similar to the large pillared vestibule, the *mazar* chamber is divided into two zones: a small area covering about one quarter of the floor space that is accessible to pilgrims and, separated by a timber trelliswork railing, a raised larger southern zone containing Nasir Khusrau's grave. Encased by a wooden enclosure, the grave is draped with cloth and fenced off by wrought-iron railing. Immediately to the south are two undecorated graves, which are believed to hold the remains of Nasir Khusrau's closest companions, including his brother Abu Sa'id. Dimly lit by small barred windows on each of its three external walls, which, together with the low ceiling height, creates an intimate atmosphere, the chamber is covered with four rows containing fifty-two wooden joists painted with verses from the Qur'an.

Above, geotechnical analysis of the site revealed that the loose conglomerate outcrop, upon which the shrine was built, required urgent structural consolidation.

Below, hillside water channels were constructed as part of preventative measures taken to stop the seepage of water into the foundations of the shrine.

Conservation work entailed the removal of debris and re-roofing of the shrine, a delicate measure considering the highly decorated woodwork used to construct its ceiling.

The shrine is built using traditional, locally available materials and its load-bearing walls are made with flat river stones set in mud mortar and reinforced with timber ties. Wooden columns and rafters provide the structure for the roof, which is finished with a mud-straw plaster set to falls to help shed rainwater and snowmelt.

### WORK UNDERTAKEN

Detailed physical surveys of the shrine were conducted in 2011, followed by a geotechnical study of the site that identified key areas requiring urgent structural consolidation and conservation. The most critical area of concern centred on the condition of the coarsely grained conglomerate stone outcrop on which the shrine is built. The base of the outcrop was found to have been extensively damaged by erosion and water penetration, resulting in the formation of fissures and cavities that had caused large sections of the loose conglomerate to become detached. Given the history of significant seismic activity in the region, the eroded state of the outcrop represented the most significant long-term threat to the shrine. In order to address this concern, an extensive network of stone breast walls, reinforced by treated timber posts, was constructed on three sides at the base of the outcrop. Large surface cavities were consolidated using hydraulic lime, applied together with a loose conglomerate in order to match the texture and colour of the outcrop. Lastly, a special mixture of hydraulic lime was injected into large cracks that had formed on the western surface of the outcrop, helping reattach loose sections of the conglomerate and seal its surface against future damage caused by water penetration. In order to protect the upper surfaces of the outcrop from erosion, the existing walkway surrounding the perimeter of the shrine was rebuilt and a wooden handrail was provided to ensure safe access for the maintenance of the roof and elevations of the shrine.

While the structure of the shrine remained largely intact, rising damp and the erosion of conglomerate foundations had caused significant settlement in the northern exterior wall. As large sections of the exterior walls were built using river stones set in mud mortar, the structure was particularly susceptible to rising damp. Analysis of the walls showed that older sections of the shrine around the *mazar*, where timber-frame ties had been used to strengthen the construction, remained intact while other areas constructed without timber inserts had become damaged. In order to stabilize the building it was decided that key sections of the northern and southern elevations, adjacent to the vestibules, would be strengthened by retrofitted structural wood-frame elements — similar to traditional techniques used in older sections of the building. Limited sections of the fragile stone masonry were carefully removed, before treated wood-frame sections were reinserted into the wall and attached to similar elements retrofitted into the walls from the interior of the vestibules. The retrofitting was carried out in one-metre segments, while hand-operated jacks were installed to bear part of the weight of the roof in the vestibules. Once the perimeter walls had been stabilized, a similar technique was employed to stabilize the internal partition wall between the small and large vestibules. Following the structural consolidation of load-bearing walls, it was decided to replace the external painted finish of the shrine with a traditional mud-straw-based plaster.

Top left, carpenters from the local community were engaged and trained in carrying out repairs to timber columns and rafters.

Top right, plasterers working to restore late-17th-century decoration added to the main vestibule of the building.

Bottom left, a timber-reinforced breast wall was designed and constructed adjacent to eroded sections of the conglomerate stone at the base of the outcrop.

Bottom right, river stone paving was laid in the open vestibules, as is customary in buildings of the region.

Right, linseed oil was applied to areas of woodwork to prevent damage from moisture.

Middle, carpenters work to repair and strengthen timber rafters damaged by penetration of moisture from the roof.

Bottom, recently applied paint was removed to provide access for conservation of mud-plaster decoration.

Compounded by the weak bond between smooth river stones and damp mud mortar in load-bearing walls, poor upkeep of the multi-levelled roof also resulted in a build-up of mud-straw plaster, which added unnecessary load to the already weakened load-bearing walls. In addition to this, several areas of the roof were found to be leaking, with particular concern focused on leaks above the *mazar* damaging the finely decorated ceiling joist with painted verses from the Qur'an. With minor conservation work required within the *mazar*, most of the activities related to the careful cleaning and consolidation of the intricate decorative elements: the most significant and complex intervention within the shrine was related to the reconstruction of the roof. More than fifty-five centimetres of accumulated earth was removed from the roof, with subsequent inspection of the wooden rafters revealing only minor decay in the material. In order to ensure appropriate slopes for shedding rainwater and snowmelt, it was decided to construct a secondary lightweight roof structure. This ensures that the resulting void enables the appropriate levels of ventilation above the decorated ceiling, which also received a second layer of waterproofing material. The final intervention in this section of the shrine was the laying of durable flooring within the *mazar*, which would reduce dust pollution and enable worshippers to use the space.

The internal elevations of the large vestibule were examined and inappropriate interventions that had been made recently were carefully removed. On the northern wall additional sections of the gypsum plaster decoration were revealed, which, together with other remaining areas, were consolidated and repaired. In order to protect the stone-masonry wall, a final new durable layer of fine mud-based plaster (*simgil*) was applied and left unpainted so as to differentiate it from older areas of decoration. The wooden perforated screen to the east of the vestibule required repair and strengthening. Sections of the missing lattice screens were removed by the local community in 2003 when it became apparent that they would be further damaged.

As part of the work to repair the screen, these sections were returned to the site, repaired and installed in their original locations. A finely decorated wooden door leading to the *mazar*, carved with geometric and floral patterns and inscriptions from the Qur'an, was carefully cleaned and treated with natural oils.

While a small landscaped garden was established around the shrine in 2003, the site remained in a general state of disarray and an ad hoc water distribution network constructed for irrigating the landscaping threatened further damage to the shrine building. A large unlined water channel that passes in a north-south direction above the site of the shrine and is used to irrigate agricultural lands north of the site posed a serious problem due to the penetration of water into the ground behind the shrine. In winter, the internal sides of the channel freeze and the overspill of water into the perimeter of the shrine posed a serious long-term hazard for visitors and for the structural integrity of the building. Critical upgrading work was carried out on a surface water channel running the length of the site to the east of the shrine. The channel was lined with a stone-masonry wall that will ensure that water does not spill onto adjacent terraces and ultimately down into the level of the shrine. Provisions were made for enabling the controlled use of water from this channel for irrigation of the landscaping of the site. Existing horticulture and planting on the site were surveyed and provisions for irrigation were made through the redirection of surface channels. Additional trees and plants were planted in key areas of the site and along the steep slopes to help prevent soil erosion. The destroyed *langar khana* and outbuildings on the northern perimeter of the site were reconstructed using traditional materials and techniques in order to provide important facilities for visitors and worshippers.

Visitors to the shrine previously had to walk along narrow, unpaved and precipitous pathways that were regularly affected by landslides and other weather-related damage that rendered access to the site unsafe. As part of the physical conservation work, an unpaved pathway leading to the first gate of the shrine from the perimeter of the Hazrat-e Sayyed village was upgraded. Work included the construction of extensive areas of retaining walls required both for the delineation of the pathway and, in some areas, for the protection of the route from rocks falling from the steep slopes above. The whole length of the pathway was paved using river stone and a surface drain was provided in order to redirect water away from the walking surfaces.

**Above, external elevations were cleaned and repaired, before being finished with a mixture of mud-gypsum plaster.**

**Left, the restored shrine and consolidated stone outcrop, as seen from the village below.**

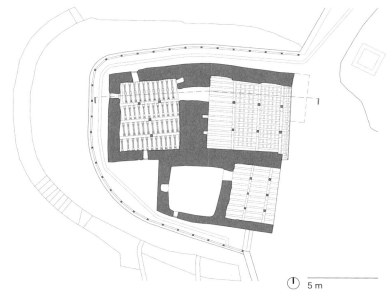

**Top, site plan and ground-floor reflected ceiling plan.**

**Above, left, a precarious trail leading to the shrine was replaced by a pathway paved with river stones and protected by a low retaining wall.**

**Right, timber railings were constructed along a pathway behind the shrine used for maintenance of the building.**

Upon the completion of project activities in 2013, the shrine was returned to the custodianship of the community and a permanent plaque, documenting the site as a registered historic monument, was installed in coordination with local authorities and the Department of Historic Monuments. While an exact estimate of users of the Nasir Khusrau Shrine is not available, the conservation and landscaping work and the provision of visitor facilities will improve and make visitor access to the site safer. Skilled and unskilled labour was engaged from Hazrat-e Sayyed and neighbouring villages, providing an important opportunity for employment (19,200 workdays). On-the-job training provided in crafts and traditional building techniques ensure that an experienced local workforce is available to undertake maintenance and repairs to the shrine in the future.

Above, the restored shrine was handed back to local custodians, who continue to maintain the building — as they have done for almost a millennia.

Left, section.

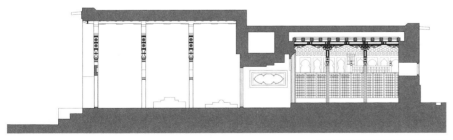

5 m

# Mullah Barat Mosque

Above, community participation in restoration work became an effective way to advocate for wider conservation measures and provide training for those responsible for the future upkeep of historic sites.

Below, as part of training local craftsmen, a pilot restoration project was undertaken on the mid-19th-century Mullah Barat Mosque.

## HISTORY AND CHARACTERISTICS

As part of the wider initiative to restore the shrine of Nasir Khusrau, local representatives of Hazrat-e Sayyed identified the Mullah Barat Mosque for urgent restoration work. Located in the centre of the village, the historic mosque had served as the main communal prayer space until a modern concrete-frame mosque was built to replace it in 2008. Since that time, the historic mosque had remained unused and had become dilapidated, with settlement damage in the *qibla* wall due to seepage of water into its foundations from a channel redirected to irrigate farmland behind the structure.

Believed to date from the 1940s, the mosque was built in the local vernacular tradition entailing the erection of a timber-frame structure with mud-brick infill covered by a flat roof constructed with uncut timber poles, compacted mud, and finished using mud-straw (*kahgil*) plaster. The building consists of a single large internal space used for congregational prayer and communal gatherings, adjoined on two sides by a deep-set elevated veranda supported by carved timber columns. A separate prayer niche (*mihrab*) had been built into the external wall of the mosque for outdoor prayers during warmer months. The internal and external elevations of the building were decorated with simple floral painted motifs, which is unusual for a mosque. A separate block of rooms used for ablutions and to provide a living space for the custodian of the site were extensively damaged at the time physical surveys were conducted by AKTC. The mosque rests beneath a large plane tree set in a small garden enclosed by a rough stone wall built using river stones.

## WORK UNDERTAKEN

Conservation work was undertaken over a three-month period in 2011, commencing with structural repairs of damaged sections in the stone foundations of the western *qibla* wall. Once the foundations and walls of the mosque had been stabilized, the repairs were carried out on the roof of the building. Timber joists damaged by the build-up of moisture were replaced before wooden boards were installed, covered with compacted-mud insulation, and the roof protected using *kahgil* plaster. Teams of carpenters worked simultaneously to repair and clean the original timber door-frames and windows. In order to preserve the painted floral decoration, sections of the gypsum plaster base that had become detached from the walls were carefully consolidated using traditional techniques. Additional work was undertaken to reconstruct the service rooms to the north of the mosque, rendering the mosque usable by the local community. In order to improve access to the mosque, the veranda and

garden pathways were paved and the perimeter wall was repaired. The restoration of the Mullah Barat Mosque provided an important opportunity to engage and train local craftsmen ahead of the more complex restoration of the Nasir Khusrau Shrine.

Top left, the restored mosque continues to be used for communal gatherings.

Top right, structural repairs were carried out to the timber roof structure prior to re-roofing the building using traditional techniques.

Above, durable stone paving being laid at the entrance veranda.

Below, ground-floor plan and section.

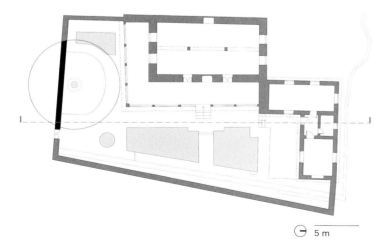

5 m

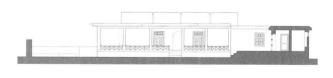

# Mir Yar Beg Shrine and Garden

The Mir Yar Beg Shrine was in a poor state of repair and its surrounding landscape inaccessible to the community.

### HISTORY AND CHARACTERISTICS

The shrine of Mir Yar Beg is a small (one-room) stone-masonry building with a fired-brick dome, located on a hillside in the Chatta area of eastern Faizabad. Mir Yar Beg inherited the throne as *mir* of Badakhshan (1815–44) from his father, who had levied taxes and expanded his rule into Kashgar and part of the Chinese province of Xinjiang. Having initially lost his father's territories, including Faizabad to rivals, Mir Yar Beg regained the town in 1822 and rebuilt his fort, where he lived until poisoned by a rival in 1844. Mir Yar Beg's Shrine is one of few remaining monuments, outside the vicinity of the old town of Faizabad, that is registered on the national database of historic monuments. The site of his grave is highly symbolic for the population of Faizabad, who credit him with reviving the fortunes of the town.

The shrine is located under a large plane tree on a raised platform area, accessed via an informal pathway from the street. Carved marble gravestones in the vicinity of the shrine identify additional burial sites, which may contain the remains of relatives of Mir Yar Beg or important figures in the area. Entry to the shrine is from the east, through narrow steps descending into a partially submerged room with small openings in its walls covered with traditional timber screens. Believed to have been built shortly after Mir Yar Beg's death, the shrine has had ad hoc repairs on at least two previous occasions, which entailed the use of loose debris applied with mud mortar on the upper sections of walls. As a result, the shrine has had extensive structural damage, including the formation of a large fracture in its masonry dome, caused by settlement in foundations and seepage of water into areas of backfill above the wall.

Further to requests by local authorities and based on the findings of a socio-economic survey carried out by AKTC, which identified a shortage in public green spaces in the town, conservation designs entailed the creation of a public park as part of the restoration of the shrine.

### WORK UNDERTAKEN

The first stage of conservation work on the shrine focused on the stabilization of its brick-masonry dome and load-bearing walls. Thick layers of mud-plaster backfill on the roof, applied by locals in order to prevent leaks, had compounded structural failures and were carefully removed. Together with the dismantling of previous areas of repair, the masonry dome was uncovered and structural repair work focused on stitching vertical fractures that had formed near the 'squinches' of the dome, using newly produced traditional square bricks. Temporary supports were constructed

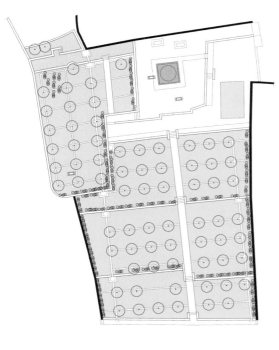

Above, the shrine as seen from the road.

Left, site plan.

Below, masons work to repair and repoint the external load-bearing walls.

10 m

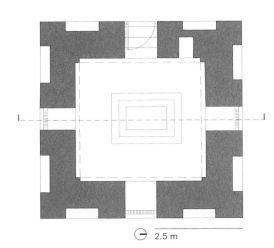

2.5 m

Top, ground-floor plan and section.

Middle, the brick-masonry dome of the shrine was repaired and metal-rod ties were installed to prevent further damage.

Bottom, interior view of the shrine with Mir Yar Beg's grave located at the centre of the space enclosed by plastered masonry walls and timber screens.

within the shrine, holding the dome in place, while teams of masons worked to repair its masonry structure. Before repairs on the dome could be completed, vertical fractures in the load-bearing walls needed to be consolidated.

Square fired bricks were fabricated to match the quality and size of the original bricks used in both the walls and dome of the shrine. Applied with lime mortar, these bricks were used to reconstruct large sections of the external walls (as had been done in the original construction), with each layer of new brickwork carefully 'woven' with remaining sections of the original brickwork. At the uppermost sections of the walls, where the circular dome 'springs' from square building walls, traditional wood reinforcements (*katiba*) were installed to structurally 'tie' walls together and provide a stable base for the transfer of lateral loads. Once the structural consolidation of the dome and walls were complete, lime concrete was applied to the roof to prevent penetration of water and finished with a durable layer of brick paving. The external elevations of the shrine, a combination of original brickwork and newly laid bricks, were left exposed and repointed with lime mortar.

Internally, the surface of the dome was cleaned and the joints between bricks were cleared of loose debris and repointed. The internal surfaces of masonry walls were cleaned and areas where the original plaster had fallen off were replastered using a composite gypsum and mud-straw plaster. The internal floor of the shrine and the grave plinth were paved using fired bricks on edge and pointed. Outside the shrine, the area around the building was paved using a combination of river and flat stones so as to prevent seepage of water into the foundations of the building.

With conservation work complete, the focus turned to transforming the external area into a public garden. In order to provide safe access to the site and incorporate the shrine as a key element of the park, the sloping landscape was terraced through the construction of low retaining walls incorporating ramps and stairs. Water from an existing channel to the south of the site was diverted into the park and linked to newly constructed channels and tanks, providing gravity-fed irrigation to more than seven hundred trees and flowers planted on the various terraces. A network of stone-paved pathways was created, linking the main entrance near the street with the upper sections of the park. In order to secure the site and prevent encroachment, a low perimeter wall was built around the entire site using stone and brick masonry. Landscaping work employed traditional planting techniques, sourcing indigenous species of plants and trees, ensuring that its upkeep and maintenance can be carried out by local custodians according to established landscaping traditions and gardening methods.

Above, visitors outside the entrance to the restored shrine, which is located on a terrace paved with river stones.

Below, the garden surrounding the shrine has been terraced and pathways paved in stone to allow safe public access.

# Hammam-e Kohna

**The Hammam-e Kohna was used as a site for dumping household waste prior to restoration.**

### HISTORY AND CHARACTERISTICS

One of the key issues to emerge from the socio-economic survey conducted by AKTC in Faizabad in 2011 was the absence of adequate public facilities for the population in the old town. In a context where many families do not have access to proper washing facilities at home, a recurring theme of discussions during the survey was the importance of traditional public bathhouses (hammams) — few of which survive in the old town.

Located in western quarters of the old town, the Hammam-e Kohna follows a typical configuration of semi-underground rooms grouped around two major masonry domed spaces (which would have been kept at different temperatures) making up the communal bathing areas. A series of open tanks are placed in these spaces from which warm water would be scooped by bathers using the facility. Sourced from a well on the site, water is heated in a large copper vessel situated over an open fire in a subterranean space (*atish khana*) under one of the outer walls of the bathhouse. Heat and smoke from the *atish khana* is led through a hypocaust system of masonry ducts running under the main spaces of the hammam that serves to maintain the temperature and humidity that is characteristic of such traditional bathhouses. At the time of surveys prepared by AKTC, the building was partially ruined and used as a dumping ground for domestic waste. The potential to improve family health and hygiene in one of the poorest segments of the population led to the restoration of the ruined Hammam-e Kohna, one of only a handful of traditional bathhouses in the old town.

### WORK UNDERTAKEN

At the onset of stabilization work, accumulated waste and infill was removed from the roof and the perimeter of the building in order to reveal the masonry stone and brick structure of the hammam. Stable parts of the existing masonry were consolidated, while ancillary spaces that were destroyed over the course of the past half century were rebuilt in a traditional manner. With the structure of the building consolidated, work commenced on the restoration of internal areas. The flooring of the hammam was removed and the hypocaust system was rebuilt using fired brick and lime mortar. Large sheets of stone were laid above the hypocaust cavity and internal paved areas were reconstructed using new and original marble tiles.

The outflow of wastewater was connected to a newly built drainage channel and a fresh water supply was provided through the construction of a deep well. Prior to undertaking restoration work, an agreement with the private owners of the hammam stipulated that the building would be managed and operated as a public facility.

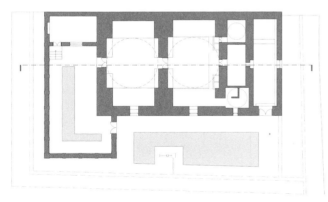

 5 m

Above, the restored hammam provides an essential service to the local community, where many homes do not have proper bathing facilities.

Middle, site plan and section.

Left, constructed using brick and stone masonry, extensive repairs were undertaken on the dome and walls of the building.

Right, marble being laid over a traditional hypocaust heating system.

# Wakhan Heritage Inventory

**A Kyrgyz shrine near the village of Ishkashim at the entrance to the Wakhan Corridor.**

## INTRODUCTION

Based on stylistic evidence from the many petroglyphs in the area, the Wakhan Corridor and the Pamirs have been settled or crossed by humans since the Lower Palaeolithic era, around 100,000 years ago. Research in the Upper Amu Darya region confirms some form of habitation from this era, and there is evidence that the Silk Road, which linked the trading centres of western China with the Mediterranean and Europe, existed for some 1700 years between 329 BC and 1400 AD. Chinese accounts mention the Wakhan region as early as the seventh century, when both Tang and Tibetan rulers tried to benefit from this 8000-kilometre trade route that linked Yarkand and Merv via Bactria, passing through the Little Pamir and the Wakhan Corridor.

One of the earliest known accounts of the Pamirs is by a Chinese pilgrim Hsuan Tsang (or Xuanzang), who travelled for seventeen years to India via Afghanistan, returning to China in AD 644. Passing through Badakhshan and the Pamirs (the Po-mi-lo), he describes the Pamirs as: "Six thousand li from east to west, and a hundred li from south to north. It is situated between two snowy mountains. The cold is glacial, and the wind furious. Snow falls even in spring and summer, day and night the wind rages. Grain and fruit cannot grow there, and trees are few and far between. In the middle of the valley is a large lake, situated in the centre of the world on a plateau of prodigious height (from *The Great Tang Dynasty Record of the Western Regions*, AD 646)."

The province of Badakhshan lies in the north-east of the country and is bordered to the north by the Pamir range of Tajikistan and to the south by the Hindu Kush in Pakistan. Wakhan district occupies a narrow finger of land running 360 kilometres east from Ishkashim, towards the Chinese frontier. Although administratively defined as a single district of Wakhan, the Afghan Pamirs are usually referred to as a separate geographic entity. The Wakhan Corridor, which is deeply incised as a result of the action of the Panj River, is in parts divided into upper and lower sections along the south side of the Panj and the Wakhan Rivers. The Lower Wakhan comprises an area along the course of the Panj between Ishkashim and Qala-e Panja. The Upper Wakhan, on the other hand, comprises the area beyond Goz Khon (where the Panj turns north-east into the Great Pamir) along the Wakhan River to Sarhad-e Broghil, which is the most easterly village before the Little Pamir range. Both the upper and lower parts are between two and three kilometres wide (although much narrower in parts of the Upper Wakhan), and are primarily settled by Wakhi communities, which are believed to comprise sixty-seven settlements ranging in size from three to 138 households.

AKTC undertook a survey in the Wakhan and the Pamir areas in Badakhshan province, as part of wider efforts to document cultural and architectural heritage in Afghanistan. Building on earlier research work in this remote region, the survey has enabled the preparation of an inventory of one hundred sites, including petroglyphs, shrines, mosques, forts and burial structures, as well as examples of indigenous architecture. The results illustrate the rich built heritage of the area, and have enabled identification of sites that might be at risk from looting or natural deterioration. The inventory has been made available to the Ministry of Information and Culture and other relevant institutions in Afghanistan, for use in further research and possible conservation of key heritage sites. The inventory also contains material that could potentially contribute to the promotion of tourism and the safeguarding of heritage sites in the context of wider infrastructural development initiatives in the Wakhan and Pamirs.

## BUILT FORM AND BUILDING TECHNIQUES

The form and construction techniques employed in the domestic vernacular architecture of Afghanistan are influenced by environmental conditions, the availability of materials and building skills, as well as specific social practices. The most common form of dwelling in the Wakhan area is a series of rectangular rooms grouped around

Above, horsemen play a game of Buzkashi on the flood plains at Sarhad-e Broghil with the Little Pamir mountains in the distance.

Following pages, Barnaz Pass, Little Pamir — many petroglyph sites survive in remote areas of the mountain chain.

329

an enclosed yard, which both provides a focus for family activities during the summers and also serves as an area for the stabling of animals.

In the Wakhan, rough and river-smoothed stone, as well as slate, are widely used both in the walls of homes or in enclosure walls, while the availability of earth in some parts allows for the production of mud bricks or compacted mud (*pakhsa*). Mud plaster mixed with straw (*kahgil*) is also widely used for external and internal render for homes and other structures. Most homes have massive flat roofs supported on timber joists, which ensure adequate insulation for the extreme winters. As with the external walls, the roofs are finished using *kahgil*.

A Wakhi home in the village of Chihil Kand serves to demonstrate the richness of the built heritage of the area. This single-storey dwelling lies within a courtyard that also gives access to a series of outbuildings and stables. Inhabited by up to twenty people, at the centre of the dwelling is a communal space (*dukan*), with raised areas on three sides (forty to sixty centimetres above the level of the central floor), with no external openings apart from a single door. In the centre of the space, located over the hearth, is a skylight constructed through a series of five timber frames placed diagonally above each other. This opening acts as a chimney, but also allows light into this inhabited space. The highly insulated space of the *dukan* serves to minimize the fuel needed to warm the dwelling during the harsh Wakhan winters.

### RELIGION AND BURIAL IN THE WAKHAN

The commemoration of forebears continues to be an important part of cultural and religious expression for communities in the Wakhan, where the landscape is dotted with individual graves and cemeteries, shrines and other funerary structures. There are also numerous natural sacred sites. The man-made structures take on a variety of architectural forms and styles, and primarily use locally available materials, such as stone and earth, while reflecting the burial practices of a range of ethnic and religious

**Below, left, stone dwelling in Sarhad-e Broghil.**

**Right, prominent conical 'burial domes' at Bozai Gumbaz facing south towards the Wakhjir River valley.**

groups who inhabit or have crossed the Wakhan over the ages. A diverse range of these sites, from sizeable mud-brick domed mausolea to simple marked graves, were documented during the course of the AKTC inventory in 2007.

The most common form of marking graves is a simple head and footstone, sometimes enhanced with an oval enclosure of upright stones. Elsewhere, burial sites of prominent individuals are enclosed by mud-brick walls or even covered by a roofed structure, which may have carved wooden doors or external decoration. In Khandud, domed tombs with internal niches were documented, while many other villages have one or more enclosed shrines (*mazars*), which are places of prayer and pilgrimage within a larger cemetery. Other documented burial sites have trees, hills or large boulders as the focus for a 'sacred' location. The use of ibex horns, either over a simple grave or over the entrance of a *mazar*, probably has origins in pre-Islamic belief systems.

One of the more unusual burial complexes is Bozai Gunbad, or "domes of the elders". Situated beside the Wakhan River on the route to Lake Chaqmaqtin, the site comprises fourteen, one-room, domed mausolea, constructed from mud bricks, in an extensive graveyard. Traces of more than eleven collapsed structures can still be made out on the site. While mud-brick domed structures are not uncommon in the region, the conical shape of the domes seems to be unique to Bozai Gunbad. Visited, among others, by Lieutenant J. Wood in 1838, little is known about the precise history

Above, stone and compacted-mud courtyard houses in Khandud.

Below, multiple tombs located within a mud enclosure in Khandud.

Above, left, rock carving on the Sang-e Navishta, Aqbelis Pass, Little Pamir.

Right, a hunting scene depicting an ibex (Pamir Arghali) and a hunter with bow, one of a number of recently discovered rock carvings in the foothills at the east of the Wakhan Corridor.

of these structures, and none of the graves seems to bear a name or date. Bozai Gunbad is one of several sites in the Wakhan that may benefit from detailed investigation in the future.

## PETROGLYPHS IN THE WAKHAN

Petroglyphs, or rock markings, represent the single most widespread evidence of human activity in the Wakhan region. During the course of the survey by AKTC in 2007, nearly a quarter of all sites identified from written records or pointed out by inhabitants were petroglyphs. Dating from the Upper Palaeolithic period (c. 15,000–10,000 BC) through to the fourteenth century AD, the petroglyphs are carved or chiselled onto rock surfaces through the valleys of the Wakhan and Pamir. The most common base for such images are hard granite boulders, but carvings were also documented on softer outcrops of slate in the Panj and Wakhan river valleys and the Little Pamir mountains. The most common subjects are stylized images — in some cases as many as forty — of the horned Pamir *aghali*, popularly known as "Marco Polo sheep".

In some cases, layers of petroglyphs are over-cut on earlier images, suggesting that sites retained their significance over millennia. A number of hunting scenes, depicting men on foot using bows and hunting dogs, were documented during the course of surveys. In one case, a group of mounted riders are shown hunting wild yak, which has been extinct in the Wakhan since the late nineteenth century (the animals currently used by the Kyrgyz are a domesticated species). Elsewhere, hands, abstract symbols and unidentifiable animals appear in petroglyphs. The most extensive documented collection can be found in the Sang-e Navishta (literally translated as "writings on stone") in the Ab-e Badjins Valley in Little Pamir, where multiple ibex images, symbols and sections of text have been cut into a group of large granite boulders.

### KYRGYZ YURTS

There are reported to be some 1400 Kyrgyz living between the Great and the Little Pamir mountains, mostly inhabiting traditional yurts (*oey*). Made up of three elements, the yurts have a lattice-wall wooden framework (*kerege*) and doorframe (*eshik*) forming a cylindrical support under a roof of forty to sixty willow struts (*uq*) at the centre of which lies a ring (*tunuk*). The top and sides of this structure are covered by a heavy woollen felt covering (*namad*), the outer layer (*chegh*), which is often embellished with inlaid designs in a range of colours. The pattern of decoration is said to relate to the specific clan of the owner of the dwelling. Within the yurt is a screened kitchen area and a central hearth under the *tunuk*; bedding and other portable property is stored against the lattice framework.

### WAKHI MYTHS AND LEGENDS

As part of preparing a Heritage Inventory, it was possible to document the rich oral folklore of villages throughout the Wakhan. A collection of short folktales, including "The Shy Wizard of Ishkashim" and "Malek and Mehran" (a tale of love, endurance — and parrots), was published by AKTC in Dari and English in *Tales from the Wakhan: Folklore and Archaeology of the Wakhan Corridor*. The first part of the book presents several folktales recounted by members of the pastoral Wakhi and nomadic Kyrgyz communities, followed by a section of illustrated summaries of key archaeological and architectural sites that were recorded as part of the Wakhan Heritage Inventory.

Below, a family from Chihil Qand participating in the Pamir Music and Sport Festival in Sarhad-e Borghil.

Bottom, left, Kyrgyz yurt with a low profile and wide roof ring (*tanuk*) in Kasch Goz, Little Pamir.

Right, traditional skylight and vent (*riczn*) located above living quarters in Chihil Qand.

BADAKHSHAN

# THE CHALLENGE OF PLANNING

Preceding pages, the main road through the old town of Faizabad showing one of the only remaining sections of historic timber-fronted shops with grass-covered roofs that once lined both sides of the bazaar.

Above, flash floods are a common occurrence, affecting communities along the Kokcha River.

Right, an increase in migration into Faizabad has spurred formal and informal development, with commercial investments being focused in areas along the main road and the river's edge.

## PLANNING

The old town of Faizabad contains large areas of residential quarters stretching along the northern bank of the Kokcha River. Bisected by the main road to Baharak, traditional one-storey timber-shuttered shops lined both sides of the road until the 1970s, when road expansion work resulted in the demolition of key sections of the bazaar. More recently, further expansion of the Taloqan-Baharak road has destroyed additional areas of these shops, giving way to the construction of ubiquitous and nondescript concrete structures resembling commercial centres in towns across Afghanistan. Sections of the once extensive bazaar, adjacent to the Pul-e Kheshti Bridge where road works have not yet occurred, represent the most significant traditional wood-frame architecture remaining in Faizabad. While approximately 14% of the 65,000 inhabitants of Faizabad live in the old town, modern areas to the southwest continue to grow as rural populations relocate to the administrative centre of the province in search of economic opportunities. Lacking resources to buy or rent property in more formal areas, migrants have built ad hoc informal settlements along the hillsides of the once scenic valley. Without access to basic services and utilities, these areas contain some of the poorest communities (living in abject conditions) in a province where the poverty rate (more than 57%) is considered one of the highest in Afghanistan.

In this context, where infrastructural development activities have discounted the value of preserving built heritage and unplanned urban settlements continue unabated in the absence of regulatory or planning frameworks, the identification and preservation of key historic sites and the provision of socio-economic training and employment opportunities have become the focus of AKTC's programmes in Faizabad. In order to identify buildings and sites of historic value, a physical survey was conducted in 2011–12 in the old town and adjacent areas in collaboration with local authorities. Detailed architectural drawings were prepared for structures that were considered to represent valuable examples of traditional construction. Local architects and draughtsmen were engaged, enabling them to develop documentation skills and become familiar with traditional building techniques and materials.

Over the course of the exercise, more than eighty buildings and sites in the old town of Faizabad were visited by survey teams, of which fourteen were assessed to contain excellent examples of local building traditions and surveyed in detail by hand. Public and religious sites of historic significance were also identified and incorporated in the plan. Locations of documented buildings were plotted on a map of the

Storm-water drains in the old town are poorly maintained and often become blocked due to dumping of commercial waste.

old town, enabling the survey team to identify larger clusters of traditional constructions and generate additional information on patterns of historic growth. Drawings prepared on the remaining sections of the traditional timber-shuttered shops formed part of wider documentation used to inscribe the buildings as registered national monuments. In addition to taking stock of Faizabad's remaining heritage, physical surveys enabled the formulation of detailed designs for the restoration of key sites in urgent need of repair. Surveys and ongoing physical conservation activities are conducted jointly with local authorities and the community, who actively participate in identifying priorities and supporting implementation of projects.

In parallel with the physical documentation of heritage sites in Faizabad, AKTC carried out an extensive socio-economic Quality of Life Assessment survey in 2011 with a sample size of approximately eight hundred households or 15% of the population in the town. The survey covered all municipal districts of Faizabad including the old town, planned residential areas to the west and informal hillside settlements. The findings of the survey were partially encouraging, highlighting areas where significant progress had been made (education rates and home ownership) and others where further support was required (employment generation, upgrading of public services, provision of healthcare and environmental improvements). The average family size (7.5) was made up mainly of those under eighteen years of age (50% of the population), who, together with others of working age (15–64), contributed towards providing subsistence (dependency ratio of 73) for their families. While Faizabad has established one of the highest youth literary rates (86%) in Afghanistan (national average 39%), the town is significantly behind in labour force participation (36%) as compared to the national average (67%), that is, those aged fifteen or above who are economically active. The division in participation in the labour workforce is particularly acute between men (61%) and women (12%). More than 67% of the respondents indicated that they lived in 'fair' conditions, with a further 24% describing their living conditions as 'poor to very bad'. Furthermore, approximately 80% of the population obtains its potable water from public shallow wells, which

**Above, surveyors undertaking a socio-economic household survey in poor informal communities on the hillsides of Faizabad.**

**Right, in the provincial capital, unregulated residential and commercial constructions increasingly encroach upon public spaces — damaging the natural landscape of Faizabad.**

are vulnerable to contamination from household waste (98% of which is deposited on open ground or in the river). Respondents (94%) also pointed out a lack of public green space and safe areas for children to play.

The findings of the Faizabad socio-economic survey provided important baseline information on the livelihood and living conditions of the population and enabled the planning and implementation of a multi-year conservation programme aimed at creating employment and training for local youth, particularly women, in trades that help generate sustainable income for households. Additional focus was placed on rehabilitating public open spaces, particularly parks and gardens, which provided safe environments for children and families.

Cohesive planning and urban management strategies are required to balance public and private investment in the town.

# SOCIO-ECONOMIC ACTIVITIES

Above, vocational training programmes are undertaken in tandem with conservation projects, providing opportunities for those in need and enabling them to improve their livelihoods.

Below, courses in tailoring, embroidery and carpet weaving (shown here) form part of the curriculum of AKTC training programmes.

## PREPARING FOR OUTREACH

Interventions that involve local communities are subject to extensive social and physical baseline surveys that are carried out prior to engagement in outreach activities.
The Aga Khan Trust for Culture (AKTC) collects and analyses data from available sources
and generally conducts its own surveys of a representative sample of local households in order to have recent information. Issues that are considered difficult to assess
in a straightforward manner, such as household income and expenditure levels, are
approached from various angles in order to arrive at better estimates. Neighbourhood
walks with knowledgeable individuals, discussions with key informants and focus
group meetings with community members usually provide the required level of quali-
tative information that is needed to better interpret quantitative data. These baseline
surveys serve a dual purpose. They provide an overview of the local needs that AKTC
can then link with available resources and know-how in the design of its intervention
programme; and they provide the benchmarks for making future comparisons to
measure progress. Follow-up studies for measuring progress against baseline data are
typically carried out at four- to five-year intervals. To a large extent, the socio-economic
baseline surveys follow the indicators set out in AKDN's Quality of Life (QoL) framework[1] with some adjustments for the built environment where AKTC tends to operate.

Given its mandate, AKTC has been addressing the direct fulfilment of basic needs
of local Afghan communities, such as education, health, water and sanitation, to
only a limited extent. Instead, it has paid more attention to two other dimensions of
poverty alleviation that are directly linked to AKTC's day-to-day engagement in the
historic built environment in Afghanistan: providing community members with access
to means that can bring welfare; and helping to establish a secure social and physical
environment.

## DIRECT AND INDIRECT CONTRIBUTIONS

The outreach approach pioneered by the Historic Cities Programme (HCP) of AKTC,
whereby socio-economic development and physical rehabilitation are both integral
elements of activities aimed at improving the built environment, has now become the
standard strategy for nearly all major HCP interventions and is generally referred to
as the "Multiple Input Area Development Approach". Over the years, socio-economic
outreach of AKTC in Afghanistan has focused on vocational training and skills development, as well as infrastructural improvements, such as construction of retention
walls, street paving, construction of covered drains, providing access to drinking

**A thriving local market in the production of
traditional clothing will provide graduates an
opportunity to generate sustained income
from their craft.**

1 — The QoL system for impact measurement
includes forty indicators related to health,
education, employment, housing conditions
and direct interpretations of QoL. AKTC uses
additional indicators for measuring household
income and expenditure levels, collects more
data on housing conditions and also measures
the experiences of park visitors and the impact of parks on the immediate surroundings.

Top, courses in carpentry, woodcarving and production of architectural fenestration are aimed at supporting growth and innovation in the local construction and furniture-making industries.

Middle, produced in the region since the 14th century, courses in glazed tile making have helped revived a lost traditional craft.

Bottom, in order to ensure the continued production of high-quality traditional musical instruments, required by growing numbers of students, support for the training of apprentices was provided to a workshop in the Old City of Kabul.

water and ensuring improved levels of sanitation and hygiene. Not less important are the indirect contributions that AKTC has been making to improve community life. This is particularly the case with access to green, clean and safe open space that is created and managed by AKTC. Such open space contributes directly to social cohesion, inclusion and participation in cultural events, engagement in sports, play or any other form of purposeful infill of leisure time. Social outreach also includes rehabilitation of monumental mosques, such as those that now serve the community in Kabul's historic Asheqan wa Arefan quarter, as well as the conservation of a number of characteristic historic houses in the same area that were under serious threat. Similar initiatives have also been undertaken in Herat's historic centre and to a lesser extent also in Faizabad.

## VOCATIONAL TRAINING, SKILLS DEVELOPMENT AND EMPLOYMENT
Between 2004 and 2016, AKTC's programme for vocational training, skills development and employment in Kabul provided 5454 young apprentices with professional training and skills development, including literacy. Roughly three quarters of these former apprentices found employment within months after completing their training. The subjects covered during this period included carpentry, wood carving, masonry, traditional plastering, tailoring, embroidery, carpet and kilim weaving, and horticulture. The choice of subjects for vocational training was directly related to the outcome of data analysis carried out by AKTC in District 1 and District 7, at the onset of its intervention. While employment clearly appeared as the highest priority of most households surveyed, AKTC also noted low levels of education among the population aged twenty years and above.

Although AKTC is not directly involved in primary education as part of basic social services delivery, its training programme did contribute indirectly by providing doors and windows for a number of schools, including the local Gazurgah School where 4600 girls are taught in four shifts. The main objective of the vocational training and skills development programme, however, is to help increase family income levels by engaging younger family members to become professionally engaged in the manufacturing of marketable crafts of outstanding quality. Subsequently, training in woodwork would not just be limited to carpentry, but would come to include the making of vertically sliding *pataii* and lattice-patterned *jali* screens, as well as the construction of musical instruments such as the *rubab*, a popular Afghan string instrument made of mulberry wood. More recently, the manufacturing of complex architectural models has been added. A number of detailed wooden models of important historic monuments have been completed and are on show for visitors. It is expected that this component of the programme will help increase interest for this craft and that this will provide a commercial market for those who have been trained. In the near future, AKTC will bring all of its Kabul-based vocational training under one roof in the former industrial site of Janglak in District 7.

The vocational training and skills development programme in Herat was started when AKTC was involved in a number of important rehabilitation projects, which included the Gazurgah complex with the shrine of the poet Abdullah Ansari, the Ikhtyaruddin Citadel in the Old City and a number of historic sites in the heart of Herat's historic centre. Vocational training in Herat was carried out by the Trust over a five-year period, starting in 2006. It involved seventy-five apprentices who were trained on-the-job in a number of specific crafts that were directly related to AKTC's local rehabilitation efforts. A wood-fired kiln was set up in 2007 to produce traditional blown-glass components. Another workshop was established in the Old City for the production of incised tiles and glazed bricks.

Following the Herat experience in the manufacturing of tiles and glazed bricks, a similar kiln was set up in Balkh for the restoration of the Khwaja Parsa Shrine. An existing mid-twentieth-century kiln within the Ali Shrine in nearby Mazar-e Sharif, which produces low-quality tiles, was not considered acceptable for this project. Using cobalt, copper, manganese and lead sulphate as dyes, AKTC specialists, working together with local craftsmen, began experimenting in 2012. This initiative ultimately succeeded in producing high-quality tiles of various designs, including large multi-coloured *muqarnas* tiles. As part of the manufacturing process, AKTC took the initiative of encouraging the development of a modest, local, glazed-tile industry that now produces pieces of very high quality in a variety of coloured glazes and calligraphic designs and directly employs twelve people. An exhibition of the tiles, introducing the technique and the art form, has since been organized. Vocational training in Balkh also involved sixty-eight student trainees who were instructed in the design of arches, domes and vaults.

In Faizabad, the capital of Badakhshan province, AKTC has been engaged in vocational training in carpentry, tailoring and embroidery, educating a total of 105 young women and 148 young men over of the period 2014–16 for direct employment in the local economy.

## PHYSICAL IMPROVEMENTS OF NEIGHBOURHOODS:
## HOUSES, MOSQUES AND INFRASTRUCTURE

Following its first household survey in Asheqan wa Arefan (District 1) and Gazurgah (District 7) in 2004, AKTC had first-hand information at hand about actual living conditions in both areas. Housing conditions and overall sanitation levels were found to be extremely poor and employment levels and family incomes well below average.

Above, training in hand-blown Herati glass, produced since the mid-14th century, focused on improving the quality of materials and techniques used in the process.

Below, a Herati glass-blower working at a furnace prepared by AKTC in the Old City of Herat.

Above, large glazed-tile panels being prepared at a workshop supporting conservation of historic monuments in Balkh.

Below, geometric designs are prepared and used to guide the assemblage of mosaic tiles cut to size.

Right, commercial demand for glazed-tile products has enabled the programme to reinvest proceeds towards further training activities.

Asheqan wa Arefan proved particularly depressed, with per capita incomes on average 15% lower than the poorer part of Gazurgah, which itself was already known as one of the more depressed areas of Kabul. As Asheqan wa Arefan is also home to the original settlement that later became Kabul and contains a number of houses and mosques of historical value, an early decision was made to rehabilitate mosques and a critical number of historic houses where people, many of whom were recent arrivals, were living in overcrowded and highly unsanitary conditions. This intervention eventually led to the upgrading of the entire quarter, directly benefiting all residents. The installation of additional toilets in courtyards and the construction of covered drains throughout Asheqan wa Arefan had a major impact on sanitary conditions. All physical aspects of this project were formally completed by 2011. Since then, the maintenance of houses and the upkeep of streets and drains is being carried out by local residents in an exemplary way. AKTC still has a minor presence in the area through an ongoing component of its vocational training programme for women.

In the upper part of Gazurgah, that is, the area surrounding Babur's Garden east of the Kabul River, housing improvement was kept to a minimum. Instead, the focus of AKTC's outreach to the community was on water supply, construction of retaining walls to prevent rock falls, construction of storm drains, street repair and street pavements. AKTC's intervention directly benefited all residents of the area, which has since grown to around 28,000 people as Kabul has expanded.

AKTC's interventions in Herat, although predominantly aimed at the preservation and reuse of historic buildings and improving drainage, did help to directly improve living conditions in sixty houses in the city's historic centre and indirectly benefited 65,000 people. The rehabilitations of major public buildings, such as the Ikhtyaruddin Citadel, the Chahar Suq Cistern and the Malik Cistern and Mosque, have been of direct benefit to the entire population of the city.

The rehabilitation and reuse of Faizabad's oldest hammam in the city centre provides a continuing and direct benefit to all residents of the adjacent quarter. AKTC has also assisted the public through rehabilitation of the Pule-Khesti Bridge, a landmark in Faizabad, which now allows easy entry to the centre of town.

## ACCESS TO CLEAN, GREEN AND SAFE OPEN SPACE

The creation of public parks in Kabul and Faizabad is perhaps the best example of AKTC's efforts to provide people with access to a secure social and physical environment. The largest park to date, Bagh-e Babur (Barbur's Garden) in Kabul, has proven so successful that it sparked interest from external funders requesting that AKTC rehabilitate the even larger, somewhat dysfunctional Chihilsitoon Park, which is also located in District 7. Work on this last park is currently underway and is expected to be completed by early 2018. Although parks in Afghanistan are barely used during the winter months, that shortfall in visitation is largely made up during the spring, summer and autumn. A benchmark in visitation of public parks created or restored by AKTC and operated through a 'Public-Private Partnership' is that 10 to 14% of the metropolitan population visits the park during the course of a calendar year. For Cairo's Al Azhar Park, the figure is 12%, for Bamako's Parc National du Mali it is 11% and

Apprentices prepare a horizontal loom, used to make flat-weave kilims, in a workshop located in a historic house restored by AKTC.

**Students enrolled in a masonry course learn to apply their training on the building site of a traditional structure.**

for Humayun's Tomb in Delhi the figure is also 11%. For Kabul the figure has over the years consistently been 12%. By checking each arriving visitor for weapons or explosives, Bagh-e Babur guarantees the public a level of safety that is unprecedented in Kabul for major public open spaces. The public has been expressing its appreciation for the clean, green and safe surroundings that the park offers by continuing to visit Bagh-e Babur in substantial numbers.

Bagh-e Qazi, a smaller and less well-known green open space between the quarters of Asheqan wa Arefan and Chindawol, which AKTC developed following its completion of the nearby housing project, is also attracting appreciable numbers of visitors, albeit mostly from the neighbourhood. This park, which is directly operated by Kabul Municipality in close collaboration with neighbourhood committees, has a football and cricket ground that is in constant use, in addition to picnic areas for families. The park is fenced and while access is free, it is semi-restricted through one main gate and an additional emergency exit.

Following a request from the local population, AKTC for some time considered up-grading Faizabad's existing polo ground into an urban park. However, with acute land shortages in the centre of town and uncertainty whether the integrity of a centrally located urban park could be secured for the future, a decision was made to instead develop the surrounding landscape of the shrine of Mir Yar Beg, the founder of Faizabad. Although located away from the centre of Faizabad, this new urban park is proving highly popular with the public and, being the only major green open space in Faizabad, it caters directly for at least half of the city's population.

## EFFECTIVENESS AND IMPACT OF AKTC'S INTERVENTION

Measuring the effectiveness and ultimately the impact of AKTC's interventions in Afghanistan requires regular monitoring and evaluation over the medium and longer term. For vocational training, skills development and literacy, it concerns the monitoring of job permanence for the initial months after graduation. Indications are that more than 65% of AKTC's graduates are able to continue in new-found employment. Continued AKTC presence at the local level, such as in Asheqan wa Arefan and Gazurgah, ensures permanent monitoring of housing conditions and improvements made to the local social and physical infrastructure. For interventions in Herat and Faizabad, AKTC monitors the condition of its interventions through regular field visits. Indications from such monitoring missions and from AKTC's permanent presence in other intervention areas are that the maintenance of improvements made by AKTC to the built environment are holding well — particularly in areas where AKTC has been able to mobilize local committees for maintenance and for carrying out small repairs. The effectiveness and impact of AKTC's involvement as co-operator of Bagh-e Babur is continuously monitored through PIMS (the Parks Impact Measurement System). Although the main quality of the park experience is very positive and social bonding at the family level is seen as a major element, the male/female balance of park visitors still appears to be biased towards male visitors. This is above all a reflection of local culture, rather than a lack of willingness of park operations to achieve a more equitable gender balance.

**Left, continued collaboration with established Afghan artists have resulted in innovative approaches to producing glazed-tile panels.**

**Right, an apprentice works to complete a hand-carved timber panel.**

# CAPACITY BUILDING AND INSTITUTIONAL SUPPORT

Above, university students receive field training in conservation and building archaeology on the site of a pilot restoration project in the Old City of Kabul.

Below, left, joint planning workshop with staff of the Commission for the Protection of Historic Cities, Ministry of Urban Development.

Right, advocacy and awareness activities have been a critical aspect of AKTC's conservation programmes.

## CAPACITY BUILDING AND INSTITUTIONAL SUPPORT

A key priority for AKTC's programme activities in Afghanistan has been to support the development of technical and managerial capacity within counterpart institutions. This effort is aimed at ensuring the sustainable long-term development of local competencies. The transfer of knowledge and skills in conservation, planning and project management has entailed working closely with local authorities within their respective institutional mandates, providing focused support for policy and implementation mechanisms, while directly engaging their staff and personnel on physical conservation projects where they learn first-hand and build practical experience. In addition to engaging official counterparts, support for the development of a broader educational curricula and provision for formal instruction at the Department of Architecture in Kabul University has enabled the Aga Khan Trust for Culture (AKTC) to invest in the education of a generation of future architects and planners. Furthermore, on-the-job training, internships and employment opportunities have been provided to Afghan professionals and craftsmen alike, enabling a better understanding of building techniques, architectural typologies and issues critical to safeguarding built heritage.

AKTC's Area Development Programmes and conservation projects in Kabul, Herat, Balkh and Badakhshan are formulated jointly with local authorities and relevant institutions in Kabul. In this process, priorities are identified and criteria established with a focus on balancing preservation needs with improvements to the physical environment, provision for vocational training, and the generation of direct employment and indirect economic opportunities that lead to an improvement in the livelihoods of communities living around heritage sites. Upon the selection of a conservation project, partner institutions are required to introduce key personnel who will work closely with AKTC staff on preparing surveys and technical documents, followed by further involvement in the supervision of implementation activities. Staff of the Department of Historic Monuments (DoHM) of the Ministry of Information and Culture have been regularly seconded on conservation projects being implemented by AKTC since 2002. Where archaeological investigations were required, as was the case during the rehabilitation of Babur's Garden, staff of the Institute of Archaeology worked closely with project consultants from the German Archaeological Institute (DAI) in carrying out the work. In addition to field exercises and training, AKTC regularly engages in providing desk-based training to civil servants responsible for monitoring and maintaining Afghanistan's vast stock of heritage and archaeological sites.

Above, a joint exercise with staff and students of the Archaeology Department at Kabul University on a pilot conservation project in the Old City of Kabul.

Below, master-planning and landscaping consultants working with young Afghan architects on the rehabilitation of the Chihilsitoon Garden.

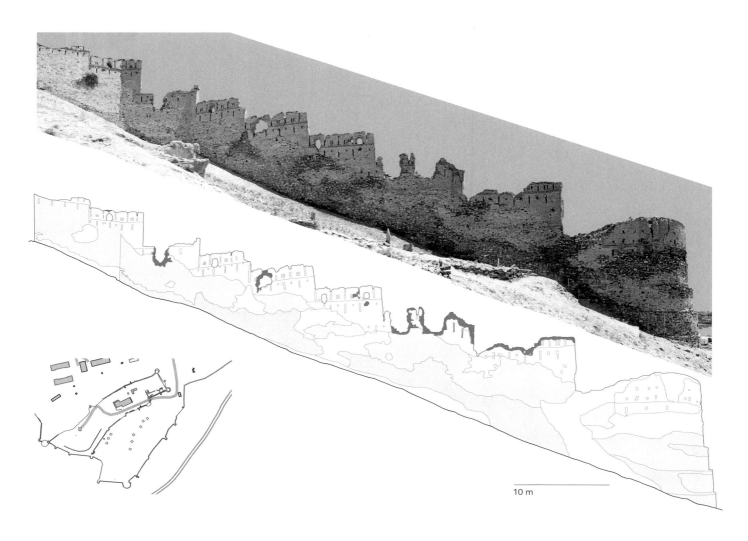

10 m

**Bala Hissar fortifications, Kabul. A joint survey prepared with the Department of Historic Monuments.**

///  Fired brick
▨  Good condition / heavily pointed stone
▓  High-priority areas requiring attention
⊹⊹⊹  Mud brick
- · - Pakhsa
▨  Unpointed stone — secure
▨  Unpointed stone — fragile

In 2008, a joint programme of surveys of heritage sites was launched together with the Ministry of Information and Culture, which has to date resulted in the preparation of physical surveys for more than 250 sites across Afghanistan. Having commenced as an exercise in taking basic measurements and preparing drawings by hand, the process now entails the scanning of monuments using the latest three-dimensional laser-scanning technology. This method enables teams of surveyors to record accurate information on site in a fraction of the time previously spent taking measurements by hand, followed by the preparation of CAD-based drawings by a team of draughtsmen. Preparation of architectural documentation and surveys of Afghanistan's vast historic landscape is fundamental to ensuring safeguarding of the country's cultural heritage. Previous attempts by external consultants at preparing surveys using this technology resulted in documents that could not be easily accessed or used by local professionals to implement project activities. In addressing this concern, AKTC has pioneered the day-to-day use of three-dimensional laser-scanning technology in Afghanistan by providing training for field survey teams and staff responsible for processing this data and generating accurate drawings. As a result, dozens of remote historic sites that would otherwise have been impossible to survey by hand have been documented.

Encouraged by the wealth of information generated through physical surveys, a project was launched with the Ministry of Information and Culture in 2011 involving the digitization of 650 monument registration dossiers (kept in hard copy only since

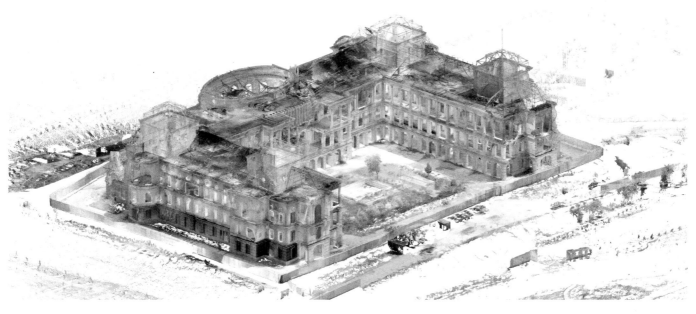

the 1950s) and the establishment of a digital archiving system capable of stream-lining the registration of historic sites. As a second phase of the training, personnel of the DoHM were tasked with preparing new monument registration dossiers (for previously undocumented historic sites) based on documentation gathered through physical surveys and over the course of AKTC's conservation activities. During this programme 550 new registration dossiers were prepared, containing key information

Above, Babur's Garden, Kabul, laser-scan survey. Part of an initiative with the Department of Historic Monuments to prepare registration dossiers for historic monuments. Below, Darulaman Palace, Kabul, laser-scan survey. A joint exercise with staff of the Ministry of Urban Development.

Above, field visits and guided tours are regularly provided for architecture and planning students.

Below, hundreds of monument plaques were prepared and installed on historic sites as part of a joint project with the Department of Historic Monuments.

Right, students of Kabul University and Kabul Polytechnic University visiting Babur's Garden.

on each monument's location (province, district, village), date of construction, key architectural elements, and current condition, which can be used to monitor future developments and prepare maintenance schedules. In addition to providing training for the DoHM staff on data archival systems, lessons provided by AKTC in graphic design programs enabled them to prepare a large public exhibition on conservation and maintenance work being carried out directly by their personnel.

While the full extent of Afghanistan's built heritage remains unclear, estimates place the number of historic structures (above ground) to well above 10,000 individual sites. Of these, 1408 are currently registered with the government — providing some measure of protection under existing preservation laws. Over the course of AKTC's conservation programmes, it became apparent that one of the key reasons why heritage sites were being damaged or destroyed was a lack of awareness on the part of the public. Many of the structures restored by AKTC had undergone some form of transformation, often through religious endowments provided by local communities for the upkeep and repair of sites in active use. This meant that people often undertook to protect their built heritage without understanding that their interventions might cause further damage. What they lacked was information that established theses sites as historic monuments and guidance on how interventions could be undertaken. In order to address this concern and raise public awareness, a project to prepare and install monument plaques was launched in 2011. Undertaken jointly with the DoHM, plaques were designed so as to clearly identify each monument, provide essential information (referencing cultural preservation laws), and encourage local communities to contact the DoHM for further guidance. By the conclusion of the project, more than 920 monument plaques had been produced for 784 registered monuments in thirty provinces and installed on site by the DoHM. On average, the Department receives up to fifteen requests each month for guidance from local communities interested in maintaining their built heritage.

In response to the crisis that faces most urban centres in Afghanistan, where unregulated development continues to destroy historic quarters, adversely affects the natural environment and contributes to the deterioration of living conditions, AKTC remains engaged with local authorities and universities in providing support for the formulation of planning and conservation policy and training. In order to address the lack of capacity required to manage challenges posed by rapid urban growth, AKTC has provided training in planning and conservation in the Department of Architecture at Kabul University and Kabul Polytechnic University since 2008. Courses are designed to supplement the existing curriculum by providing lectures, seminars and design studios delivered by Afghan and international practitioners. Class-based training in theory and design is further enhanced by survey activities, field visits, and practical training exercises in conservation and building archaeology conducted on projects in the Old City of Kabul. With the aim of ensuring that a new generation of Afghan professionals are competent in effectively addressing the critical issues that they are likely to encounter in subsequent professional practice, these programmes have benefited 1035 male and female students, some of whom have gone on to receive post-graduate degrees and now hold senior positions in municipalities and urban planning institutions.

Further direct support to local institutions for planning and management activities has been provided though the establishment of Old City Commissions in Kabul and Herat as part of AKTC's conservation programmes. Bringing together a wider range of stakeholders, including representatives of local communities, these forums have established a productive dialogue between policy makers, planners and residents on appropriate forms of redevelopment in heritage areas. While the focus of the Commissions was to establish a mechanism to address urgent challenges directly, working processes developed in this context were incorporated into the mandates of official bodies, such as the Department for the Protection of Old (Historic) Cities established under the auspices of the Ministry of Urban Development. In order to facilitate a wider process of planning and development, AKTC has participated in the collection of baseline data and preparation of analytical reports focused on synthesizing the patterns of growth and transformation in Kabul. Undertaken jointly with Kabul Municipality and the Ministry of Urban Development, these exercises enable planners and policy makers to better understand the complexity of issues and challenges that affect the built environment. Furthermore, through participation in advisory forums and technical committees established by the government, AKTC personnel have joined other national and international institutions in supporting the development of Afghan capacity and in establishing best practices.

When considered in a larger context and from a long-term perspective, support provided by AKTC has been instrumental in identifying issues critical to safeguarding Afghanistan's heritage and, through its active and consistent engagement, building the local capacity required to address these challenges. Along the way, it has been important to ensure local ownership of the process and to remain committed to assisting Afghan institutions and professionals alike in the long term.

**Above, workshops, seminars and design studios on architecture, conservation and planning have been undertaken as part of a programme to support professional development.**

**Below, Kabul University Architecture Department students working on projects devised as part of a long-term capacity development initiative.**

# REVITALIZING MUSICAL HERITAGE

# THE AGA KHAN MUSIC INITIATIVE

Above, public recital of AKMI musicians.

Below, music training at the AKMI school in Kabul. Reviving the practice of master-apprentice is a priority for the Music Initiative.

## REVITALIZING MUSICAL HERITAGE

Afghanistan's musical heritage encompasses the artistic legacy of many peoples, cultures and civilizations whose cultivation of song, poetry, dance and performance on musical instruments is documented from early antiquity. Ghandaran-style friezes dating from the Kushan Empire (second century BC–third century AD) depict dancers and musicians playing instruments that resemble the long-necked lutes and frame drums of our own time.

Later empires also cultivated poetry and music, in particular the Samanids, who ruled the territory of present-day Afghanistan in the ninth and tenth centuries and served as patrons to the poets of Khorasan and Transoxania: Ferdowsi, author of the *Shahnameh* (Book of Kings), and Rudaki, who during his lifetime was celebrated as a singer and harp player.

In the late fifteenth century, the Timurid ruler of Khorasan, Sultan Husayn Mirza Bayqara, turned the city of Herat into a *locus* of artistic patronage centred around the poet-polymath Ali Sher Nawai (1441–1501), whose verse has been set to music by generations of singers and remains popular today.

Following the conquest of Kabul in 1504 by Babur, who would subsequently conquer Delhi and found the Mughal dynasty, eastern Khorasan was drawn increasingly into the cultural orbit of Hindustan. Cultural ties between Kabul and India persisted in the wake of the Mughal Empire's decline and eventual demise, and were reanimated in the mid-nineteenth century when the ruler of Kabul, Amir Sher Ali Khan, brought a number of classically trained musicians from India to perform at his court. He gave them residences in a section of the Old City adjacent to the royal palace so that they could easily be summoned to court when needed, and this area, known as Kuche Kharabat, became the musicians' quarter of Kabul. For more than a century, musicians thrived not only in Kabul, but throughout Afghanistan, performing a large variety of regional repertories, styles and genres at weddings, in tea houses, and, beginning in the 1940s, on the radio.

This active and very audible and visible musical life became one of the many casualties of the political and social turbulence that enveloped Afghanistan during almost two decades of internecine conflict and war, culminating in the Taliban's rise to power and takeover of Kabul in 1996. The Taliban banned musical instruments and live musical performances at weddings, and made the playing of music cassettes in shops, hotels and vehicles illegal. A 2001 report on musical censorship in Afghanistan produced by John Baily, an ethnomusicologist who had conducted extensive fieldwork

Detail of the Airtam Frieze (a musician). Bactria, the Kushan period, 1st century AD, limestone.

1 — John Baily, *"Can you stop the birds singing?" The Censorship of Music in Afghanistan.* Freemuse (The World Forum on Music and Censorship), 2001. Online at: http://freemuse.org/graphics/Publications/PDF/Afghanistansats.pdf.

in the country in the early 1970s, summarized the devastating effects of total music censorship: "In the past, music was part of *normal* life... Today, the lack of music is symptomatic and indicative of an *abnormal* life. Normality, almost by definition, can never return to Afghanistan as long as the ban on music continues."[1]

By the time the Aga Khan Music Initiative (AKMI) began its work in Afghanistan, in 2003, the Taliban yoke on the country had been broken, and the ban on music lifted, but the teaching and transmission of music had been seriously disrupted. As a congeries of orally transmitted traditions, Afghan music has depended for its survival on lineages of tradition-bearers, who pass on their musical knowledge to subsequent generations through a form of oral pedagogy known as *ustad-shagird* ("master-apprentice" or "master-disciple"). *Ustad-shagird* pedagogy has been conventionalized and ritualized in a variety of local forms throughout the Persianate world of Central Eurasia and the subcontinent, but all of these forms share the essential features of close and abiding contact between a master teacher and apprentice-disciples with whom the teacher meets individually or collectively on a regular basis. In early twenty-first-century Afghanistan, with many master musicians deceased or living in exile, a dearth of usable musical instruments and dim prospects for earning a livelihood as a musician, the country presented daunting challenges to institutional efforts to reanimate the *ustad-shagird* system and revitalize musical life.

## THE AGA KHAN MUSIC INITIATIVE

The Aga Khan Music Initiative is the youngest programme of the Aga Khan Trust for Culture (AKTC). Launched in 2000 by His Highness the Aga Khan to support talented musicians and music educators working to preserve, transmit and further develop their musical heritage in contemporary forms, the Music Initiative began its work in Afghanistan, Kazakhstan, Kyrgyzstan, Tajikistan and Uzbekistan. In each country, the Music Initiative developed a country specific strategy that reflected the overall

**Left, a joint musical rehearsal between second semester students of courses in *tabla* and harmonium in the AKMI school in Kabul.**

**Right, a number of female students have graduated from the AKMI programme.**

priorities of the Aga Khan Trust for Culture and the Aga Khan Development Network, as well as the recommendations of a needs assessment study conducted by a knowledgeable music specialist.

For the needs assessment study in Afghanistan, the Music Initiative turned to Professor John Baily, author of the 2001 FreeMuse report on music censorship, and one of three Western ethnomusicologists who had conducted sustained fieldwork in Afghanistan in the 1960s and 1970s (the other two are American ethnomusicologists Hiromi Lorraine Sakata and Mark Slobin). For the first phase of what was conceived as a long-term cultural development project, Professor Baily recommended establishing a small music school in Kabul that would operate according to the traditional system of *ustad-shagird* pedagogy. Baily was hired as a consultant to organize the launch of the school and oversee its initial year of operation. Four *ustads* were initially appointed as teachers: Ustad Salim Bakhsh, Ustad Ghulam Hussain, Ustad Amruddin and Ustad Wali Nabizadeh — all from Kuche Kharabat, the hereditary musicians' community in Kabul's Old City. Baily arranged for use of a single teaching room on the premises of the Foundation for Culture and Civil Society, and managed to acquire a small number of musical instruments for the students' use. The *ustads* taught a combination of musical styles and genres: North Indian *ragas* performed on the Afghan *rubab* and *tabla*, which had become the *de facto* Kabuli art music tradition; *ghazal* singing; and instrumental folk music from various regions of Afghanistan.

**As part of their training programme, students practice vocal compositions using hand-operated harmoniums.**

Right, the Goldaste Kharabat Orchestra rehearsing in a historic house restored by AKTC.

Below, in addition to training provided on classical instruments, courses are held regularly on traditional instruments used in Afghan folk music — such as seen here on the *ghaychak*.

Bottom, a master's course in music being delivered by an established artist.

Opposite page, promotion for traditional music has resulted in collaboration with a wide range of cultural institutions.

The school's activities expanded in 2005, under the supervision of a full-time coordinator. Classes were moved to a house adjacent to the grounds of the AKTC building in Gozergah Street, and additional musical instruments were acquired for the students. The Indian ambassador to Afghanistan, His Excellency Rakesh Sood, kindly facilitated the donation of a cache of Indian instruments, including harmoniums, *tablas*, *dilrubas* and Kashmiri *rubabs*. Six *ustads* from Kuche Kharabat joined the four teachers already working in the school, and this group was supplemented by Ustad Asif Mahmoud, a master *tabla* player who had emigrated to London but made periodic visits to Kabul to teach.

In 2006, the Music Initiative opened a second school in Afghanistan — this one in Herat, where AKTC's Historic Cities Programme was engaged in a number of major conservation projects. The school was located in Karbasi House, a privately owned property in the Bar Durrani quarter that had been rehabilitated by the Historic Cities Programme. The musical focus of the Herat school differed from that of the Kabul school, with its Indian instruments and *ghazal* singing. By contrast, in Herat, students learned the instrumental repertoire performed on the long-necked *dutar* lute under the tutelage of legendary master musicians Ustad Mahmud Khushnawaz, Ustad Abdul Karim Hassanpoor and Ustad Karim Herawi, an innovative performer who transformed the two-stringed *dutar* into a fourteen-stringed instrument, including sympathetic strings, modelled after the Afghan *tanbur* and *rubab*.

In all, more than a thousand students, both male and female, have received training in the Aga Khan Music Initiative's two Afghan schools. In addition to performance training, the Music Initiative also launched a programme to train young luthiers in instrument making — an urgent need in a country where demand for high-quality instruments far outstrips supply.

## MUSIC DOCUMENTATION

In 2009, with support from the governments of Norway and the United States, the Music Initiative started a project to document folk music in rural regions of northern and western Afghanistan. Toronto-based Afghan singer-composer Wahid Qasemi was engaged to travel to Badakhshan, Balkh, Badghis and Herat, accompanied by a Music Initiative team, to identify, interview and document traditional musicians.

**Above**, public recital of the Goldaste Khara-bat Orchestra, composed of *ustads* and select students of the AKMI programme.

**Below**, group portraits of recent graduates from the AKMI programme in Herat, together with their trainers (*ustads*).

Some ninety-five musicians were filmed, recorded and interviewed, and from this initial group, the most outstanding tradition-bearers were selected to travel to Kabul to record their music and present public performances. These live recitals were filmed, producing more than forty-two hours of video footage that was broadcast through local media. The principal objective of this initiative was threefold: first, to raise awareness among a cross-section of the Afghan public — especially the younger generation — about their traditional musical heritage; second, to build on the training regime provided through the Music Initiative's schools to encourage the emergence of a new generation of Afghan musicians with an understanding of traditional performance styles; and third, to foster links between far-flung and little-known rural musicians whose skills might otherwise remain unrecognized, and who might benefit from interaction with one another.

Since 2002, a significant re-awakening of interest in Afghan music has stirred people throughout the country, creating a demand for public recitals and for music instruction. To address this demand, the Music Initiative has organized many concerts, including regional concerts, often in partnership with the French Institute of Afghanistan, Kabul's Radio Kilid, and the AKTC's Afghan Cultural Initiative.

On the international front, the Aga Khan Music Initiative has been active in presenting Afghan music through the performances of two remarkable musicians, Afghan *rubab* master Homayoun Sakhi and *tabla* virtuoso Salar Nader, both of whom reside in the United States but return to Afghanistan periodically to teach and present concerts. Sakhi appears on three of the ten CD-DVDs in the Music Initiative's anthology *Music of Central Asia*, released worldwide by Smithsonian Folkways Recordings between 2005 and 2012: *Homayun Sakhi: The Art of the Afghan Rubab* (vol. 3); *Rainbow: Kronos Quartet with Alim & Fargana Qasimov and Homayoun Sakhi* (vol. 8); and *In the Footsteps of Babur: Musical Encounters from the Land of the Mughals* (vol. 9). Salar Nader appears on the later two releases. In addition to their recording activities, Homayoun Sakhi and Salar Nader have taken part in numerous interregional musical projects conceived and curated by the Music Initiative, joining their Afghan *rubab* and *tabla* with musical instruments and styles from the Middle East, Central Asia and South Asia to which they are historically related. Through these projects, the Aga Khan Music Initiative honours Afghanistan's musical heritage and places it front and centre on the world's most prestigious stages.

Above, Afghan *rubab* master Homayoun Sakhi and *tabla* virtuoso Salar Nader performing an AKMI-curated concert at the Ismaili Centre in London.

Left, a traditional music recital performed in Babur's Garden.

# CULTURAL SUPPORT ACTIVITIES

Above, visits by school groups to Babur's Garden are regularly prepared as part of AKTC's cultural support activities.

Below, in collaboration with the Ministry of Education and private schools, secondary-school visits have been prepared to key cultural sites, such as the National Museum (seen here) and the National Archives.

## CULTURAL SUPPORT ACTIVITIES

As in any other society, the notion of culture is an important aspect of local and national identity for Afghans. Along with tradition, which can mean anything from religious or social customs to certain uses of language, culture serves as a mirror by which Afghans express and understand what it means to belong to the diverse community that is their nation. For many Afghans who have witnessed their rich cultural traditions and practices — linked to diverse ethnicities — exploited negatively as a source of divisiveness and conflict, cultural recovery is intrinsically connected with the objective of post-war recovery, healing and, ultimately, with national unity. It is, therefore, vital that cultural recovery be integrated into the wider process of reconciliation and reconstruction and be used as a platform for promoting pluralism and mutual understanding.

While significant support has been forthcoming during the last decade for the more conventional and tangible aspects of Afghan culture — physical conservation of monuments and sites — less attention has been paid to activities that provide a bridge between traditional customs and the arts, the potential for culture to be more integrated into formal education, or the links between Afghan culture and activities in the wider region, especially in South and Central Asia.

The genesis of AKTC's support for wider cultural initiatives in Afghanistan lies in its focus on rehabilitating public spaces and monuments with the potential to be actively used for cultural and educational events. A key example of this has been the restoration of Babur's Garden, which has, since its completion in 2008, been used for more than thirty cultural programmes on average each year. The opportunity to establish the Queen's Palace of Babur's Garden as a venue for cultural programmes came in 2006, during its rehabilitation, when a French-Afghan theatrical group staged a Dari language performance of Shakespeare's *Love's Labour's Lost* for an audience of young students and local craftsmen involved in the restoration work. The precedent was established and the site continued to be used for cultural and educational programmes over the subsequent decade.

In 2010, in partnership with the British Library, AKTC prepared a public exhibition of more than 130 drawings, prints and photographs entitled *Afghanistan Observed* at the Queen's Palace in Babur's Garden. The material on show sparked the imagination of the public, attracting more than 16,000 visitors in a single month. More than three years later, a follow-up exhibition of facsimiles of Mughal miniature paintings from various international collections, including those of the British Library, attracted more than 85,000 visitors over a five-month period.

Above, a public exhibition being prepared at the Queen's Palace in Babur's Garden.

Below, visitors to an exhibition of photographs and illustrations of Afghanistan from the late 19th century.

Based on significant public interest and AKTC's vast experience in preparing and managing cultural programmes, its support for cultural activities has evolved to include: the arrangement of traditional music recitals; planning of educational cultural tours and public exhibitions; staging of theatrical performances and film festivals; preparation of research and publications on culturally relevant material; and commissioning of documentary films and mobile cinema programmes. Outreach and the dissemination of cultural programmes have taken on many forms, from small musical recitals to public broadcasts through Afghanistan's state and private media, reaching hundreds of thousands of spectators.

Over the course of a decade, AKTC's cultural initiatives — along with those of other organizations — have resulted in the recovery of traditional cultural practices. Folk songs and classical instrumental music, which had been banned prior to 2002 and since declined in popularity, have been revived and form the basis of a new fusion of genres by a younger generation of musicians. This was partially achieved through folk music research and recording projects implemented in tandem with outreach activities. A multi-year research programme focusing on identifying practitioners of traditional forms of music was launched in 2010 with the aim of recording and promoting their work. Teams of musicologists travelled to outlying districts of Badakhshan,

Top left, a three-year field research on regional folk music resulted in the recording and production of a large collection of Afghan folk music, followed by a series of public recitals.

Top right, artists from Badghis province perform a variation on the traditional *attan* dance, entailing the use of short wooden sticks.

Bottom left, support for the performing arts, including theatre, music and dance, forms part of AKTC's cultural support programmes.

Bottom right, a training programme for Afghan theatre performers ended with a performance of "Fools and Feather".

A public recital of folk music from Badakhshan at the restored Queen's Palace in Babur's Garden.

Balkh and Herat provinces, areas believed to contain the last vestiges of the Pamiri, Moqaam and Qasida Khani traditions of folk music within Afghanistan. There they met with and interviewed more than a hundred artists considered to be the last of their generation of folk musicians. Pamiri music can be traced back to its roots in Uzbek and Turkic music and has been passed on through generations of inhabitants of the Pamir regions of Badakhshan. The most common form of Pamiri music is the *falak*, which contains both slow (*rafter falak*) and fast (*paran falak*) rhythms that evoke various aspects of life in the Pamir. From contemplative ballads to laments and raucous choruses of celebration, Pamiri *falak* is performed by both men and women and set to simple musical instruments, such as drums and the six-string Pamiri *rubab*. The three-year research programme resulted in the recording of more than seventeen hours of broadcast-quality musical compilations. Together with videos prepared during live performances in Kabul, this recorded music continues to be popular and is disseminated through local radio and television.

Organization of cultural and educational events within restored heritage sites, together with music and training programmes implemented by the Aga Khan Music Initiative (AKMI), enabled AKTC staff to better understand the fine grain of Afghanistan's rich and varied cultural practices. Aimed at contributing to the wider process of recovery and in order to promote an understanding of Afghanistan's rich and varied heritage, both inside the country and internationally, a sustained long-term programme of support for cultural initiatives was set in motion in 2011. Focus

Above, training programmes devised under AKTC's cultural support programmes have focused on developing new skills in areas generally not associated with traditional crafts, such as in the production of architectural models.

Below, a large wooden model of the Timur Shah Mausoleum.

was placed on support for activities aiming to foster creative linkages and synergies between those actively working in the realms of traditional architecture and crafts, fine arts and social history, with groups and organizations practicing contemporary art, dance and theatre among others. The purpose was to promote interaction and collaboration between craftsmen, artists, writers, poets, musicians and other practitioners from Afghanistan and the region. In order to engage groups outside the cultural mainstream, the programme also encouraged and assisted in the production and dissemination of literature, poetry, oral history, research and academic study of cultural issues.

Under the auspices of this programme, a joint initiative with the Ministry of Education has resulted in the participation of more than 65,000 children from primary and secondary schools in an ongoing cultural education initiative that gives them access to Babur's Garden, the National Museum and the National Archives. Transported to these sites along with their teachers, school groups are provided with specially designed learning materials and accompanied by experienced and knowledgeable staff on an in-depth tour of the sites. During the programme, children learn about the general history of Afghanistan, experience its natural environment, and are able to see its historic monuments and artefacts. Tours of the National Archives, where some of the country's most important documents are kept, include sessions where illuminated manuscripts from the seventeenth century are brought out from storage areas and presented to the children by staff. The programme has enabled first-hand encounters and a chance to learn for children who would otherwise not have had the opportunity to visit the National Archives or the National Museum.

Considered by many to be outside the skill-sets of local craftsmen, the construction of detailed and complex architectural models is an art form in its own right. An important educational tool for museums, galleries and academic institutions across the world, architectural models convey the ingenuity of architects and builders while providing inspiration for younger generations. As part of support for crafts education, documentation of built heritage and architectural education, AKTC undertook to produce detailed large-scale wooden architectural models of some of Afghanistan's key historic sites and monuments. Requiring close interaction between students, architects and craftsmen, the project was intended to raise public awareness and enable a better understanding of historic sites and monuments. With key exhibitions currently being planned in Kabul and Balkh, it is expected that the display will generate significant public and commercial interest — providing sustained economic opportunities for the teams of craftsmen and architects that collaborated on preparing these models.

Research projects and publications prepared though cultural activities managed by AKTC have been able to document and further expand upon a body of knowledge relating to Afghanistan's cultural heritage. Collaboration between Islamic art scholar Bruce Wannell and researchers from the Department of Literature of Kabul University enabled the publication of two books on the heritage of elite burials in Kabul and Herat. The books document finely carved marble gravestones within the royal grave enclosures in Babur's Garden and near Timur Shah's Mausoleum, as well as in private burial plots on the outskirts of Bagh-e Qazi in the Old City. The gravestones analysed span the Mughal and Barakzai periods, and include the notable graves of Zahir-ud-Din Muhammad Babur, the founder of the Mughal Empire, and Ruqaiya Sultana Begum, the daughter of Mirza Hind-al and the first wife of Emperor Akbar. In Herat, the gravestones documented were located primarily inside the shrine of Khwaja Abdullah Ansari in the village of Gazurgah. The highly decorated box-cenotaphs cover graves

from the Taimuri, Safavi and Chingizi periods, dating from as early as 1433. Inscriptions analysed included the fine *haft qalam* (seven chisels) carving on the gravestone of Shah Gharib Mirza, the son of Sultan Husayn Bayqara. The publication also includes descriptions of the cippus and headstone of Abdullah Ansari's tomb and the inscription found on the gravestone of the great miniature painter Behzad. Detailed transcriptions of religious and poetic inscriptions (delicately carved on the gravestones) are included in the publication, while photographs and hand-drawn illustrations

**Support has also been extended to independent or state-run crafts and training programmes, such as the tile workshop in the Jami Mosque in Herat.**

**Documentation of craft practices and dissemination of information through publication and film have been at the centre of AKTC's promotional activities.**

highlight the damage many of these finely crafted stones have suffered due to years of fighting and neglect. As with other publications prepared by AKTC, the books on elite burials have been disseminated widely.

Film has become one of the most important forms of documentation of historic and cultural environments in Afghanistan. The archives of the Institute of Afghan Film contain a rich legacy of moving images, including the first locally produced feature films as well as movies and historic documentaries from the 1920s onwards. Threatened with destruction on many occasions, the thousands of partially digitized 8 mm and 16 mm films represent a major resource on the social, cultural and economic development of the country over a remarkable ninety-year period. This treasure of moving images was made available for the first time to the public during a film festival organized jointly between the Institute of Afghan Film and AKTC. The three-day public festival was held outdoors in Babur's Garden and included screenings of fifteen films on topics ranging from documentaries on tourism promotion, historic sites, and state-sponsored development projects to full-feature films intended for commercial purposes. A separate collaboration with the Film Institute in 2015 enabled the preparation of a mobile cinema programme that aimed to make documentary and educational films on historic and cultural subject matter available to communities in rural villages. Four mobile teams, travelling with film equipment, visited nine provinces and staged 120 public screenings in schools, cultural centres or other state-owned buildings, attracting more than 35,000 participants. Encouraged by the success of the initiative, additional mobile cinema programmes are being planned for the year ahead.

In addition to screening material from film archives, AKTC has commissioned several documentary films on the social and cultural traditions of Afghanistan. As part of wider documentation activities in the Wakhan Valley in north-eastern Afghanistan, a fifteen-minute documentary film was prepared in collaboration with local and international filmmakers focusing on the Wakhi and Kyrgyz communities. Filmmakers travelled to the region in the brief summer months when it is possible to access the remoter areas of the Wakhan occupied by these communities and documented their cultural practices, traditions and living environments. A follow-up collaboration with French TV 5 resulted in the preparation of three separate films on cultural heritage in Afghanistan, as part of TV 5's "Escapade — The Heritage Magazine", which was broadcast locally and to international audiences in 2015.

Since 2011, eighty-nine distinct projects, fostering 102 cultural initiatives involving more than 120 individuals or partner organizations, were supported through cultural programmes implemented directly by AKTC. These included twenty-three public lectures on cultural topics and a further twenty training initiatives in photography, ethnomusicology, theatre, glazed-tile manufacturing, calligraphy and management of historic public sites. In total, sixteen publications were prepared under the programme and seven public culture festivals were organized, including an International Women's Film Festival, the National Theatre Festival and the Nauroz Music Festival. Through both direct participation and broadcasting on public media, these programmes have benefited tens of thousands of people and have helped raise local and international awareness of the rich cultural traditions of Afghanistan.

Above, collaboration with the Institute of Afghan Film resulted in a mobile cinema project that enabled thousands of Afghans access to historic films and documentaries from the Institute's archives.

Below, a project to record oral history in the Old City of Kabul has resulted in the publication of several pamphlets containing stories passed down over generations.

Left, support has been extended to cultural organizations and civil society groups promoting traditional arts and crafts.

# Acknowledgements

The Aga Khan Trust for Culture would like to extend special thanks for the financial support of the Norwegian Government towards the preparation of the illustrations and texts that are used in this publication, which is intended to make information about Afghanistan's built heritage and historic areas available to students, researchers and professionals. This support was granted to the Afghan Cultural Initiative, a multi-year project aimed at supporting the documentation, dissemination and promotion of cultural traditions and practices in the country.

NORWEGIAN EMBASSY

**AKTC MANAGEMENT**
Luis Monreal, General Manager; Cameron Rashti, Director, HCP (2006 to present) / Stefano Bianca (until 2006); Fairouz Nishanova, Director, Aga Khan Music Initiative; Jurjen van der Tas, Deputy Director, HCP; Ajmal Maiwandi, CEO, AKTC Afghanistan (2010 to present) / Jolyon Leslie (2004–10) / Karel Bos (2003–04).

**AKDN RESIDENT REPRESENTATIVES**
The Trust has received valuable support from fellow colleagues within the Aga Khan Development Network and from the Ismaili community. The Trust is grateful for this support and would like to thank the following: Nurjehan Mawani, AKDN Resident Representative to Afghanistan (2013 to present) / Aly Mawji (2004–13); Mir Ahmad Joyenda, National Council President, Afghanistan (2014 to present) / Sherbaz Hakimi (2004–14).

**CONSULTANTS**
Shukurullah Baig, Kerstin Brautegam, Daoud Breshna, Nathalie Bruhiere, Benedict Bull, Pietro Calogero, Brendan Cassar, Noah Coburn, Dave Cousins, Nick Danziger, Jean Dippenaar, Deborah Dunham, Ute Franke-Vogt, Sher Ghazi, Beatriz Gomez Martin, Zahra Hassan, Pam Hunte, Daniel Ibled, Corinne Jaber, Hadi Jahanabadian, Vaheed Kaacemy, Bashir Kazimee, Mona Khechen, Ebba Koch, Fanny Kurzenne, Beat Laubli, Guido Licciardi, Andy Miller, Koukaba Mojadidi, Babar Mumtaz, Pavel Neugebauer, Noriko Osada, Francois du Plesiss, Hartmut Pliett, John Pott, Simone Ricca, Rafi Samizay, Markus Schadl, Anna Seidel, Mohammed Shaheer, Amund Sindig-Larsen, Sophia Sprenger, Niloufar Taheri, Ugo Tonietti, Thomas Urban, Anthony Wain, Bruce Wannell.

**PROJECT MANAGEMENT**
Fazil Karim Ahmadi, Farkhod Bagirov, Arash Boostani, Birte Brugmann, Ertugrul Erbay, Jamshid Habib, Katrin Lotz, Shahla Naimi, Abdul Wasay Najimi, Ratish Nanda, Abassin Nessar, Habib Noori, Mustafa Nouri, Salim Rafik, Mario Ragazzi, Francesca Reccia, Mohammad Daud Sadiq, Ghulam Sakhizada, Sekander Ozod-Seradj, Mirwaiss Sidiqi, Anna Soave, Maggie Stevenson, Naeem Wahidi, Susanne Wik.

**PROJECT STAFF**
Mohammed Rafi Ahadi, Aziz Ahmad, Bashir Ahmad, Rashed Ahmad, Mustafa Ahmadi, Mohammad Amil, Sayed Farhad Alavi, Nael Ameen, Wahid Ahmad Amini, Mohammad Aqa, Mustafa Asghari, Abdul Saboor Atrafi, Mohammad Hakim Aziz, Mohammad Basir, Basira, Razaq Bator, Abdul Mahmood Jan Doost, Esmatullah, Homayoon Etifaq, Farhad, Fraidoon, Obaidullah Furqani, Mustafa Ghaznawy, Shah Wali Ghaznawy, Habiburahman, Hameedullah, Mohammed Hanbal, Mohammad Hanif, Diana Hanifi, Navid Hatef, Mohammad Yasin Hejrat, Abdul Hamid Hemat, Reza Ibrahimi, Mohammad Ikram, Mohammed Iqbal, Ahmed Jalil, Mohammad Firooz Jami, Jowshan, Maliha Karimi, Medhi Keramatfar, Mohammad Khalid, Jawad Khan, Nabat Khan, Abdul Latif Kohistani, Abdul Hasib Latifi, Abdullah Mahmood, Mohammad Marouf, Mohammad Shafiq Mashal, Meena, Khan Mohammad, Payam Mohammad, Wali Mohammad, Allah Mohammed, Muneebullah Mosamim, Shahab Mushref, Toofan Nabizada, Abdul Sami Najimi, Ahmad Naveed, Mohammad Navid, Nematullah Nayab, Peer Nazar, Haroun Omar, Mohammed Omar, Sulaiman Popal, Mohammad Waris Qaimizada, Abdul Hamid Rahimi, Fazel Rahman, Abdul Ghani Rahmani, Rahmatullah, Mohammad Ramin, Ahmad Rashid, Abdul Jalil Rayan, Khadim Hussain Rohani, Farzana Saber, Abdullah Safi, Safiullah, Abdul Ghani Sahibzada, Amanullah Sahibzada, Soraya Salem, Abdul Samad, Samiullah, Shaiq Sarwary, Serajuddin Seraj, Shafiqurahman, Omid Shams, Zakia Shams, Sharifullah, Najibullah Stanikzai, Wahidullah Stanikzai, Mohammad Taher, Turyalay, Wahidullah, Ahmed Walid, Ramazan Walizada, Ahmad Shah Wardak, Yama, Nasir Ahmad Yawar, Bahram Zondai.

**AKMI CONSULTANTS AND STAFF**
Theodore Levin, AKMI Senior Project Consultant (2003 to present); Mirwaiss Sidiqi, AKMI Coordinator, Afghanistan (2005–14); Abdul Zarif, AKMI Assistant Coordinator (2009 to present); Ahmad Shoaib Saljoqe, Zubair Saljoqe.

**SURVEYORS**
Adila, Ramin Afshar, Zahoor Ahmad, Imtiaz Ali, Nek Ali, Fatima Alikhani, Nafisa Azimi, Aqeela Bano, Jamal Bebe, Farida Bibi, Farida, Fawzia, Geti, Abdul Habib, Habiba, Hafisa, Hela, Huma, Husna, Mohammad Iqbal, Enjilla Irfan, Jalaludin, Latifa, Malalai, Manija, Marzia, Amir Mohammad, Muska, Najia, Najiba, Narges, Nasrin, Nelma, Niloufer, Leena Omid, Abdul Rahim, Abdul Hameed Rahimi, Sheima Rahimi, Malika Rahmani, Mohammad Ramin, Rokhsareh, Fardin Roshanfar, Ruqia, Shafia, Shahriwer, Shahwali, Shaima, Morsal Shams, Roya Vahdat, Abdul Wadood, Wesna, Zainab, Zakira.

**INTERNSHIPS**
Omid Ahmadi, Sayed Arif Akbari, Naqibullah Alimi, Sheragha Aminzai, Kashif Essa, Sabuhi Essa, Hadia, Haseenullah, Ayaz Hosham, Ahmad Javid, Mohammad Khalid, Ahmad Massod, Mohammad Nasir, Hamida Panjshiri, Sadaf, Mohammad Zaher Shewa, Currim Suteria, Rohid Wahidi.

**ADMINISTRATIVE SUPPORT**
Jamila Afzalyar, Salim Ahmad, Andisha Ahmadi, Fazal Ahmad Ahmadi, Bilal Alam, Waheed Ullah Alizoi, Rahimullah Amani, Ghowsuddin Amirian, Sheela Anwari, Qais Aseel, Mohammad Asif, Baryaly Babakarkhail, Batool, Humayon Bavar, Farida Durrani, Ahmed Farid, Sharifa Hekmat, Ezatullah Imran, Khalil Ahmad Islamzada, Aziza Jami, Abdul Khalil, Roshan Khudabakhsh, Lida, Gulnaz Majid, Farzana Mansoori, Ahmad Sayed Muhibullah, Mustafa Muneer, Najimulah Najimi, Ahmed Nasir, Amanullah Nasrat, Narges Nemat, Khalid Ahmad Noori, Helay Rahimi, Abdul Latif Ramin, Haseeb Rasooli, Zekeria Roohi, Abdul Sattar Rustami, Ahmadullah Safay, Abdul Azim Saleh, Ahmad Shoaib Saljoqe, Samiullah, Mohammad Tariq Saqib, Sarajuddin, Mohammad Shafi, Nauroze Shah, Ahmed Javed Stanekzai, Mohammad Waiss Tabish, Tahera, Mohammad Owais Tokhi, Gita Tolo, Farahnaz Yousufi, Zakiullah, Abdul Zarif, Ziba, Zohal.

**PARTNERSHIP AND CO-FUNDING**

FEDERAL REPUBLIC OF GERMANY (FEDERAL FOREIGN OFFICE, ICOMOS GERMANY)
**Kabul:** Babur's Garden, Burj-e Wazir, Qala-e Moeen Afzal Khan, Chihilsitoon Garden, Bagh-e Qazi Park; **Herat:** Malik Mosque and Cistern Complex, Hazrat-e Bilal Mosque, Mukhtarzadah House, Akhawan House, Attarbashi House, Qandahari House, Karbasi House, Posteendoz House, Entezari House, Chahar Suq Cistern and Market Complex, Wazir Cistern, Hariva School, Arbabzadah Serai, Abdullah Ansari Shrine, Namakdan Pavilion, Zarnegar Khanaqa; **Balkh:** Khwaja Parsa Mosque and Park, Subhan Qoli Madrasa Gate, Dehdadi Mosque, Khwaja Nizamuddin Shrine, Mir Ruzadar Shrine, Sultan Ahmad Khezraviah Shrine, Chahar Gunbad Shrine, Khwaja Bajgahi Shrine, Tanga-e Shadian; **General:** Socio-Economic Vocational Training, Capacity Building and Institutional Support, Cultural Support Activities.

INDIA (MINISTRY OF EXTERNAL AFFAIRS)
**Kabul:** Stor Palace Rehabilitation.

UNITED STATES OF AMERICA (STATE DEPARTMENT, AMBASSADORS FUND FOR CULTURAL PRESERVATION, USAID)
**Kabul:** Babur's Garden, Goldasta Mosque, Ulya Madrasa, Bagh-e Qazi Park; **Herat:** Khwaja Rokhband Mosque and Cistern Complex, Shash Nal Mosque, Ikhtyaruddin Citadel; **Balkh:** Noh Gunbad Mosque; **General:** Capacity Building and Institutional Support, Music Training, Cultural Support Activities.

NORWAY (MINISTRY OF FOREIGN AFFAIRS)
**Kabul:** Asheqan wa Arefan Shrine, Shanasazi Mosque and Hammam Complex; **Balkh:** Takhta Pul Mosque; **Badakhshan:** Nasir Khusrau Shrine, Mir Yar Beg Shrine and Garden, Hammam-e Kohna; **General:** Socio-Economic Vocational Training, Capacity Building and Institutional Support, Music Training, Cultural Support Activities.

SWITZERLAND (SWISS AGENCY FOR DEVELOPMENT AND COOPERATION)
**General:** Cultural Support Activities.

UNITED KINGDOM (FOREIGN AND COMMONWEALTH OFFICE)
**Kabul:** Chahardah Masoom Shrine, Pakhtafurushi Madrasa, Shutorkhana Hammam.

SAVE THE CHILDREN
**Kabul:** Babur's Garden.

FOUNDATION OPEN SOCIETY INSTITUTE
**General**: Cultural Support Activities.

PRINCE CLAUS FUND (NETHERLANDS)
**Kabul**: Milma Pal Mosque; **Herat**: Yu Aw School.

CANADA (CIDA)
**General**: Cultural Support Activities.

THE WORLD BANK
**General**: Capacity Building and Institutional Support.

## PARTNER ORGANIZATIONS

GOVERNMENT OF AFGHANISTAN
The projects presented in this publication have been implemented by the Aga Khan Trust for Culture in partnership with the Municipalities of Kabul, Herat, Balkh and Faizabad, as well as the Government of the Islamic Republic of Afghanistan's Ministries of Information and Culture, Urban Development and Housing, Religious and Foreign Affairs, Education (Afghan National Institute for Music) and Higher Education.

NON-GOVERNMENTAL PARTNERS
French Archaeological Delegation in Afghanistan (DAFA), German Archaeological Institute (DAI), KfW Development Bank (Germany), Islamic Museum in Berlin, British Library, French Institute in Afghanistan, Goethe Institute, Hollis Library (Harvard University), Afghanistan Centre at Kabul University (ACKU), Associazione Giovanni Secco Suardo (AGSS), World Monuments Fund (WMF), British Museum, British Council, and United Nations Educational, Scientific and Cultural Organization (UNESCO).

## EDITING CREDITS

The Trust would like to thank in particular Philip Jodidio, Markus Eisen (Prestel), Harriet Graham, Torsten Köchlin, AKTC Afghanistan: Ajmal Maiwandi, Katrin Lotz, Sharifa Hekmat, Hamid Hemat, Wahid Amini and Mustafa Ghaznawy, and AKTC Geneva: Shiraz Allibhai and Lobna Montasser.

## PHOTO CREDITS

Aga Khan Music Initiative: pp. 362 (bottom), 369 (top right)
Aga Khan Trust for Culture-Afghanistan: pp. back cover bottom, back cover flap, 2, 12, 14 (bottom), 17, 19 (bottom), 21 (left), 22 (left images), 36 (top, centre), 38, 39, 40, 42, 43, 44, 45 (left, bottom right), 48, 49 (top, bottom left), 50, 51 (top images), 52, 53 (top), 54, 55, 56, 57, 59, 60, 61, 62, 63, 64 (left), 65, 67, 68, 69, 70, 71, 72, 74, 75, 76, 78, 79, 80, 81, 83 (top), 84, 85, 86–87, 88, 89, 90 (bottom), 92 (bottom), 93 (left, top right), 94, 95, 96, 97 (bottom right), 99, 100 (bottom), 102, 103, 104, 105 (left, bottom right), 108, 109, 110, 111, 112, 113 (right images), 114, 115, 116, 117, 118, 119 (bottom images), 121 (bottom), 122 (left, centre, bottom right), 123, 131 (bottom), 132, 133 (left, top right) 136, 137, 139 (bottom), 140, 141, 143, 144, 145 (top, bottom right), 146–147, 148, 149, 150 (left, bottom left), 151, 160, 161, 163, 165, 166, 168, 169, 170 (top, bottom left), 171, 172, 173, 174 (left), 176, 177, 178, 179, 180, 181 (top), 182, 183 (top left, bottom images), 184, 185 (top), 186, 187, 189 (bottom right), 192, 193, 194, 195 (top, bottom left), 196, 197, 198, 199, 200, 201, 202 (bottom), 203, 205 (top right, bottom images), 210 (bottom), 211, 212, 213, 215, 216 (bottom left, bottom centre), 218, 219, 220, 221 (top), 222, 223, 225, 226, 227 (bottom images), 231, 233 (right), 236, 237, 238, 241, 242–243, 245, 246, 247 (bottom left), 252, 254 (top), 255 (middle, bottom), 256–257, 262, 263, 266 (bottom), 267, 268, 270, 271 (bottom right images), 274, 275, 276, 277 (bottom left), 278, 279, 281 (bottom), 282, 283 (bottom right), 284, 285 (top left images), 286, 287 (bottom images), 288, 289, 290, 291, 292, 293, 294, 295, 296–297, 299, 300, 301, 306, 307, 308, 309, 310–311, 312, 313, 314, 315, 316, 317, 318, 319, 320, 321, 322, 323, 324, 325, 326, 327, 328, 329, 330–331, 332, 333, 334, 335, 336–337, 338, 339, 340, 341, 347 (bottom), 348, 349, 350, 351, 354, 355, 358, 359, 362 (top), 364 (bottom right), 365, 366, 367, 368 (top), 369 (bottom), 372, 373, 374, 376, 377, 378, 379
British Library: pp. 28 (bottom), 35, 121 (top), 131 (top), 139 (top)
Andrea Bruno: p. 28 (top)
John Burke: p. 47
Commercial Satellite Image: pp. 164, 254 (bottom)
Courtesy of the Office of the President, Islamic Republic of Afghanistan: p. 9
Joseph Kassel: p. 266 (top)
Jolyon Leslie: pp. 19 (top), 66
Romano Martini: p. 105 (top right)
Oskar von Niedermayer: pp. 29, 157, 202 (top), 230 (top), 240
Simon Norfolk / Aga Khan Trust for Culture: pp. front cover, front cover flap, back cover top, 4, 10, 11, 23 (bottom), 31 (bottom), 36 (bottom), 41 (top, centre), 46, 51 (bottom), 73 (left), 83 (bottom), 106–107, 119 (top), 120, 122 (top right), 124, 125, 126–127, 129, 130, 133 (bottom right), 135, 174 (right), 175 (top), 183 (right), 185 (bottom), 188, 189 (top), 208–209, 214, 221 (bottom), 228, 232, 233 (left), 234, 235, 239, 247 (bottom centre, bottom right), 255 (top right), 258, 261, 264, 265, 271 (top), 272–273, 277 (top, bottom right), 280, 281 (top), 283 (top, bottom left), 285 (bottom), 287 (top), 304–305, 344, 345, 346 (top, centre), 368 (bottom images), 375
Gary Otte / Aga Khan Trust for Culture: pp. 7, 49 (bottom right), 53 (bottom), 64 (right), 92 (top), 98, 100 (top), 138, 150 (bottom right), 346 (bottom)
Photographer unknown: p. 210 (top)
Josephine Powell / Fine Arts Library, Harvard University: pp. 23 (top), 230 (bottom), 250–251, 253, 260
Christian Richters / Aga Khan Trust for Culture: pp. 14 (top), 16, 18, 21 (right), 22 (right), 26–27, 32–33, 34, 41 (bottom), 45 (top right), 73 (right), 77, 82, 90 (top), 91, 93 (bottom right), 97 (left, top right), 101, 113 (left), 142, 145 (bottom left), 154–155, 158–159, 170 (bottom right), 175 (bottom), 181 (bottom), 189 (bottom left), 190–191, 195 (bottom right), 205 (top left), 216 (bottom right), 217, 224, 227 (top), 347 (top), 364 (bottom left)
Wilhelm Rieck: p. 31 (top)
The State Hermitage Museum, St. Petersburg / © The State Hermitage Museum / photo by Dmitry Sirotkin: p. 363
Victoria and Albert Museum, London: p. 13

## 3D SCAN AND DRAWING CREDITS

Aga Khan Trust for Culture-Afghanistan: pp. 20, 30, 37, 40, 45, 48, 54, 57, 58, 61, 63, 64, 67, 69, 71, 72, 76, 79, 83, 87, 89, 90, 93, 95, 97, 99, 102, 105, 109, 111, 113, 115, 117, 128, 134, 135, 140, 144, 148, 156, 162, 167, 171, 174, 177, 180, 183, 185, 188, 193, 195, 199, 201, 204, 206–207, 216, 219, 221, 224, 227, 231, 232, 234, 239, 241, 244, 255, 263, 264, 269, 270, 277, 280, 283, 285, 287, 289, 291, 293, 295, 298, 318, 319, 321, 323, 324, 327, 356, 357
British Army: p. 157